G000253288

Probate Practitioner's Handbook

Third Edition

Probate Practitioner's Handbook

Third Edition

General Editor

Lesley King *Solicitor*
Principal Lecturer at The College of Law

law society publishing

All rights reserved. No part of this publication may be
reproduced in any material form, whether by photocopying,
scanning, downloading onto computer or otherwise without
the written permission of the Law Society except in accordance
with the provisions of the Copyright, Designs and Patents Act 1988.
Applications should be addressed in the first instance, in writing, to
Law Society Publishing. Any unauthorised or restricted act in relation to
this publication may result in civil proceedings and/or criminal prosecution.

Solicitors in private practice may use the material in this book for
the purposes of private practice as a solicitor and may reproduce
the forms and checklists contained in it for those purposes.
Anyone wishing to use the material for any other reasons
must first obtain the Law Society's consent in writing.

© The Law Society 1999

First published 1991
2nd edition 1995
3rd edition 1999

ISBN 1 85328 517 X

The Solicitors' (Non-Contentious Business) Remuneration Order 1994
reproduced in Chapter 2 is Crown copyright.

Published by the Law Society
113 Chancery Lane, London WC2A 1PL

Typeset by York House Typographic, London
Printed by Thanet Press Limited, Margate

Contents

Foreword

When I originated and planned the first edition of this Handbook, I was sure a book of its kind would prove useful to the profession. It did so, and the Handbook also went on to set the style and tone for other Law Society publications. So I was particularly pleased when Lesley King agreed to take over the general editorship for this third edition, both because of her pre-eminence in the field and because of the continuing place a further edition showed the Handbook to have.

Mrs King has fully recast, revised and updated the Handbook and I am delighted it looks like living on into the new millennium.

Alison Plouviez
Secretary of the Law Society's
Employment Law Committee

PART ONE

Probate and the Professional Rules

This Part covers the interaction of the professional rules with probate and estate administration work and deals particularly with some of the aspects of those rules which have caused difficulty to practitioners in the past.

The Professional Ethics Division of the Law Society (address in Chapter 30) may be able to help with difficult matters. You can write or phone and help is confidential.

Please note that in this Handbook references are made to *The Guide to the Professional Conduct of Solicitors 1996*. A new edition of the Guide is due to be published in summer 1999.

Chapter 1

Solicitors and instructions

WHO IS MY CLIENT?

Personal representatives (PRs)

1.1   In probate and estate administration, the solicitor's clients are the personal representatives. Problems can arise if a PR is elderly and a son or daughter offers to 'act for' him or her. Here, as in other legal work, a solicitor's instructions should come direct from the client – otherwise the PR should be considering renunciation. A PR may be replaced under Administration of Justice Act 1985, s.50 or passed over under Supreme Court Act 1981, s.116.

As an alternative to renunciation, one of two or more executors may choose to have 'power reserved' to him or her which gives the option to get involved later (the power reserved process is simpler than that for renunciation). Renunciation or the reservation of power might also be considered by prospective PRs who plan to be away for long periods of time, or who clearly do not wish to be involved in the administration. If this is suggested, the pros and cons should be clearly pointed out to those concerned. (A useful article on this by Philip Rossdale appeared in the *Solicitors Journal* [1995] 13 January.)

Other problems can arise if, for example, two PRs instruct one firm and later one fails to respond to letters. If possible, grasp the nettle and clarify matters as soon as possible.

Again, one of two or more PRs may be dissatisfied and wish to go elsewhere. Some assistance with the resulting difficulty over costs may be available from the opinion at para. 14.13. See also 'Requests from Clients' at para. 14.18.

Beneficiaries

1.2   Some recent cases may point the way to an extension to the liability of professionals to third parties. (Aspects of liability are considered by

3

Steven Fennell in Chapter 6.) However, in general, beneficiaries' rights in estate administration are limited. They have the right to have the estate properly administered, but are not entitled, unless they are also PRs, to make decisions about the conduct of the administration, or to be involved in the day-to-day business of administering the estate. (Residuary beneficiaries have the right to obtain remuneration certificates – see Chapter 2.)

Beneficiaries who are not PRs are not *clients* of the solicitor acting for the PRs, so it is not their job to instruct those solicitors, but the PRs'. Where possible, of course, beneficiaries' wishes, and particularly those of residuary beneficiaries, can be taken into account. This may be of particular relevance if the beneficiary is a charity and can, for example, reclaim income tax paid or avoid capital gains tax where assets are sold on behalf of the charity as bare trustee. (Charitable beneficiaries are considered further from para. 15.27 onwards.)

Bear in mind that most beneficiaries will have no idea of how much needs to be done to complete the winding up of an estate and how long it can take to do it. They may expect payment of their legacies or to be able to take possession of their gifts within, at most, a few weeks of the death. This, together with their lack of involvement in the administration, can mean worry and uncertainty for them and may possibly result in expression of unjustified dissatisfaction with the firm involved. Accordingly, obtaining the PRs' consent to telling the beneficiaries briefly of the expected timescale for completing the administration, or how long an unexpected hold-up may take to resolve, is likely to pay dividends all round.

It is the usual practice of many firms to notify all beneficiaries of their entitlements or legacies at an early stage. (See [1995] *New Law Journal* Probate Supplement, 29 September for an interesting discussion of the cases by James Sunnucks.) Legatees may simply be informed or sent a copy of the relevant part of the will and residuary beneficiaries may be sent a copy of the whole will. Taking this action, and including an indication of the realistic likely date of payment, may put the beneficiaries' minds at rest – and lower unrealistic expectations – as well as save time and costs in unnecessary correspondence. If your anticipated timetable changes you will need to update people who are still working to the original dates.

Solicitors approached for information by beneficiaries during the administration may wish to agree with and advise the PRs on the information to be given. This will depend on factors such as the beneficiaries' status and relationship to the PRs (and the deceased), the nature of the questions and the costs which would be involved in dealing with them. Although beneficiaries are not clients, the Office for Supervision of Solicitors (OSS) would expect replies to letters of enquiry to be reasonably informative and to be sent reasonably promptly.

More information about trustees and beneficiaries, and the information which beneficiaries are entitled to have, is available in works such as Underhill and Hayton: *Law Relating to Trusts and Trustees* (see Booklist, Chapter 29).

INSTRUCTIONS

General reminders

1.3 Generally, see *The Guide to the Professional Conduct of Solicitors 1996* (the Guide), Chapter 13 on client care.

You need to be sure that the person purporting to instruct you has authority to do so (are the next of kin to be administrators or might there be an as yet untraced will appointing others as executors?) and that you know what they want you to do (agree precisely what is possible and what your firm can do). Making a summary of your instructions for the front of the file can be a useful reminder of the extent of your original retainer, particularly if more than one person is likely to be working on the file. Extensions or alterations to the retainer can be dealt with in the same way, together with the date. As a matter of routine, instructions and alterations should, of course, be confirmed in writing as soon as possible. See Chapter 13 of the Guide on client care.

The case of *Cancer Research Campaign* v. *Ernest Brounec* [1997] S.T.C. 1425 illustrates the importance of identifying the scope of the retainer.

At this stage also consider what information clients need from you. This Handbook contains some specimen materials which solicitors in private practice may adapt or adopt for the purpose set out on page iv but not for any other purpose. They are intended to cover certain basic points relating to succession and estate administration work.

Other materials for clients can be obtained from the Law Society (address in Chapter 30). The Booklist (Chapter 29) contains details of what is available.

Difficulty with instructions

1.4 Light may be shed upon some difficulties by going back to the beginning and finding exact answers to the questions:

- 'Who is my client?' (Usually, but not always, the same as 'Who will pay my bill?')'
- 'What have I been instructed to do?'
- 'What is my role – professional, legal, practical?'

The answer to the first question will help disentangle conflicts in areas where these might arise; contradictory or unacceptable instructions can be revealed by the answer to question two; and the answer to the third question can pinpoint where the difficulty lies.

Some other problems which can arise in the course of estate administration are dealt with in Chapter 14.

CONFLICTS AND DISPUTES

1.5 Conflicts usually arise for clients between their roles as beneficiary and PR. PRs who are not able to put that duty above their own interests should consider renunciation. Another problem, particularly where an intestacy and a step-relationship are involved, is that one PR may feel left out or that the other is being 'favoured', especially if the firm acting is the other PR's usual solicitor.

Both PRs should be involved in the decision-taking and it may be helpful, in these sensitive situations, to ensure that the content of conversations and correspondence with one PR is fully and promptly reported to the other.

Disputes can, of course, arise on any number of grounds – because a will is challenged, through disappointment on the part of the family about the disposition of the estate, or about the identity of the PRs. It may be appropriate to advise the client what steps the other side may take, whether counsel's or a specialist solicitor's opinion or even litigation may be involved, and about the costs and time implications. Clear preliminary instructions need to be obtained and confirmed in writing.

Family companies can be a fertile source of difficulty. Firms who have acted for the founder and members of his or her family personally and on behalf of the business may find that the various parties are at loggerheads after the death. This may mean the firm having to cease to act for some or all of those involved.

The Guide deals extensively with conflicts of interest, principally in Chapter 15.

Independent advice

1.6 From time to time, beneficiaries or PRs may seek independent advice about their position, perhaps because they think a lay or co-PR is mishandling an administration, or because they consider a solicitor's firm is working too slowly. Such a move creates some practical difficulties.

The main one usually relates to costs. The opinion set out in para. 14.13, although it relates to PRs seeking independent advice only, may be of interest in this connection. In any event, you may like to discuss the costs issue with those involved early on. It may also be appropriate to discuss the implications for the administration of what has happened.

Another difficulty may relate to access to papers, particularly if the disagreement centres on dissatisfaction with the firm of solicitors handling the administration. The solution of these problems is difficult, but dealing with the following questions may shed some light on the matter:

- 'Who is the firm's original client?'

- 'Has the retainer been terminated? By whom?'

- 'To whom will duties, such as the duty of confidentiality, be owed?'

- 'To whom should reports be made?'

- 'If a conflict appears to have arisen, is there a conflict for the firm, or is it in fact a conflict for the PR?'

The Guide deals with termination of retainers in Chapter 12.

You may have to advise a client to seek independent advice if you have made a mistake or there is concern that a mistake may have been made by you: see para. 14.24. You have a *discretion* to advise the Solicitors' Indemnity Fund about circumstances which you believe may result in a claim – it is advisable to take advice from the Indemnity Fund in such circumstances. However, you have a *duty* to notify them of claims which *have been made* against you, or which you learn *will be made*: in both cases, if the amount exceeds £500. (See Rules 19.1 and 19.2 of the Solicitors' Indemnity Rules 1995.)

Solicitors as witnesses

1.7   Solicitors may be drawn into disputes about a will after a death, for example if it is questioned whether the testator or testatrix had capacity.

Some years ago the Council of the Law Society obtained the opinion of leading counsel on the duty of a solicitor who had acted for a testator in drawing up his will which, after the death, had been the subject of a dispute.

It was decided that a solicitor should make available a statement of his or her evidence regarding the execution of the will and circumstances surrounding it, to a person who is either a party to probate proceedings or whom the solicitor believes to have a reasonable claim under the will but who is not yet a party to any proceedings, whether or not the solicitor acted for those propounding the will. Further guidance on the position of a solicitor who may be a material witness can be found in the Guide, Principle 21.12. (Also see Chapter 11 of this Handbook on Contentious Probate.)

While the facts of each matter will differ, the principle that the available information should be made accessible impartially to both sides is likely to be of value.

The advice of the Professional Ethics Division (address in Chapter 30) on all such points may be sought.

EXECUTORS IN THE OFFICE

Retired and non-practising solicitors

1.8   Many solicitors take up executorships during retirement or during a period in which they are consultants to their previous firms. As far as charging clauses are concerned, these will need to be interpreted to see whether they are wide enough to cover charging by a person not involved in any business. A person may not act as a solicitor, of course, unless he or she holds a current practising certificate. Solicitors merely on the Roll, i.e. non-practising and retired solicitors not holding practising certificates, may not describe themselves as 'solicitors' or act as such, by, for example, making an application for the grant of representation as a solicitor.

Fee earners about to retire or move firms

1.9 When a fee earner leaves your firm, you may wish to resolve the question of their appointment as executor or executrix. What is to happen? Was the appointment of the individual personally (so that the testator or testatrix will probably want the fee earner to continue to act after going to the new firm) or in effect of the firm (so that someone else in your firm should now be appointed)? Ideally the client's instructions should be obtained. Making contact in this way can also usefully remind the client that other aspects of the will may need review and revision. You should, from a marketing point of view, include an invitation to make an appointment for this; why not send a copy of the firm's brochure too? (For more on marketing, see Chapter 20.)

Supervision of employee PRs

1.10 The following (updated) guidance was first issued in 1991 by the Property and Commercial Services and the Standards and Guidance Committees of the Council of the Law Society.

'Solicitor's clerk appointed executor of a client's will: Duty of supervision

The Solicitors Complaints Bureau [as it then was] has recently had to deal with a case involving the misappropriation of trust funds by an unqualified employee of a solicitor who drafted a will for a client and was appointed under that will as sole executor. The clerk in that case administered the estate through the firm by which he was employed but the monies were held outside the firm. The Standards and Guidance Committee, in conjunction with the Property and Commercial Services Committee and the Wills and Equity Committee [not the Land Law and Succession Committee], wish to remind solicitors of their obligation to supervise both their admitted and unadmitted staff. Principle 3.01 of the Guide states, "A solicitor is responsible for exercising proper supervision over both admitted and unadmitted staff."

Further, Principle 3.13 of the Guide states that, "As a matter of conduct a partner is prima facie responsible for the acts or omissions of the firm and this extends to the acts or omissions of staff."

In particular a solicitor should take special care when exercising these functions in circumstances where a clerk is an executor or executrix whether alone or with a lay person and is administering the estate through the firm, but the money involved is being paid into an account which is outside the Accounts Rules.

Firms may wish to consider whether it would be appropriate to prohibit unqualified staff from being appointed executor or executrix for clients of the firm by inserting appropriate clauses into the contracts of employment of those staff. However, the solicitor's duty to act in the best interest of the client may mean that such a blanket prohibition would be inappropriate. Therefore consideration should be given to clauses restricting unqualified staff from being named as executor or executrix unless prior approval of a partner is obtained. Any such restrictions must not prejudice the interest of the firm's client. The contract could also provide that where an unqualified member of staff became executor or executrix on the death of a client, all estate monies should be paid into the firm's client account.

Similar points should be borne in mind where an unqualified member of staff is appointed attorney or enduring attorney for a client.'

It is worth noting that the Solicitors' Accounts Rules 1998 impose some record-keeping requirements where money is held outside a firm's client bank account (e.g. where a client's own bank account is operated). See Chapter 5 for a fuller discussion.

Chapter 2

Costs and charging

SOURCES OF INFORMATION

2.1 More information about costs and charging can be found in the Guide and publications produced from time to time by the Law Society.

Textbooks such as *Cordery on Solicitors* and works on practice management may also be of interest in this connection (the Booklist includes details of a number of general works – see Chapter 29).

In probates the client is the lay executor. Problems arise where the solicitor is the executor.

Residuary beneficiaries have rights to obtain remuneration certificates. Details of the Solicitors' Remuneration Order are given at para. 2.4 onwards.

In December 1998 the Council of The Law Society made the Solicitors' Costs Information and Client Care Code which is incorporated into the Solicitors' Practice (Costs Information and Client Care) Amendment Rule. The existing Rule 15 will be deleted and replaced. The Code and new Rule are not however yet in force. They are likely to come into effect during 1999. However we have included them in this chapter and in Chapter 3 as they do embody the Law Society's current thinking on best practice.

The Code will replace the existing written professional standards on costs information to be provided by the client and the detail currently in Practice Rule 15 regarding client care. It seeks to be more specific as to what is meant by giving the best information possible on costs.

COSTS AND THE CLIENT

2.2 The Law Society wants openness about costs. The final charge for the administration of an estate may be difficult to predict at the outset, but most clients will not understand why and are likely to interpret vagueness and uncertainty about costs as a signal that they will be enormous or that the firm is not being frank. Either way it is in the firm's interests (as well as in accordance with the obligations imposed by the Law Society) to give clients the facts as far as is possible. If you cannot give an idea of the cost for the whole administration, you can tell the client why, as well as what work you will have to do before you can estimate the total costs and how much it will cost the client for you to reach that point. If nothing else, clients can be told the hourly charging rate of the person handling their work, and given an idea of the number of hours involved, plus details of any known disbursements.

Such evidence as is available indicates that most clients feel they get good value from solicitors. So do not shrink from discussing fees and do include everything the client is likely to have to pay for, including disbursements. Clients expect to go to a supermarket and see prices clearly marked for each item, with no surprises at the check-out. They expect the same simplicity and straightforwardness from other services they purchase. Plain speaking about costs is in everyone's interests. (See para. 2.24 and also Chapter 3 on client care.)

Solicitors should always remember Practice Rule 1 when it comes to billing. Solicitors should never put their own interests before those of the client. This is particularly important in a contentious probate when a client is proposing to spend a lot of money on legal work when there may be very little at stake.

CHARGING FOR WILLS

2.3 Although this Handbook is primarily about estate administration, will drafting is, of course, closely related. A number of general points about wills are included in Part Five. As with estate administration, there is a need to be open with clients and potential clients about the cost involved. However, it is often feasible to quote a definite fee for drafting a will.

Many firms offer will preparation at a price lower than or similar to the commercial will-selling services; making this known will encourage clients to consult solicitors. If your firm's charges are higher, be open about the cost and explain the good value your service offers. Explain all the reasons why seeing a solicitor is worth the extra amount.

Some clients can still get help with will drafting under the Green Form Scheme. The relevant form indicates who is eligible and details are included at para. 27.5.

THE SOLICITORS' (NON-CONTENTIOUS BUSINESS) REMUNERATION ORDER 1994

2.4   (The rest of this chapter is based on an article which originally appeared in [1994] *Gazette*, 28 September, 31.)

The main text of the order is set out in para. 2.5. An article-by-article commentary starts at para. 2.6. A specimen of the information you must give entitled persons is given at para. 2.21. A statement entitled 'Relevant factors when giving costs information for non-contentious work' appears at para. 2.24 and draws together and updates existing guidance about giving costs information to clients.

2.5   *Made – – – –*   *5th October 1994*

     Laid before Parliament   *10th October 1994*

     Coming into force   *1st November 1994*

The Lord Chancellor, the Lord Chief Justice, the Master of the Rolls, the President of the Law Society, the president of Holborn Law Society and the Chief Land Registrar (in respect of business done under the Land Registration Act 1925 [1925 c.21], together constituting the committee authorised to make orders under section 56 of the Solicitors Act 1974 [1974 c.47, as modified by the Administration of Justice Act 1985 (c.61), Schedule 2, paragraphs 22 and 23], in exercise of the powers conferred on them by that section and having complied with the requirements of section 56(3), hereby make the following Order:

Citation, commencement and revocation

1. (1) This Order may be cited as the Solicitors' (Non-Contentious Business) Remuneration Order 1994.

(2) This Order shall come into force on 1st November 1994 and shall apply to all non-contentious business for which bills are delivered on or after that date.

(3) The Solicitors' Remuneration Order 1972 [S.I. 1972 no. 1139] is hereby revoked except in its application to business for which bills are delivered before this Order comes into force.

Interpretation

2. In this Order:

'client' means the client of a solicitor;

'costs' means the amount charged in a solicitor's bill, exclusive of disbursements and value added tax, in respect of non-contentious business or common form probate business;

'entitled person' means a client or an entitled third party;

'entitled third party' means a residuary beneficiary absolutely and immediately (and not contingently) entitled to an inheritance, where a solicitor has charged the estate for his professional costs for acting in the administration of the estate, and either

(a) the only personal representatives are solicitors (whether or not acting in a professional capacity); or

(b) the only personal representatives are solicitors acting jointly with partners or employees in a professional capacity;

'paid disbursements' means disbursements already paid by the solicitor;

'recognised body' means a body corporate recognised by the Council under section 9 of the Administration of Justice Act 1985 [1985, c.61];

'remuneration certificate' means a certificate issued by the Council pursuant to this Order;

'residuary beneficiary' includes a person entitled to all or part of the residue of an intestate estate;

'solicitor' includes a recognised body;

'the Council' means the Council of the Law Society.

Solicitors' costs

3. A solicitor's costs shall be such sum as may be fair and reasonable to both solicitor and entitled person, having regard to all the circumstances of the case and in particular to:

(a) the complexity of the matter or the difficulty or novelty of the questions raised;

(b) the skill, labour, specialised knowledge and responsibility involved;

(c) the time spent on the business;

(d) the number and importance of the documents prepared or perused, without regard to length;

(e) the place where and the circumstances in which the business or any part thereof is transacted;

(f) the amount or value of any money or property involved;

(g) whether any land involved is registered land;

(h) the importance of the matter to the client; and

(i) the approval (express or implied) of the entitled person or the express approval of the testator to:

(i) the solicitor undertaking all or any part of the work giving rise to the costs or

(ii) the amount of the costs.

Right to certification

4. (1) Without prejudice to the provisions of sections 70, 71 and 72 of the Solicitors Act 1974 (which relate to taxation of costs), an entitled person may, subject to the provisions of this Order, require a solicitor to obtain a remuneration certificate from the Council in respect of a bill which has been delivered where the costs are not more than £50,000.

(2) The remuneration certificate must state what sum, in the opinion of the Council, would be a fair and reasonable charge for the business covered by the bill (whether it be the sum charged or a lesser sum). In the absence of taxation the sum payable in respect of such costs is the sum stated in the remuneration certificate.

Disciplinary and other measures

5. (1) If on a taxation the taxing officer allows less than one half of the costs, he must bring the facts of the case to the attention of the Council.

(2) The provisions of this Order are without prejudice to the general powers of the Council under the Solicitors Act 1974.

Commencement of proceedings against a client

6. Before a solicitor brings proceedings to recover costs against a client on a bill for non-contentious business he must inform the client in writing of the matters specified in article 8, except where the bill has been taxed.

Costs paid by deduction

7. (1) If a solicitor deducts his costs from monies held for or on behalf of a client or of an estate in satisfaction of a bill and an entitled person objects in writing to the amount of the bill within the prescribed time, the solicitor must immediately inform the entitled person in writing of the matters specified in article 8, unless he has already done so.

(2) In this article and in article 10, 'the prescribed time' means:

    (a) in respect of a client, three months after delivery of the relevant bill, or a lesser time (which may not be less than one month) specified in writing to the client at the time of delivery of the bill, or

    (b) in respect of an entitled third party, three months after delivery of notification to the entitled party of the amount of the costs, or a lesser time (which may not be less than one month) specified in writing to the entitled third party at the time of such notification.

Information to be given in writing to entitled person

8. When required by articles 6 or 7, a solicitor shall inform an entitled person in writing of the following matters:

    (a) where article 4(1) applies:

(i) that the entitled person may, within one month of receiving from the solicitor the information specified in this article or (if later) of delivery of the bill or notification of the amount of the costs, require the solicitor to obtain a remuneration certificate; and

(ii) that (unless the solicitor has agreed to do so) the Council may waive the requirements of article 11(1), if satisfied from the client's written application that exceptional circumstances exist to justify granting a waiver;

(b) that sections 70, 71 and 72 of the Solicitors Act 1974 set out the entitled person's rights in relation to taxation;

(c) that (where the whole of the bill has not been paid, by deduction or otherwise) the solicitor may charge interest on the outstanding amount of the bill in accordance with article 14.

Loss by client of right to certification

9. A client may not require a solicitor to obtain a remuneration certificate:

(a) after a bill has been delivered and paid by the client, other than by deduction;

(b) where a bill has been delivered, after the expiry of one month from the date on which the client was informed in writing of the matters specified in article 8 or from delivery of the bill if later;

(c) after the solicitor and client have entered into a non-contentious business agreement in accordance with the provisions of section 57 of the Solicitors Act 1974;

(d) after a court has ordered the bill to be taxed;

(e) if article 11(2) applies.

Loss by entitled third party of right to certification

10. An entitled third party may not require a solicitor to obtain a remuneration certificate:

(a) after the prescribed time (within the meaning of article 7(2)(b)) has elapsed without any objection being received to the amount of the costs;

(b) after the expiry of one month from the date on which the entitled third party was (in compliance with article 7) informed in writing of the matters specified in article 8 or from notification of the costs if later;

(c) after a court has ordered the bill to be taxed.

Requirement to pay a sum towards the costs

11. (1) On requiring a solicitor to obtain a remuneration certificate a client must pay to the solicitor the paid disbursements and value added tax comprised in the bill together with 50% of the costs unless:

(a) the client has already paid the amount required under this article, by deduction from monies held or otherwise; or

(b) the solicitor or (if the solicitor refuses) the Council has agreed in writing to waive all or part of this requirement.

(2) The Council shall be under no obligation to provide a remuneration certificate, and the solicitor may take steps to obtain payment of his bill if the client, having been informed of his right to seek a waiver of the requirements of paragraph (1), has not:

(a) within one month of receipt of the information specified in article 8, either paid in accordance with paragraph (1) or applied to the Council in writing for a waiver of the requirements of paragraph (1); or

(b) made payment in accordance with the requirements of paragraph (1) within one month of written notification that he has been refused a waiver of those requirements by the Council.

Miscellaneous provisions

12. (1) After an application has been made by a solicitor for a remuneration certificate the client may pay the bill in full without invalidating the application.

(2) A solicitor and entitled person may agree in writing to waive the provisions of sub-paragraphs (a) or (b) of articles 9 or 10.

(3) A solicitor may take from his client security for the payment of any costs, including the amount of any interest to which the solicitor may become entitled under article 14.

Refunds by solicitor

13. (1) If a solicitor has received payment of all or part of his costs and a remuneration certificate is issued for less than the sum already paid, the solicitor must immediately pay to the entitled person any refund which may be due (after taking into account any other sums which may properly be payable to the solicitor whether for costs, paid disbursements, value added tax or otherwise) unless the solicitor has applied for an order for taxation within one month of receipt by him of the remuneration certificate.

(2) Where a solicitor applies for taxation, his liability to pay any refund under paragraph (1) shall be suspended for so long as the taxation is still pending.

(3) The obligation of the solicitor to repay costs under paragraph (1) is without prejudice to any liability of the solicitor to pay interest on the repayment by virtue of any enactment, rule of law or professional rule.

Interest

14. (1) After the information specified in article 8 has been given to an entitled person in compliance with articles 6 or 7, a solicitor may charge interest on the unpaid amount of his costs plus any paid disbursements and value added tax, subject to paragraphs (2) and (3) below.

(2) Where an entitlement to interest arises under paragraph (1), and subject to any agreement made between a solicitor and client, the period for which interest may be charged may run from one month after the date of delivery of a bill, unless the solicitor fails to lodge an application within one month of receipt of a request for a remuneration certificate under article 4, in which case no interest is payable in respect of the period between one month after receiving the request and the actual date on which the application is lodged.

(3) Subject to any agreement made between a solicitor and client, the rate of interest must not exceed the rate for the time being payable on judgement debts.

(4) Interest charged under this article must be calculated, where applicable, by reference to the following:

(a) if a solicitor is required to obtain a remuneration certificate, the total amount of the costs certified by the Council to be fair and reasonable plus paid disbursements and value added tax;

(b) if an application is made for the bill to be taxed, the amount ascertained on taxation;

(c) if an application is made for the bill to be taxed or a solicitor is required to obtain a remuneration certificate and for any reason the taxation or application for a remuneration certificate does not proceed, the unpaid amount of the costs shown in the bill or such lesser sum as may be agreed between the solicitor and the client, plus paid disbursements and value added tax.

Application by solicitor

15. A solicitor, when making an application for a remuneration certificate in accordance with the provisions of this Order, must deliver to the Council the complete relevant file and working papers, and any other information or documentation which the Council may require for the purpose of providing a remuneration certificate.

EXPLANATORY NOTE

(This note is not part of the Order)

Section 56 of the Solicitors Act 1974 establishes a Committee with power to make general orders regulating the remuneration of solicitors in respect of non-contentious business. Paragraph 22(2) of Schedule 2 to the Administration of Justice Act 1985 modifies the section so that references to solicitors include references to recognised bodies (solicitors' incorporated practices recognised under section 9 of the Administration of Justice Act 1985). This Order sets out the rights of solicitors' clients and residuary beneficiaries of certain estates to require the solicitor charging the client or estate to obtain a certificate from the Law Society as to the reasonableness of his costs. The Order prescribes requirements in relation to information to be given in writing to clients and beneficiaries who are entitled to require a solicitor to obtain a certificate, and lays certain obligations on clients, beneficiaries and solicitors.

THE LAW SOCIETY'S COMMENTARY ON THE 1994 ORDER

Article 1 – Citation, commencement and revocation

2.6 The Order came into force on 1 November 1994. It applies only to matters for which bills are delivered on or after 1 November 1994; the Solicitors' Remuneration Order 1972 applies to bills delivered previously. The Solicitors' Remuneration Order 1972 is revoked from 1 November 1994 in respect of all bills delivered on or after that date.

Article 2 – Interpretation

2.7 Although it is not stated, the Interpretation Act 1978 applies in the new Order where article 2 is silent.

'Client', 'paid disbursements', 'recognised body', 'remuneration certificate', 'solicitor' and 'the Council' are defined.

'Costs' is defined as the amount charged *exclusive* of VAT and disbursements.

'Residuary beneficiary' is defined as *including* a person entitled to all or part of the residue of an intestate estate.

'Entitled third party' is defined as a residuary beneficiary who is entitled to ask the solicitor to obtain a remuneration certificate. The definition has the following effect:

- A residuary beneficiary of an estate where there is at least one lay executor or executrix is *not* an entitled third party.

- A residuary beneficiary of an estate in which all the personal representatives are solicitors *would* be able to ask the solicitor billing the estate to obtain a remuneration certificate, even if the bill is from another solicitor (not a personal representative) instructed by the personal representatives to do the work.

- A residuary beneficiary who will become entitled only upon the happening of some event – for example a person entitled subject to a life interest, or a minor entitled only on majority – is *not* an entitled third party.

'Entitled person' is defined as a person entitled to a remuneration certificate – a client or an entitled third party.

Article 3 – Matters taken into account 'in particular'

2.8 Note the importance of an entitled person's express or implied approval, or a testator's or testatrix's express approval, of the amount of the costs or any particular work giving rise to the costs. If, for example, the file shows compliance with the written professional standards, recorded discussions with the client authorising unusual work, or an express provision in a will or in a document referred to in a will, it could operate in a solicitor's favour in assessing the reasonableness of the costs.

Article 4 – Right to certification

2.9 Note the £50,000 limit.

Article 5 – Disciplinary and other measures

2.10 Note the reference to the general disciplinary powers of the Society.

Article 6 – Obligation to give information before suing on a bill

2.11 Note the information required to be given. [See the specimen 'Notice of Rights' in paras 2.21–2.23.]

Article 7 – Obligation to give information when costs have been taken by deduction

2.12 Note there is no *automatic* obligation in deduction cases to send out the information which a solicitor must send to a client before suing on an unpaid bill. There is an obligation, where costs have been taken by deduction from money held by the solicitor on behalf of a client or on behalf of an estate, and an entitled person (client or residuary beneficiary) raises written objections to the amount of the costs within three months, that information must be given 'immediately' to the person raising the objections.

The normal time which must be allowed for the entitled person to raise objections is three months. The solicitor may, however, stipulate a shorter time when sending the bill or notification of costs. The shorter time must not be less than one month.

Article 8 – The information to be given to the entitled person

2.13   If required to do so under article 6 or 7 the solicitor must inform the entitled person:

- of the right to ask for a remuneration certificate;

- that the entitled person must ask for a remuneration certificate within one month of receipt of the information about their rights, or within one month of receipt of the bill or notification of the costs if later;

- that the client may apply to the Society for a waiver of the requirement to pay half the amount of the bill, VAT and paid disbursements, when requesting a remuneration certificate, if exceptional circumstances apply. (The solicitor can, of course, waive the advance payment. This may reduce delay in obtaining the certificate and eventual payment of costs);

- of the entitled person's rights in connection with taxation of the bill; and

- of the solicitor's right to charge interest on the outstanding bill.

Article 9 – Loss by client of the right to a remuneration certificate

2.14   Note the situations in which a client loses this right and, in particular:

- where there is a non-contentious business agreement; and

- where the client has not paid half the costs in advance of the application as required by article 11, and has not obtained or applied in writing for a waiver.

Article 10 – Loss by entitled third party of the right to a remuneration certificate

2.15   The provisions of this article are, with the appropriate modifications, the same as those applying in respect of clients, except that there is no mention of the bill being delivered and paid, or of the requirement that half the costs be paid, as costs will have been taken by deduction from the estate. There is no mention of a non-contentious business agreement; normally there could be no such agreement as a person cannot enter into a contract with himself or herself.

Article 11 – Requirement to pay a sum towards the costs

2.16   As a prerequisite to obtaining a remuneration certificate a client who has not already done so must pay half the costs and all the VAT and paid disbursements before the solicitor is obliged to apply for a remuneration certificate. The requirement may be waived by the solicitor or by the Society on application by the client if the solicitor has refused to do so, providing exceptional circumstances exist to justify waiving the requirement. The Society will have regard to the fact that a remuneration certificate rarely reduces the solicitor's costs by more than half, so normally a client will in the end pay at least half of the costs.

Article 12 – Miscellaneous

2.17   This article sets out various provisions which are not easy to classify. Note in particular that:

- if the application for a certificate has been made the client can pay the bill without invalidating the application;

- if the solicitor and client agree in writing, the client will *not* lose his or her right to a remuneration certificate by paying the bill or by asking 'out of time' for the solicitor to obtain a remuneration certificate;

- the solicitor has the right to take security for the payment of costs (this provision mirrors article 6 of the old Order).

Article 13 – Refunds of money due to an entitled person, and interest on refund moneys

2.18   This article is new; it specifies the implied duty to refund any overpayment arising from a remuneration certificate being issued for a smaller sum than that shown on the certificate, where costs have already been paid in full. The solicitor must make the refund immediately unless he or she 'appeals' the certificate by applying for taxation of the bill within one month of receiving the certificate.

The article also flags up the possibility that the refund may carry interest under the Solicitors' Accounts Rules or under trust law, since the money to be refunded will have been held by the solicitor for a period 'on behalf of' the client or the estate.

Article 14 – Interest payable on unpaid costs

2.19 The provisions of this article mirror article 5 of the old Order, with additions. Since in estate cases money will have been taken by deduction these provisions only apply in respect of clients who have not paid the whole of the bill. As with the old Order a solicitor who has given a client the information required before suing on the bill may charge interest at the judgement debt rate on the unpaid amount from one month after delivery of the bill. Note in particular:

- the solicitor and client may agree that interest will run from before or after the date of delivery of the bill, or that interest will be charged at a higher or lower rate than the judgement debt rate (interest runs from one month after the date of delivery of the bill unless the solicitor and client agree otherwise);

- if the solicitor delays in applying for a remuneration certificate interest may not be charged for the period between one month after the client's request and the date on which the solicitor makes the application to the Law Society;

- interest is chargeable on the amount certified unless either the application is withdrawn or there is a taxation of the bill; in which case it is chargeable on the full amount in the bill or the taxed amount respectively.

Article 15 – Applications

2.20 This article requires the solicitor to supply the file and any other information or documentation required for the purpose of providing a remuneration certificate.

SPECIMEN 'NOTICE OF RIGHTS'

2.21 This specimen information for entitled persons is not part of the Order and you may use any form of words which complies with the requirements of the Order.

Remuneration certificates

2.22 (1) If you are not satisfied with the amount of our fee you have the right to ask us to obtain a remuneration certificate from the Law Society.

(2) The certificate will either say that our fee is fair and reasonable, or it will substitute a lower fee.

(3) If you wish us to obtain a certificate you must ask us to do so *within a month* of receiving this notice.

(4) We may charge interest on unpaid bills and we will do so at [the rate payable on judgement debts, from one month after delivery of our bill].

(5) (a) If you ask us to obtain a remuneration certificate, then, unless we already hold the money to cover these, you must first pay:

- half our fee shown in the bill;

- all the VAT shown on the bill;

- all the expenses we have incurred shown in the bill – sometimes called 'paid disbursements'.

(b) However, you may ask the Law Society [at 8 Dormer Place, Royal Leamington Spa, Warwickshire CV32 5AE] to waive this requirement so that you do not have to pay anything for the time being. You would have to show that exceptional circumstances apply in your case.

(6) Your rights are set out more fully in the Solicitors' (Non-Contentious Business) Remuneration Order 1994.

Taxation

2.23 You may be entitled to have our charges reviewed by the court. (This is called 'taxation'.) The procedure is different from the remuneration certificate procedure and it is set out in Solicitors Act 1974, ss. 70, 71 and 72. Where appropriate it refers to the new Practice Rule 15.

Relevant Factors when Giving Cost Information for Non-Contentious Work

Introduction

2.24 The rest of this chapter draws together and updates the existing guidance available to the profession about giving costs information to clients, particularly with regard to estimates, quotations, or other costs indications. Where appropriate it refers to the new Practice Rule.

Practice Rule 15 (PR 15)

2.25 The existing Rule 15 is designed to ensure that clients know the name and status of the person(s) responsible for both the day-to-day conduct and overall supervision of their matters, and that clients are at all relevant times given appropriate information as to the issues raised and progress of those matters.

Firms are required to maintain their own procedures for dealing with complaints about the service received and in practical terms, such complaints usually manifest themselves at the time of billing.

The new Rule requires that in addition to the requirement to inform the client of the name of the person handling the case and to operate a complaints handling procedure, solicitors will also be required to give 'appropriate' information as to the costs of any matter (both professional fees and disbursements). The full text of the new Rule is set out in Chapter 3.

What is 'appropriate' is explained in the code incorporated into the new Rule.

Written professional standards on costs (WPS)

2.26 The current standards were issued in February 1991 and set out clearly what is expected of practitioners in relation to the giving of information on costs. The new Rule has the advantage of presenting all the information in one place and will replace the existing written professional standards on costs information and the detail currently in Rule 15.

The current practice management standards

2.27 The standards were issued in 1993, and a copy sent to all practitioners. The standards, *inter alia*, encourage compliance with the WPS and PR 15.

Client care letter

2.28 The best way of ensuring compliance with PR 15 and the WPS is to send the client, as soon as possible after instructions are taken, a comprehensive client care or terms of business letter.

The Law Society has designed a series of sample letters to assist with compliance with the new Rule. There is no reason why practitioners should not devise their own letter to suit the particular needs or circumstances of the client. From the Committee's standpoint, the existence of such a letter is prima facie evidence of compliance with PR 15 and WPS.

Agreements under Solicitors Act 1974, s.57 (as amended)

2.29 Solicitors who enter into a written agreement signed by the client concerning their costs or remuneration (including hourly rates) will find that these can only be challenged through the courts as they are outside the scope of the remuneration certifying procedure.

However, to qualify as such an agreement, the terms must be precise and unambiguous (*Chamberlain* v. *Boodle & King* [1982] 3 All E.R. 188).

Depending on the wording used, solicitors may find that if the client signs and returns a client care or terms of business letter of the type referred to above, then a section 57 agreement may have been entered into.

If a solicitor is involved in a costs dispute, care should be taken by the solicitor to make sure there is no section 57 agreement in existence. If there is, then the solicitor may be inviting further difficulties with the client by telling them about remedies which are not, in fact, available.

'An Approach to Non-Contentious Costs'

2.30 This booklet contains useful information and guidance on non-contentious costs and generally forms the basis upon which remuneration certificate assessments are made. The booklet is available from the Law Society.

Estimates, quotations or other indications of cost

2.31 The word 'indication' is used where appropriate to include quotations and estimates.

It is advisable that indications are given by an authorised responsible member of a firm and that a standard procedure for giving indications is adopted within the firm. All such indications should be readily visible on the file.

The WPS expect all indications to be confirmed in writing to the client. The final amount payable should not vary substantially from the relevant indication unless the client has been informed in writing at the time that there was a change of circumstances.

If a solicitor wishes to give a qualified indication, e.g. by stating that it may be reviewed if the matter develops in an unforeseen manner or turns out to be more complex or difficult than originally envisaged, then such an indication will still be binding on the solicitor unless he informs the client immediately and in writing of the change in circumstances. The solicitor should point out that the original indication no longer stands and/or the client's instructions to proceed should be sought.

In cases where the solicitor's fee is to be paid by a third party, it may be that the indication has only been given to the third party and not to the solicitor's client. In such cases (depending on the overall circumstances) the same principles as set out above in relation to solicitor and own client indications will generally apply.

Consumer Protection Act 1987, Part III

2.32 Practitioners are reminded that indications could fall within section 20 of this Act. Section 20 sets out the circumstances in which a misleading indication could give rise to a criminal offence. Further details are contained in *An Approach to Non-Contentious Costs*.

Solicitors'(Non-Contentious Business) Remuneration Order 1994 and remuneration certificates

2.33   Article 3 states that a solicitor's remuneration in non-contentious business 'shall be such sum as may be fair and reasonable having regard to all the circumstances of the case'.

The normal practice of the Appeals and Adjudication Committee would be to regard any indication of the likely cost of the matter as a material consideration to be taken into account in the giving of a certificate if it appears that the indication was given as an incentive to the client to give instructions to that solicitor, or that the client relied on the indication.

The Committee will therefore normally hold an indication (whether oral or written) to be binding upon the solicitor giving it. Similarly, it is the policy of the Committee to view a material breach of the WPS as a circumstance to be taken into account in assessing a fair and reasonable fee under the above Order.

Where there is a dispute as to whether an oral indication has been given, the Committee will try to ascertain from the available documentation and circumstances whether the claim that an oral indication was given can be justified.

Office for Supervision of Solicitors (OSS) and IPS

2.34   A material breach of the WPS could lead to a finding (by the Committee) that the solicitor has provided inadequate professional services (IPS) or, in a serious or persistent case, a finding (after reference to the Solicitors' Disciplinary Tribunal) of professional misconduct.

Similarly, the exceeding of costs without appropriate notice or warning could, depending on the particular circumstances of the case, result in the fee being reduced to the indication figure if the matter is subject to an IPS investigation.

It therefore follows that the principles applied to remuneration certificates apply equally to IPS investigations in the context of costs indications.

Change of circumstance

2.35 A solicitor is required to notify the client immediately, and in writing, if a change of circumstances has occurred so that the original qualified indication no longer applies. It is appreciated that some special circumstance, e.g. a contract race, may make it impractical for the solicitor to revise the indication in the way contemplated by the statement.

Solicitors should take extra care in these circumstances to ensure that the client does not rely on the indication if it has become misleading.

Split transactions

2.36 Where a transaction has a number of parts (e.g. the purchase of a property, the creation or discharge of a mortgage or the registration of title) the indication, unless it states otherwise, will be deemed to include all of these matters. The view that an indication only covers the basic transaction and that a charge can be raised in addition for ancillary matters such as registration of title is not acceptable and this may well be (depending on the circumstances) a misleading indication.

Petty disbursements

2.37 The practice of adding petty disbursements such as postage, telephone calls and faxes to the final bill is generally unacceptable. Petty disbursements are considered to be part of the overheads of the firm. They are expenses of the firm and should be included in the calculation of the fee even if there is an indication that petty disbursements will not normally be allowed, unless there is a specific agreement to the contrary.

Where a transaction is likely to involve substantial telephone work, faxing or photocopying, it should be made clear to the client if such items are to be charged in addition to any indication of costs.

Abortive matters

2.38 In general, where an indication has been given for a completed transaction and it does not proceed to completion, the charge for the abortive work should be made on a pro-rata basis. In the context of conveyancing, an indication given for a sale will normally be held to

31

include all abortive sales unless the solicitor has revised his indication at the appropriate time.

In a purchase transaction, it is in both the solicitor's and the client's interests that the extent of the indication is revised in writing as soon as abortive matters make it clear that the original indication is no longer appropriate.

In all abortive matter cases, the Appeals and Adjudication Committee will look closely at the available evidence and decide the scope of the indication.

[See para.14.8 in connection with estates which turn out to be insolvent.]

Approximations

2.39 Where an indication is expressed in forms such as 'about £500', or 'approximately £500', it would normally be expected that the final fee charged would be within 10 per cent of the indicated figure. Any fee outside that tolerance may (depending on the circumstances) be viewed as a substantial variation resulting in the original approximation restricting the solicitor's fee.

Time-limits

2.40 When confirming an indication, it is advisable to make clear the time period within which the indication will remain valid. Failure to do so may well (depending on the circumstances of the case) result in the solicitor being held to what he considers to be an out-of-date figure, particularly where it is clear that the client still viewed the indication as an incentive to instruct the solicitor and relied upon it.

Chapter 3

Client care

Keeping Clients and other publications on client care are included in the Booklist, Chapter 29. See Chapter 13 of the Guide for details of the written professional standards and information on costs for clients as well.

RULE 15 AND SOURCES OF INFORMATION

Existing Rule 15

3.1   The existing Rule 15 reads:

1.   Every principal in private practice shall operate a complaints handling procedure which shall, inter alia, ensure that clients are informed whom to approach in the event of any problem with the service provided.

2.   Every solicitor in private practice shall, unless it is inappropriate in the circumstances:

   (a)   ensure that clients know the name and status of the person responsible for the day-to-day conduct of the matter and the principal responsible for its overall supervision;

   (b)   ensure that clients know whom to approach in the event of any problem with the service provided; and

   (c)   ensure that clients are at all relevant times given any appropriate information as to the issues raised and the progress of the matter.

New Rule

3.2   The proposed new Rule reads:

[Draft] Solicitors' Practice (Costs Information and Client Care) Amendment Rule [1999]

Rule dated [date of notification of the Lord Chancellor's approval under the Courts and Legal Services Act 1990, Schedule 4] made by the Council of the Law Society with the concurrence of the Master of the Rolls under section 31 of the Solicitors Act 1974 and section 9 of the Administration of Justice Act 1985.

On [six months after notification of the Lord Chancellor's approval under the Courts and Legal Services Act 1990, Schedule 4], **delete** Rule 15 of the Solicitors' Practice Rules 1990 (client care) and **replace** with the following:

'Rule 15 (Costs information and client care)

Solicitors shall:

(a)   give information about costs and other matters; and

(b)   operate a complaints handling procedure

in accordance with a Solicitors' Costs Information and Client Care Code made from time to time by the Council of the Law Society with the concurrence of the Master of the Rolls, but subject to the notes.

Notes

(i)   *A serious breach of the code, or persistent breaches of a material nature, will be a breach of the rule, and may also be evidence of inadequate professional services under section 37A of the Solicitors Act 1974.*

(ii) *Material breaches of the code which are not serious or persistent will not be a breach of the rule, but may be evidence of inadequate professional services under section 37A.*

(iii) *The powers of the Office for the Supervision of Solicitors on a finding of inadequate professional services include:*

(a) *disallowing all or part of the solicitor's costs; and*

(b) *directing the solicitor to pay compensation to the client up to a limit of £1,000.*

(iv) Non-material breaches of the code will not be a breach of the rule, and will not be evidence of inadequate professional services under section 37A.

(v) Registered foreign lawyers, although subject to Rule 15 as a matter of professional conduct, are not subject to section 37A. However, solicitor partners in a multi-national partnership are subject to section 37A for professional services provided by the firm.'

[Draft] Solicitors' Costs Information and Client Care Code [1999]

Code dated [six months after notification of the Lord Chancellor's approval under the Courts and Legal Services Act 1990, Schedule 4] made by the Council of the Law Society with the concurrence of the Master of the Rolls under Rule 15 of the Solicitors' Practice Rules 1990, regulating the English and Welsh practices of solicitors, registered foreign lawyers and recognised bodies in giving information to clients and operating complaints procedures.

1. Introduction

(a) This code replaces the written professional standards on costs information for clients (see paras. 3–6) and the detail previously contained in Practice Rule 15 (client care) (see para. 7).

(b) The main object of the code is to make sure that clients are given the information they need to understand what is happening generally and in particular on:

    (i) the cost of legal services both at the outset and as a matter progresses; and

    (ii) responsibility for clients' matters.

(c) The code also requires firms to operate a complaints handling procedure.

(d) It is good practice to record in writing:

    (i) all information required to be given by the code including all decisions relating to costs and the arrangements for updating costs information; and

(ii) the reasons why the information required by the code has not been given in a particular case.

(e) References to costs, where appropriate, include fees, VAT and disbursements.

2. Application

(a) The code is of general application, and it applies to registered foreign lawyers as well as to solicitors. However, as set out in para. 2(b), parts of the code may not be appropriate in every case, and solicitors should consider the interests of each client in deciding which parts not to apply in the particular circumstances.

(b) The full information required by the code may be inappropriate, for example:

(i) in every case, for a regular client for whom repetitive work is done, where the client has already been provided with the relevant information, although such a client should be informed of changes; and

(ii) if compliance with the code may at the time be insensitive or impractical. In such a case relevant information should be given as soon as reasonably practicable.

(c) Employed solicitors should have regard to paras. 3–6 of the code where appropriate, e.g. when acting for clients other than their employer. Paragraph 7 does not apply to employed solicitors.

(d) Solicitors should comply with paras. 3–6 of the code even where a client is legally aided if the client may have a financial interest in the costs because contributions are payable or the statutory charge may apply or they may become liable for the costs of another party.

(e) The code also applies to contingency fee and conditional fee arrangements and to arrangements with a client for the solicitor to retain commissions received from third parties.

3. Informing the client about costs

(a) Costs information must not be inaccurate or misleading.

(b) Any costs information required to be given by the code must be given clearly, in a way and at a level which is appropriate to the particular client. Any terms with which the client may be unfamiliar, for example 'disbursement', should be explained.

(c) The information required by paras. 4 and 5 of the code should be given to a client at the outset of, and at appropriate stages throughout, the matter. All information given orally should be confirmed in writing to the client as soon as possible.

4. Advance costs information – general

The overall costs

(a) The solicitor should give the client the best information possible about the likely overall costs, including a breakdown between fees, VAT and disbursements.

(b) The solicitor should explain clearly to the client the time likely to be spent in dealing with a matter, if time spent is a factor in the calculation of the fees.

(c) Giving 'the best information possible' includes:

  (i) agreeing a fixed fee; or

  (ii) giving a realistic estimate; or

  (iii) giving a forecast within a possible range of costs; or

  (iv) explaining to the client the reasons why it is not possible to fix, or give a realistic estimate or forecast of, the overall costs, and giving instead the best information possible about the cost of the next stage of the matter.

(d) The solicitor should, in an appropriate case, explain to a privately paying client that the client may set an upper limit on the firm's costs for which the client may be liable without further authority. Solicitors should not exceed an agreed limit without first obtaining the client's consent.

(e) The solicitor should make it clear at the outset if an estimate, quotation or other indication of cost is not intended to be fixed.

Basis of firm's charges

(f) The solicitor should also explain to the client how the firm's fees are calculated except where the overall costs are fixed or clear. If the basis of charging is an hourly rate, that must be made clear.

(g) The client should be told if charging rates may be increased.

Further information

(h) The solicitor should explain what reasonably foreseeable payments a client may have to make either to the solicitor or to a third party and when those payments are likely to be needed.

(i) The solicitor should explain to the client the arrangements for updating the costs information as set out in para. 6.

Client's ability to pay and source of funding

(j) The solicitor should discuss with the client how, when and by whom any costs are to be met and consider:

(i) whether the client may be eligible and should apply for legal aid (including advice and assistance);

(ii) whether the client's liability for their own costs may be covered by insurance;

(iii) whether the client's liability for another party's costs may be covered by pre-purchased insurance and, if not, whether it would be advisable for the client's liability for another party's costs to be covered by after-the-event insurance (including in every case where a conditional fee or contingency fee arrangement is proposed); and

(iv) whether the client's liability for costs (including the costs of another party) may be covered by another person, e.g. an employer or trade union.

Cost-benefit and risk

(k) The solicitor should discuss with the client whether the likely outcome in a matter will justify the expense or risk involved including, if relevant, the risk of having to bear an opponent's costs.

5. Additional information for particular clients

Legally aided clients

(a) The solicitor should explain to a legally aided client the client's potential liability for the client's own costs and those of any other party, including:

  (i) the effect of the statutory charge and its likely amount;

  (ii) the client's obligation to pay any contribution assessed and the consequences of failing to do so;

  (iii) the fact that the client may still be ordered by the court to contribute to the opponent's costs if the case is lost even though the client's own costs are covered by legal aid; and

  (iv) the fact that even if the client wins, the opponent may not be ordered to pay or be capable of paying the full amount of the client's costs.

Privately paying clients in contentious matters (and potentially contentious matters)

(b) The solicitor should explain to the client the client's potential liability for the client's own costs and for those of any other party, including:

  (i) the fact that the client will be responsible for paying the firm's bill in full regardless of any order for costs made against an opponent;

  (ii) the probability that the client will have to pay the opponent's costs as well as the client's own costs if the case is lost;

  (iii) the fact that even if the client wins, the opponent may not be ordered to pay or be capable of paying the full amount of the client's costs; and

  (iv) the fact that if the opponent is legally aided the client may not recover costs, even if successful.

Liability for third party costs in non-contentious matters

(c) The solicitor should explain to the client any liability the client may have for the payment of the costs of a third party. When appropriate, solicitors are advised to obtain a firm figure for or agree a cap to a third party's costs.

6. Updating costs information

The solicitor should keep the client properly informed about costs as a matter progresses. In particular, the solicitor should:

(a) tell the client, unless otherwise agreed, how much the costs are at regular intervals (at least every six months) and in appropriate cases deliver interim bills at agreed intervals;

(b) explain to the client (and confirm in writing) any changed circumstances which will, or which are likely to affect the amount of costs, the degree of risk involved, or the cost-benefit to the client of continuing with the matter;

(c) inform the client in writing as soon as it appears that a costs estimate or agreed upper limit may or will be exceeded; and

(d) consider the client's eligibility for legal aid if a material change in the client's means comes to the solicitor's attention.

7. Client care and complaints handling

(a) Every solicitor in private practice must ensure that the client:

  (i) is given a clear explanation of the issues raised in a matter and is kept properly informed about its progress (including the likely timescale);

  (ii) is given the name and status of the person dealing with the matter and the name of the principal responsible for its overall supervision;

  (iii) is told whom to contact about any problem with the service provided; and

  (iv) is given details of any changes in the information required to be given by this paragraph.

Complaints handling

(b) Every principal in private practice must:

  (i) ensure the client is told the name of the person in the firm to contact about any problem with the service provided;

  (ii) have a written complaints procedure and ensure that complaints are handled in accordance with it; and

  (iii) ensure that the client is given a copy of the complaints procedure on request.

MORE THAN A COMPLAINTS PROCEDURE

3.3 Both the existing and the new Rule refer to a complaints handling procedure. However, client care is more than setting up a means for dissatisfied clients to resolve their problems, important though that is. Client care means focusing your own and your firm's attention on clients' needs. This may be through simple steps which you can adopt immediately (like meeting clients in reception, rather than having them 'sent up' – recent research shows that seemingly minor factor is the single thing clients appreciate most). It may be through something which involves a major review of your work and how you do it, intended to improve the quality of service offered (and save you time and effort), such as practice-wide standardisation of procedures or computerisation.

References to client care crop up throughout this Handbook, explicitly and otherwise. One of the aims of the Handbook is to help reduce the time you spend on routine and repeated tasks, to free you for more satisfying and productive ones, including giving the best possible service to your clients. Examples of standard letters, leaflets and checklists for wills and probate clients have been included or are recommended. (Solicitors in private practice may adapt or adopt those included for the purpose set out on page iv but not for any other purpose.) More generally, help with assessing how you do what you do is also included (for example, the checklists on client care in this Part). Some of the dozens of inexpensive books on business management (and managing your personal workload) available in general bookshops are listed in the Booklist in Chapter 29. See also Chapter 18.

When introducing changes, it is important to recognise that any change, even for the better, is stressful; and that results are more likely to be lasting if you have a clear idea of your goal but set about reaching it in stages: consolidate progress before moving ahead.

Many practices and individual solicitors have faced enormous pressures in the last few years, particularly from changes forced on them by the last recession and clients' altered expectations. Workloads may have increased or decreased sharply. Client care need not be just another worry; it can help you stand back from what you do and where you are and offers the opportunity to make some changes you have chosen.

What does Rule 15 Mean for your Firm?

3.4   Rule 15 obliges firms to tell clients:

- who is responsible for their matter;

- the name of the supervising principal;

- the person to approach in the event of any problems with the service provided.

In addition, every principal in private practice must operate a complaints handling procedure. The OSS expects that procedure to be employed effectively and in a manner that provides the best possible opportunity for the complaint to be resolved by the firm if it is not to be asked to justify how it complied with Rule 15.

If a client raises a problem with it, the OSS will establish whether there are grounds for complaint, tell the client what the Office can and cannot do, and ask if the complaint has been put to the firm involved. The OSS generally expects clients to do this first. The OSS will return complaints to the firm if the client has not done so.

If the client remains unhappy, the OSS assesses the response from the firm and tells the client if this is satisfactory. If not, it investigates.

If the OSS does investigate a complaint, it will try to resolve it by agreement. If this cannot be done, a more formal investigation will take place and it will discuss the firm's complaints handling procedures. If appropriate, improvements may be recommended but if there are serious shortcomings, it may seek a sanction for breach of Rule 15.

COMMUNICATIONS AND CLIENT CARE

3.5 The emphasis in much of the Law Society's work in recent years has been on client care, and helping firms to provide high quality services. The OSS has a dedicated client care and compliance team who have been at the forefront of many initiatives to help firms.

Communicating clearly with clients is a vital part of good client care. Using pre-prepared information such as leaflets, brochures, information sheets and standard letters saves time, helps ensure consistency throughout the practice and provides an icebreaker for new clients.

The following checklist (originated by the OSS) includes reminders about what to do when.

Checklist: better client communication

3.6 *1. At the first appointment:*

- Cover preliminary points:

  - Identify the supervising partner.

  - Agree the objective with your client and consider, if appropriate, whether the likely outcome justifies the expense or risk involved.

  - Explain the action you will be taking, especially the next step and any action the client must take.

  - Discuss the timescale involved, including when you are next likely to contact the client.

  - Give the client the best information possible about the likely cost.

  - Run through how costs will be met – Green Form/legal aid/insurance, instalments, direct debit, etc.

  - Discuss and explain any payments on account (both initial and future).

  - Point out any other reasonably foreseeable payments the client may have to make, and when.

  - Tell the client the likely cost and/or basis of charging, and what will happen if the matter doesn't proceed or proves abortive.

  - Give the client your firm's standard costs information guide and standard information leaflet with relevant information about the firm's services.

- Point out who should be contacted about any problem with the service.

- Record the instructions.

- Note any agreed fee (+/– VAT/disbursements), and what it covers.

- Confirm oral estimates in writing.

- Mark the file if a limit on costs has been agreed.

- Set out the position in the firm's confirmatory terms of business letter.

- After the first interview confirm those instructions in a 'client care' letter.

2. During the case:

- Keep the client regularly informed of progress (and promptly return phone calls).

- If there is delay, tell the client why.

- Explain important and relevant documents.

- Tell the client if a change of staff will affect his matter.

- Explain if a costs forecast needs revising and the revised forecast. (This must be done in writing.)

- Review with the client whether the likely outcome will justify the continuing expense or risk.

- In continuing matters, report the costs incurred at least every six months.

- Review whether any agreed costs limit has been reached.

3. At the end of the matter:

- Write confirming the matter has been completed.

- Explain any continuing consequences.

- Render your bill as promptly as possible. See Principle 14.07 in the Guide.

- Account promptly for all client funds held by you (together with interest as appropriate).

- Hand over all papers and property to which the client is entitled (subject to any lien if a bill has not been paid).

- Take speedy action on any post-completion matters.

STANDARD INFORMATION

3.7   Three examples of standard information for clients, which set out basic details about what to expect, in different styles, are included here. At para. 3.8 is an example of a client information leaflet, prepared by the OSS and slightly edited. At para. 3.9 are the parts relevant to probate of the specimen leaflet in the OSS's guide, *Keeping Clients.* Finally, at para. 3.10 is a specimen letter for estate administration clients. (Solicitors in private practice may adapt or adopt these for the purpose set out on page iv but not for any other purpose.)

In addition to general information about your firm, you might want to provide specific information about wills and probate. The Law Society produces a number of publications, such as *Making a Will Won't Kill You* and the *Guide for Personal Representatives,* all available from the Law Society (see Booklist and Addresses, Chapters 29 and 30 respectively.)

In addition to providing the standard information to clients the OSS recommends issuing a copy of the client care letter to residuary beneficiaries. This is especially relevant where solicitors are themselves acting as personal representatives. The beneficiaries will then be aware of how matters are being handled and this may avoid problems.

Bear in mind that residuary beneficiaries have a right to complain about your services and if found wanting the OSS has power to award a financial penalty against you by reducing your bill. Residuary beneficiaries are also entitled to require you to obtain a remuneration certificate so questions as to costs should always be discussed and beneficiaries kept informed.

SPECIMEN CLIENT INFORMATION LEAFLET

3.8   (This is based on an example from the OSS)

A guide for our clients

We want the best relationship between us as we help you with your matter and this leaflet explains:

- the name of the person looking after your matter and/or the supervising partner;
- when our office is open;
- where people can be reached in an emergency outside office hours;
- our costs and the service we promise you;
- how you can help us; and
- what to do if you are unhappy about the way your matter is being dealt with.

Your instructions to us are being looked after by:

Mr/s _____

who is a partner/consultant/assistant solicitor/trainee solicitor/legal executive. If he or she is unavailable:

Mr/s _____

will be pleased to take a message for you.

The supervising partner is:

Mr/s _____

Our office is open from _____ to _____ each weekday and from _____ to _____ on Saturdays.

If an emergency arises when the office is closed please ring:

Mr/s _____

Our promise to you

We aim to reply to correspondence within two working days.

At the outset we will confirm in writing to you:

- your instructions to us;
- any advice we have given;

- the approximate time the matter will take to finalise;

- what action we will be taking;

- when you are next likely to hear from us;

- any action we need you to take;

- the best information we can give as to the likely cost and how it will be met; and

- any further information we need from you.

During the conduct of your matter we will:

- keep you informed of progress;

- advise you of any delays and explain the reasons;

- explain the effect of any important documents;

- inform you if a costs forecast needs revising;

- explain any changes of staff affecting your matter; and

- if you so wish, send you copies of important letters (but it will cost more if you ask for copies of all letters).

At the end of your matter we will:

- write confirming its conclusion;

- explain any continuing consequences;

- render our bill as promptly as possible;

- account to you for all money due to you; and

- you can ask for any papers and property to which you are entitled, subject to our right to retain them in certain unusual circumstances, for example if our bill has not been paid.

How you can help us

- Give us clear instructions.

- Tell us if you have any important time-limits.

- Make sure we have understood each other correctly. Ask us if you are not sure about anything.

- Deal promptly with any important questions which may arise.

- Keep in regular touch. Do not feel afraid to ask for a progress report if you are worried about anything or do not hear from us when you expect to do so.

- Help us plan our working day. For example unless it is urgent, write to us rather than telephone, and make an appointment if you want to see someone. Remember, avoiding unnecessary calls and appointments helps us keep costs down for you.

We will be pleased to give you costs information at any time. Our aim is to meet the Law Society's written professional standards and recommended good practice in their *Keeping Clients* Guide. When we write confirming your instructions we will give you the best information we can about the likely cost, including our terms for payment of bills and right to charge interest on an unpaid bill. Ask us about anything you would like amplified or explained.

Standard costs information

Our charges

When taking your instructions we will:

- discuss how your legal charges are to be met and whether you are eligible for legal aid – we can make the application for you;

- give you the best information we can about likely costs either by:

  - agreeing a fee with you;

  - providing you with an estimate of costs; or

  - explaining how our costs will be worked out.

Value Added Tax (VAT) and all the payments out which we make on your behalf (called 'disbursements') will be added to our final account.

We will confirm these arrangements in writing, explain what work they cover, tell you about other foreseeable payments which are likely to be necessary, and set out our terms of payment for bills and our right to charge interest on an unpaid bill.

You can:

- set a limit on the costs to be incurred without further agreement with you (this is not the same as an 'agreed fee'); and

- ask us for details of what costs have been run up at any stage.

We will tell you what costs have been incurred at least every six months where a matter takes some time.

Unless you are on legal aid we may ask you for a payment on account of our costs for disbursements, especially for court or tribunal work. We may need to ask you for further payments as the matter progresses.

If you think your bill is too high we will be pleased to explain how it has been worked out. If you are still unhappy after that, we can explain your rights to have the bill checked by the Law Society and/or the courts.

What to do if you are dissatisfied

Tell us if you feel you are not receiving the service you hoped for. We want to know if you are dissatisfied. We can try to put it right, and will look into it promptly and thoroughly.

Mention it first to the person looking after your matter.

If you are still unhappy after that you can complain to:

Mr/s _____

who will investigate it and contact you to talk about the problem. It will help if you put your complaint in writing (keeping a copy for yourself) explaining what action you want us to take. Afterwards he or she will write confirming your complaint, the discussion, and what we will be doing about it. This will be at no extra cost to you.

[*Note*: Only if a client complains should solicitors disclose details of their firm's complaints handling procedure and only if they fail to resolve the complaint after taking every step to do so should they inform the client of how to seek assistance from the OSS. The OSS Helpline for clients is 0870 606 6565.]

SPECIMEN LEAFLET: ESTATE ADMINISTRATION: INFORMATION FOR CLIENTS

3.9 These are the paragraphs relating to probate, slightly edited, from the specimen information leaflet for clients in the OSS's guide *Keeping Clients*.

(a) Charges

Our charges will be calculated according to:

- the time spent by solicitors and legal staff in dealing with the estate, and

- a 'value element'. This is a percentage of the gross value of the estate, as the monetary value involved is one measure of the extent of responsibility falling on the firm.

We review our charging rates [every six months/every year]. It is our practice to write to you about changes in these rates and tell you the dates after which the changes will apply.

We give below an explanation of the 'time' and 'value' factors.

Time

- For meetings, discussions and other work progressing the administration of the estate, the hourly charging rates (excluding VAT) of our solicitors and legal staff are:

	£
partners	_____
other solicitors	_____
trainee solicitors	_____
legal executives	_____

VAT will be added at the current rate.

If less than one hour is involved, we calculate the time spent in units of six minutes. (One six-minute unit equals 10 per cent of the hourly rate).

- Telephone calls and letters are treated differently:

  - telephone calls (made and received by us) are recorded in units each of six minutes;

  - short and routine letters (written and received) are counted as six minutes each.

Value

The 'value element' is calculated as follows:

- ____ per cent on the gross value of the estate (excluding the value of the deceased's home if this was owned); and

- ____ per cent on the value of the deceased's home.

Additional expense

Other expenditure will be necessary in dealing with the estate. This will include:

- Probate Registry fee (for issuing the grant)   £_____ (no VAT)

- Commissioner's fee (the charge for swearing the personal representatives' oath)   £_____ (no VAT)

- Valuers' fees (if necessary)   £_____ (plus VAT)

- Additional court copies of the grant document £_____ (no VAT)

[*Note*: It is becoming increasingly common for probate practitioners along with those practising in other areas of law to agree a fixed fee for the work at the outset. This can still include a percentage of the estate's value but a fixed fee provides simplicity with certainty for all concerned and minimises the chances of a dispute over costs.]

(b) Amount of work

It is difficult at the beginning of the administration of most estates to say how much work will be involved, but we estimate at present that about _____ hours' work, spread over several months, will be needed. We will be able to give you a more accurate estimate after we have prepared the application for the grant of representation in about ___ days' time. We will write to you immediately if it becomes clear that substantially more time will be needed than we expect.

(c) Bills

We usually submit bills at intervals during the administration of estates. This will keep you informed about charges. If you approve them, both the interim and final bills can be paid from estate funds automatically and you do not need to make payment personally.

The first interim bill is normally submitted after the grant has been obtained. If it is likely to be some time before we can finalise the tax position and complete the administration, we normally submit a second interim bill during the course of the administration. Our final bill will be presented when the administration is completed.

(d) Staff

The partner with ultimate responsibility for this matter is [   ]. It will be handled on a day-to-day basis by [   ], [a solicitor/a trainee solicitor/a legal executive]. We want to offer you and all our clients a friendly and efficient service, but if any difficulty should arise, please raise the matter first with [him] [her]. If you still have problems, please contact [   ], the partner responsible.

Should you still be unhappy with the situation please refer the matter to [   ], [address and telephone number], who will investigate and contact you to talk about the problem. [He][She] will then write to you about the matter and the action being taken.

(e) Handling the administration

(i) Grants of representation

As explained more fully in our leaflet *The Personal Representative's Guide* [see Booklist, Chapter 29], unless the estate is very small and with no freehold or leasehold property (such as a house or flat) the personal representatives will have to obtain a grant of representation from the Probate Registry showing their entitlement to deal with the estate. We will probably be able to tell you straightaway if a grant is needed, and we shall handle all the necessary paperwork for you.

If the deceased left a will, the application is to the Probate Registry for a grant of probate; if the deceased did not make a will and therefore died 'intestate', the application is for a grant of letters of administration.

If a will was left, this should set out who is to inherit the estate. If there was no will, the law sets out who is entitled to inherit and we should be able to tell you at a very early stage which members of the family are entitled to the estate and in what proportions and shares.

(ii) First steps

The first stage of our work is to prepare the papers for the application for the grant. We try to complete this promptly. You should be hearing from us within the next seven to fourteen days. We will also tell you then how quickly we expect to receive the documents from the Probate Registry.

We usually write as soon as possible to all the beneficiaries named in the will, or to those family members entitled on an intestacy, to tell them of their legacies and entitlements. When writing, we also try to indicate when we expect to be able to make payment.

We will arrange for payment of the funeral account and other bills in due course. *Would you please therefore send the funeral account and other unpaid bills and accounts to us as soon as possible?*

(iii) Inheritance tax

We do our best to tell you as quickly as possible whether or not there is likely to be any inheritance tax (IHT) to pay, and if so, advise on how the tax is to be paid. We shall deal with this when we write to you about obtaining the grant.

It may be helpful to have some very general guidance on IHT. None is payable if the value of the net estate is less than £223,000. Above this amount, IHT is payable at the rate of 40 per cent on the net value of the rest of the estate. There is no tax at all, whatever the value of the estate, on property going to a widow or widower, or to a registered charity. The value of this exempt property is deducted from the value of the whole estate before the tax calculation is done. So gifts to husbands and wives and charities can take an estate out of the tax bracket.

However, if there is likely to be a large amount of IHT to pay, either on the estate now or by the family in the future, we will discuss this with you and, if necessary, the others involved, before the grant is obtained, to consider whether or not action can be taken to reduce the amount payable either now or in the future.

If you have any questions or difficulties at any time, do not hesitate to get in touch with us. In the meantime, I await the bills and accounts and [list other documents] mentioned in para. e(ii) above.

STANDARD INFORMATION: INTRODUCTORY LETTER FOR PERSONAL REPRESENTATIVES

3.10   This is a specimen standard letter for new PR clients.

Dear

THE ESTATE OF THE LATE [Mr/s   ]

Thank you for asking this firm to carry out the administration of [Mr/s   's] estate.

When we [met/spoke on the telephone] [yesterday,] we discussed a number of the steps which have to be taken and I enclose a leaflet* which explains in more detail some of the duties you will be taking on in acting as [Mr/s   's] [executors/administrators]. Please let me know if I can add to this in any way.

(a) Questionnaire

I enclose a questionnaire** listing information I shall need to start work. Simply let me have the information in the way that is easiest for you – this will probably be by making notes on the leaflet and sending it back to me with the papers it mentions. I can photocopy any papers that you send me, and your completed questionnaire, and return these to you, if you wish.

[We may already have much of the information asked for on our files. If so, please indicate this on the form together with the name of the person here to whom I should speak.]

Please let me know if you want any help in connection with the funeral or with making property safe.

(b) [Mr/s   's will]

If you do not have a copy of [Mr/s   's] will, I shall be sending one to you very shortly. If you think there may be a later will, or codicil, please let me know as soon as possible.

(c) [Mr/s   's estate]

We will have to establish the value of what [Mr/s   ] owned when [he/she] died and the amount of money [he/she] owed in outstanding bills. The questionnaire includes suggestions about property [Mr/s   ] may have owned and which may not otherwise immediately come to mind. A similar list of bills which may be due to be paid is also included. Please let me have any relevant documents and papers you trace.

(d) The administration of the estate

It may be helpful if I briefly outline what has to be done before work is completed and the estate can finally be wound up. As the [executors/ administrators] you have the responsibility of administering the estate properly. This means establishing the extent of the estate, paying the debts and distributing the balance. The law requires that this be done with due diligence. It is my job to help you do this [with the assistance of colleagues within the firm]. We shall handle all the following steps on the basis of the information you provide:

- Estimating the value of the estate after all the bills are paid and identifying any problems there may be before the beneficiaries can be given their entitlements.

- Estimating the length of time it will take to deal with everything; we shall tell you how long we expect this to be and, as far as possible, what the cost will be.

- Dealing with any inheritance tax (IHT) due – this has to be paid before we can get the grant of representation from the Probate Registry.

- Sending copies of the grant to banks, building societies and others holding money and property. Some items may need to be sold and, of course, I will discuss this with you. (Larger and more valuable items may have to be professionally valued. Fees for this and other work for the estate will be paid from money in the estate.)

- Collecting and paying estate money into our client account (where it will be subject to the protection of the Law Society's rules regarding solicitors' firms' handling of clients' money). This also helps us to start to prepare the accounts, which will show the assets of the estate and the payments of bills and legacies. I should be able to let you know how matters stand at any particular time, should you wish it.

- Once the bills have been paid, it will be possible to start paying smaller legacies under the will. The final stages of my work involve obtaining confirmation from the Inland Revenue that no more tax is due, finalising the accounts, handing over the remaining entitlements to the beneficiaries and getting their receipts [and setting up the necessary trusts under the [will] [intestacy]].

I hope this outline of what has to be done is helpful. Please contact me if I can be of assistance in any way at any stage. If I am not available, my secretary [   ] or my colleague [   ] would be happy to take a message. Finally, I look forward to receiving the following from you [list the items] mentioned in para(s) [   ].

Yours sincerely

[*The Personal Representative's Guide and **the *Questionnaire for Personal Representative Clients* – both available from the Law Society (see address in Chapter 30) – complement this letter.]

Chapter 4

Estate administration and the Financial Services Act: a review

This review is intended to give a brief outline of the relevance of the Financial Services Act 1986 to wills and probate work and to raise the issues that should be considered. First, terminology and sources are covered, then where to find more information; finally, some of the basic points are outlined.

TERMINOLOGY AND SOURCES

4.1 The Financial Services Act 1986 (FSA) currently enables recognised professional bodies (RPBs) to authorise their members to conduct investment business. In addition, the RPBs make rules relating to the conduct of investment business. All the functions of RPBs are to be transferred to the new Financial Services Authority. It is anticipated that the draft Financial Services and Markets Bill, which will give effect to the new regulatory regime, will come into force in mid-2000. The Law Society will continue to regulate firms of solicitors until then. It is likely that a new definition of investment business will enable many firms to avoid the need for authorisation. Firms that do need authorisation under the new regime will be directly regulated by the FSA as the RPBs will no longer have this role.

The **Solicitors' Investment Business Rules 1995** (SIBR) and the **Solicitors' Practice Rules 1990** (SPR) (which form part of the framework governing solicitors' activities in this field) may be found in the Guide at Annex 27B and Annex 1A respectively.

Solicitors conducting investment business must also comply with the **Money Laundering Regulations 1993** now contained in the Guide at Annex 3B. Guidance on money laundering may be obtained from the Professional Ethics Division (address in Chapter 30). See also Annex 16D of the Guide for the text of the Blue Warning Card on money laundering.

MORE INFORMATION

4.2 Probate work is, generally speaking, the area where most solicitors come into contact with investment business, the FSA and the SIBR. It is, therefore, important that solicitors are aware of the compliance requirements and also the investment business opportunities involved.

If you wish to gain a wider knowledge of this area the following publications would be useful:

- *Solicitors and Financial Services: A Compliance Handbook* by Peter Camp, published by the Law Society;

- *Financial Services: Regulating Investment Business 1995* by Simon Morris, published by Sweet & Maxwell;

- *Rider & Ashe: Financial Services Law 1998,* by Barry Rider and Michael Ashe. Published by Butterworths.

The Professional Ethics Division (address in Chapter 30) offers confidential guidance on both the Practice Rules and the Investment Business Rules, including whether or not authorisation is required.

THE BASICS

4.3 What follows is, necessarily, a brief indication of the relevant aspects and the Guide and the Rules will give more detailed information. See also Chapter 27 of the Guide which gives an excellent overview.

Do I need to be authorised?

4.4 If you are carrying out probate and trust work, you are likely to be caught by the FSA and, if so, will need authorisation. For most solicitors that may be obtained from the Law Society. (For further information see the Guide, paras 27.04–27.21.)

What are 'investments' and what is 'investment business'?

4.5 'Investments' are defined in Part I of Schedule 1 to the FSA. (See the Guide, para. 27.02.) Examples include stocks and shares and life policies. (National Savings products are outside the scope of the FSA.) The activities constituting 'investment business' are defined in

Part II of Schedule 1 to the FSA. (See the Guide, para. 27.03: examples include dealing in investments and managing investments.) The activities of 'sending dematerialised instructions' and 'custody of investments' were added in July 1996 and June 1997 respectively. 'Custody of investments' involves safeguarding *and* administering investments and this is likely to be relevant to firms conducting probate/trust work. Further guidance is available from the Professional Ethics Division.

What do I have to do to comply with the Rules?

4.6   If you have established that you are conducting investment business, because investments are involved together with an investment activity, and you are authorised, you will then need to determine which of the SIBR apply. (If you are not authorised, it is a criminal offence to carry on investment business.) If investments are not involved or an investment activity is not involved, then you will not be conducting investment business and neither the FSA nor the SIBR will be relevant.

What is 'discrete investment business'?

4.7   The SIBR only apply to investment business. The Rules distinguish between 'discrete investment business' (DIB) and other investment business (non-DIB). All the SIBR apply to DIB, but only some rules apply to non-DIB. Essentially, DIB is 'mainstream investment business'. You cannot conduct DIB without a category 2 investment business certificate and to get such a certificate you need to employ a 'qualified person'. (See the Guide, para. 27.05.) You can avoid doing DIB by using a 'permitted third party' (PTP) or the 'incidental' exception. (See the Guide, para. 27.13.) Also, no work carried out by the solicitor *as PR* shall be DIB (SIBR, R10(1)).

Permitted third parties

4.8   Permitted third parties (PTPs) are defined in the SIBR and are, essentially, persons authorised under the FSA, exempted persons and, for overseas investments, overseas professionals – but (in relation to packaged products) they do not include life offices, operators of regulated collective investment schemes and their appointed representatives or members of their marketing group (tied agents). Solicitors Financial Services (SFS), an organisation set up by the Law Society, has created a panel of PTPs made up of the three largest firms of independent financial advisers in the country.

The 'incidental' exception

4.9 If a solicitor is involved only in winding up estates, then investment business work is likely to be 'incidental' to the main activity, which is the administration. The effect of this is that the work will be non-DIB and the requirements for compliance with the SIBR are very few: see Chapter 27 of the Guide, para. 27.13, and the Rules themselves.

Custody of investments

4.10 Solicitors providing custody services, i.e. safeguarding and administering investments, will need to consider Rule 17 of the SIBR. Appendix 8 of the SIBR contains the detailed rules relating to custody but Rule 17(2) makes it clear that solicitors who are personal representatives/trustees are not caught unless they are separately remunerated for their custody services. Further guidance on these issues is available from the Professional Ethics Division.

Trust work

4.11 The incidental exception may, not surprisingly, only be used when it can be said that the investment activity concerned is incidental to the administration of the estate. If the will creates a trust, while the incidental exception is available for the sale of the deceased's investments for inheritance tax, it is unlikely to be available for the purchase of new investments.

For continuing work, therefore, it will usually be necessary to use a permitted third party if DIB is to be avoided. Most of the detailed Rules of SIBR apply only to DIB. In particular, Chapter 6 of the SIBR applies only to DIB. However, it is necessary to check the SIBR in cases of doubt. Guidance may be obtained from the Professional Ethics Division.

Offering advice to beneficiaries

4.12 If solicitors wish to offer investment advice to beneficiaries, the incidental exception is also unlikely to be available. Solicitors will need to consider whether they are conducting DIB and which of the SIBR will apply. Remember that most of the SIBR apply only to DIB.

Investment business opportunities

4.13 If a firm decides to offer investment services to its clients, either by carrying on DIB or by using a PTP, then there are a number of investment business opportunities deriving from probate work. Examples include offering investment advice to beneficiaries and tax planning for beneficiaries.

The relevance of the SPR

4.14 Solicitors who are involved in investment business are not only bound by the SIBR, but also by the Solicitors' Practice Rules (SPR). As with any aspect of a solicitor's practice, the SPR will apply, but of particular relevance to probate work and investment business are Rules 2, 3, 5, 10 and 12. (See the Guide, paras 27.19 onwards.)

The relevance of the Accounts Rules

4.15 Solicitors are also subject to the Solicitors' Accounts Rules 1991 and the Accountant's Report Rules or the Solicitors Accounts Rules 1998. The Solicitors' Accounts Rules 1998 may be implemented in full before 1 May 2000 but all firms must implement the 1998 Rules no later than 1 May 2000. Brief guidance on these is included in Chapter 5.

Chapter 5

The Solicitors' Accounts Rules 1998

THE NEW RULES

5.1 The 1998 Rules were made by the Council of the Law Society with the approval of the Master of the Rolls on 22 July 1998. You must implement them by 1 May 2000 at the latest. Until then you can continue to operate the Solicitors' Accounts Rules 1991, or can opt to implement the 1998 Rules. Once you opt for the 1998 Rules you must implement them in their entirety. You cannot pick and choose.

The 1998 Rules replace the Solicitors' Accounts Rules 1991, the Solicitors' Accounts (Legal Aid Temporary Provision) Rule 1992 and the Accountant's Report Rules 1991. They include explanatory notes which are part of the Rules.

WHY REWRITE THE RULES AT ALL?

5.2 The Rules were rewritten for three main reasons:

- the old Rules had been subject to many piecemeal amendments over the years and as a result were becoming more and more difficult to interpret;

- the Professional Ethics Division of the Law Society received more questions on the old Rules than on any single other subject;

- a number of gaps in the old Rules had been identified.

The aims of the rewrite were as follows:

- to rewrite the Rules in plain English;

- to ensure they made sense and could provide answers to the questions which commonly arose;

- to ensure they provided a cohesive whole contained in a single document;

- to make a number of substantive changes to limit the risks arising from gaps in the old Rules.

SUBSTANTIVE CHANGES TO SOLICITORS' ACCOUNTS RULES 1991

5.3 The substantive changes introduced are set out below.

Extension of rules to liquidators, etc.

5.4 Liquidators, trustees in bankruptcy, Court of Protection receivers and trustees of occupational pension schemes are brought within the Rules to a limited extent (Rule 9).

The reason for this extension of the Rules is to protect the vulnerable against defalcations and to protect the profession from claims on the Indemnity and Compensation Funds.

Provided liquidators, etc. comply with their own statutory rules and regulations, they will be deemed to have complied sufficiently with the Solicitors' Accounts Rules so long as they also comply with the limited record-keeping requirements of Rule 9:

- a central record of bills to be kept;

- any records kept under the statutory rules to be retained for at least six years;

- such records to be kept or registered centrally;

- such records to be available for monitoring and inspection by the Law Society;

- such records to be produced to the reporting accountants to enable them to check compliance.

Joint accounts

5.5 Joint accounts are brought within the Rules to a limited extent (Rule 10).

Again the change is because the Law Society sees a danger of fraud, particularly where an account is held with a lay person who leaves the solicitor to operate the account alone. The Rules in general do not apply but various record-keeping requirements do. These include:

- a central record of bills to be kept;

- statements and passbooks to be retained for at least six years;

- such statements and passbooks to be kept or registered centrally;

- the records to be available for monitoring and inspection by the Law Society;

- the records to be produced to the reporting accountants to enable them to check compliance.

Client's own account

5.6   Solicitors operating a client's own account (for example, under a power of attorney) are brought within the Rules to a limited extent (Rule 11) to protect against fraud.

The Rules in general do not apply but various record-keeping requirements do. These include:

- solicitor to receive and keep statements and passbooks for at least six years;

- such statements and passbooks to be kept or registered centrally;

- the records to be available for monitoring and inspection by the Law Society;

- the records to be produced to the reporting accountants to enable them to check compliance.

Controlled trust money

5.7   The treatment of controlled trust money is made much more similar to the treatment of client money as the present limited regulatory regime leaves controlled trust money open to fraud (Rule 8). A number of changes are introduced:

(a)   You must pay controlled trust money without delay into:

- *either* a separate designated client account reserved for money of that trust;

- *or* a general client account;

although, as under the old Rules, there are circumstances when controlled trust money may be withheld from a client account (Rule 18).

(b) You must keep full records of all dealings with controlled trust money unless you use an outside manager to run the trust on a day-to-day basis. In such a case the manager must keep and retain appropriate accounting records available for inspection by the Society.

(c) Normally you must prepare bank reconciliations at least every five weeks. However, where you keep controlled trust money in a passbook-operated separate designated client account, you need only prepare one for that money every 14 weeks. There is no requirement to check that interest has been credited since the last statement or entry in the passbook.

(d) Trustees are subject to the legal duty not to profit from their trust and must obtain the best reasonably obtainable rate of interest. You have three options in respect of controlled trust money:

- you can place the money in a separate designated client account in which case all interest earned belongs to the trust;

- you can set up a general client account just for controlled trust money. The interest will be credited to the office bank account in the normal way but you must immediately allocate it to each controlled trust;

- you can continue to mix controlled trust money with client money in a general client account **so long as** you are able to comply with your legal duty (Rule 15 note (vi)).

Unpaid professional disbursements

5.8 Money for unpaid professional disbursements can be paid into the office bank account for a limited period (Rule 19(1)(b)) where the money is received in payment of a solicitors' bill, and the disbursement has been incurred.

You can pay money received for unpaid professional disbursements (client money) into your office bank account provided by the end of the second working day following receipt you either pay the disbursement or transfer the sum required for its settlement to your client account.

The advantage of this change is that it simplifies dealing with receipts of costs allowing more to be paid straight into the office bank account and resulting in fewer transfers between client and office bank account.

'Professional' disbursements include the fees of counsel, other lawyers, and other professional or other agents or experts instructed by the solicitor – this will include interpreters, translators, process servers, surveyors and estate agents instructed by the solicitors. It does not include travel agents' charges.

Special rule for legal aid practitioners (Rule 21)

5.9 There are two special dispensations for money received from the Legal Aid Board:

(a) Provided the Board gives instructions in writing, advance payment for work to be carried out may be paid into the office bank account.

(b) A payment for costs may be paid into the office bank account even when mixed with client money for unpaid disbursements provided the disbursements are paid or money representing them transferred to the client bank account within 14 days of receipt.

There is a special rule for payments from a third party.

Where the Board has already paid any costs to a solicitor (or has paid professional disbursements direct) and costs are subsequently settled by a third party, the entire third party payment must be paid into the client bank account.

Any balance belonging to the solicitor must be transferred to the office bank account within 14 days of the solicitor sending a report to the Board containing details of the third party payment. The amount retained in the client bank account must be recorded as held for the Board (either on the individual client's ledger account or on a separate ledger in the Board's name).

It must be kept there until the Board informs the solicitor that it has recouped an equivalent sum from subsequent legal aid payments due to the solicitor. The retained sum must be transferred to an office bank account within 14 days of notification.

Time-limit on transfers

5.10 A standard 14-day time-limit has been introduced on all transfers needing to be made from the client bank account (Rules 19–21).

Under the old Rules there were a variety of different time-limits. There was no time-limit at all under Rule 5 for mixed cheques representing office and client money; legal aid practitioners had a 14-day period to sort out payments from the Board; and there was a seven-day period under R5A where office money had been paid into the client bank account.

There is now a standard 14-day period for all transfers (apart from the two-day period for unpaid professional disbursements under Rule 19(1)(b)).

Changes to the Rules on interest (Rules 24–27)

5.11 As before you must account to a client for all interest earned on separate designated client accounts. You are required by Rule 25(1) to aim for a reasonable rate of interest on such money.

The main changes are in respect of sums in lieu of interest.

Where money is not held in a separate designated client account the general rule is that you **must** account to the client for a sum in lieu of interest. However, there are the following exceptions where there is no need to account:

(a) if the amount calculated is £20 or less;

(b) (i) if the amount held does not exceed the amount and the time for which it is held does not exceed the period set out in the table:

Amount £	Time / (Weeks)
1,000	8
2,000	4
10,000	2
20,000	1

   (ii) if the amount held exceeds £20,000 but is held for one week or less, unless it is fair and reasonable to account having regard to all the circumstances;

(c) on money held for the payment of counsel's fees, once counsel has requested a delay in settlement;

(d) on money held for the Legal Aid Board;

(e)   on money held in the client account as a result of an advance from the solicitor to the client to cover a payment for which the client had insufficient funds;

(f)   if there is an agreement to contract out of the interest provisions of the Rules.

You are still allowed to retain any interest earned on client money held in a general client account over and above the amount you are required to pay out. It is expressly provided in Rule 13 that interest earned in this way is office money.

A client may fail to present a cheque for payment promptly. Note (vii) to Rule 24 states that whether or not it is reasonable to recalculate the amount due will depend on all the circumstances of the case. You can make a reasonable charge for any extra work carried out but only if you are legally entitled to make a charge for such work.

When calculating the amount due to a client in lieu of interest, Rule 25(1) requires you to account for a 'fair' sum. It need not necessarily reflect the highest rate of interest available but it is not acceptable to look only at the lowest rate of interest available. Rule 25(2) provides that the sum must be calculated:

• on the balance(s) held over the whole period for which cleared funds are held;

• at a rate not less than whichever is the higher of:

   • the rate payable on a separate designated client account for the amount(s) held; or

   • the rate payable on the relevant amount(s) if placed on deposit on similar terms by a member of the business community;

   • at the bank or building society where the money is held.

Substantive Changes to Accountant's Report Rules

5.12   The Accountant's Report Rules 1991 (ARR) were amended by the Council of the Law Society in December 1995 with effect from 1 September 1998. The ARR are incorporated into the 1998 Solicitors' Accounts Rules (SAR). Where your practice has not yet adopted the new

Solicitors' Accounts Rules, you will have to comply with the Accountant's Report Rules 1991 as amended.

The changes made in December 1995 stem from the Law Society's attempts to reduce the costs of default. It became apparent from the reports of the then Monitoring Unit and from inspections carried out by the then Solicitors' Complaints Bureau's Investigation Accountants that some reporting accountants were not carrying out their duties effectively and that serious breaches of the Rules and in some cases fraud had not been identified.

The amendments to the Rules require that reporting accountants must have registered auditor status together with membership of one of the accountancy bodies currently listed in the ARR. You will, therefore, have to make sure that any accountants making reports to be delivered on or after 1 September 1998 have the appropriate status. To enable the Law Society to maintain accurate records you must inform the Society of any change in the reporting accountant.

You have to produce a letter of engagement for accountants incorporating the terms set out in the second schedule to the ARR. The letter (and a copy) have to be signed by the solicitor (or a partner or director) and by the accountant. The letter has to be kept for three years and produced to the Law Society on request.

Accountants are also required to report on any substantial departure from the Guidelines for Procedures and Systems for Accounting for client money.

In addition to the requirements for testing already contained in the ARR, reporting accountants as from 1 September 1998 will have to complete and sign a Law Society checklist which the solicitor must keep for three years and produce to the Law Society on request. The checklist is intended to be an assurance to the solicitor and to the Law Society that the work required to be done has indeed been done. It does not impose any additional obligations on accountants.

The SAR include the above rquirements. In addition, a solicitor who has operated a client's own account as signatory must deliver an accountant's report for the accounting period within six months of the end of the period (SAR Rule 35).

The reporting accountant will have to check that records, statements and passbooks are being kept as required by liquidators, Court of Protection receivers, etc. (SAR Rule 9). The reporting accountant will also check the new requirements for joint accounts (Rule 10). There is a useful article on the new Report Rules by Amanda Reade in [1997] *New Law Journal*, 15 August.

AN OUTLINE OF THE SOLICITORS' ACCOUNTS RULES 1998

Who is governed by the Rules?

5.13   The rules apply to solicitors, registered foreign lawyers and recognised bodies. They do not apply to solicitors who are employed by, for example, a local authority or to a solicitor when carrying out the function of a coroner or other judicial office or a sheriff or under sheriff.

As explained above certain record-keeping requirements are extended to liquidators, Court of Protection receivers, etc. Reporting accountants are regulated by Part F of the Rules.

All of the partners in a practice are required to ensure compliance with the Rules by fellow partners and everyone else in the practice. (This duty extends to directors of recognised bodies.) The recent case of *Weston* v. *The Law Society, The Times*, 15 July 1998 is a reminder that solicitors are under a heavy obligation in securing compliance with the Rules. The Court of Appeal confirmed that it was appropriate to strike off a solicitor where no dishonesty was alleged but the partner in question was guilty of breaches through his partners' activities of which he was unaware. Lord Bingham referred to 'the duty of anyone holding anyone else's money to exercise a proper stewardship in relation to it'.

The Law Society's Guidelines – published as Appendix 3 to the Rules – state that compliance with the Rules is the equal responsibility of all partners. Responsibility for day-to-day supervision may be delegated to individual partner(s) but it is not acceptable to delegate total responsibility to a cashier or bookkeeper.

Classification of money (Rule 13)

5.14   All money held or received in the course of a practice falls into one of the following categories.

Client money

5.15 This is money held or received for a client and all other money which is not controlled trust money or office money.

A 'client' is defined by Rule 2 as a person for whom the solicitor acts. However, client money includes money held for non-clients as a bailee, agent, or donee of a power of attorney. It also extends to money held as stakeholder or liquidator.

Client money also includes money received:

- for unpaid professional disbursements – for definition see para. 5.8 above;

- for other unpaid disbursements where the solicitor has not incurred a liability to pay them;

- on account of costs;

- as commission paid in respect of a client unless the solicitor is entitled to retain it.

Controlled trust money

5.16 This is money held or received for a 'controlled trust'. A controlled trust is one where the solicitor is the sole trustee or co-trustee only with one or more of his partners or employees. Note that if the trust is not controlled, for example because there is a lay co-trustee, the money is client money. There is no longer a category of 'trust' money.

Office money

5.17 This is money which belongs to the solicitor or practice. It includes:

- money held or received in connection with running the practice, for example PAYE or VAT on the firm's fees;

- interest on general client accounts;

- money received for profit costs where a bill or written notification of costs has been sent;

- money received to repay the solicitor for disbursements already paid;

- money received for disbursements which are unpaid but for which the solicitor has incurred a liability to pay (e.g. items settled by an account such as Land Registry search fees, taxi fares) – however, unpaid professional disbursements are expressly excluded and money received for them is client money;

- money received for an agreed fee;

- money held in the client account but earmarked for costs and awaiting transfer.

USE OF CLIENT ACCOUNT

5.18 A solicitor who holds or receives client money and/or controlled trust money must keep one or more client accounts.

What is a client account? (Rule 14)

5.19 A client account is an account of the practice kept at a bank or building society in England or Wales. It must include the word 'client' in the title. There are two types of client account:

- a separate designated client account which is a deposit account for a single client or a current or deposit account kept for a single controlled trust;

- a general client account which is any other client account.

What money goes into the client bank account? (Rule 15)

5.20 Rule 15(1) states that you must pay all client money and controlled trust money without delay into the client account. As with the old Rules there are some exceptions, for example when a client instructs you not to pay in money (Rule 16(1)) or where a controlled trustee operating in accordance with his/her powers pays money into a non-client account or retains it as cash.

Rule 15(2) states that no other money may be paid into the client account. Again there are exceptions so, for example, you can use your own money to open or maintain the client account and can advance money to the client where you are holding too little money for a client or controlled trust to fund a payment.

When can money come out of the client account?

5.21 This is governed by Rule 22. The Rules are similar to the old Rules and the situation in which you can withdraw client money and controlled trust money include:

- making payments on behalf of the client or trust;

- paying disbursements on behalf of the client or trust;

- reimbursing yourself for money spent on behalf of the client or trust;

- transferring to another client account.

The money you take out of a general client account must not exceed the total you hold for that client or controlled trust in all the general client accounts.

There is one exception to this which is where you hold money in a separate designated client account for a client or trust. You can withdraw from a general client account in excess of the amount held there for the client or trust provided you make a transfer from the designated client account immediately.

Mixed receipts (Rule 20)

5.22 Where you receive office money mixed with either client or controlled trust money, you either split the cheque or pay the whole amount into the client account.

If you pay it all into the client account you must transfer all office money out of the client account within 14 days.

Special rules for dealing with money received for bills (Rule 19)

5.23 There are four possibilities:

(a) *Identify the type of money received and deal with it appropriately*

- If the money is all office money put it all in the office account.

- If the money is all client money put it all in the client account.

- If the money is a mixture deal with it under Rule 20 – either splitting it or paying it all into the client account.

(b) *Where the money is all office money and/or client money in the form of unpaid professional disbursements for which you have incurred a liability to pay*

This is the new possibility allowed by the 1998 Rules. You can pay the whole amount into the office account but the disbursements must be paid or the required sum transferred to the client account by the end of the second working day following receipt.

(c) *Irrespective of the type of money*

Pay it all into the client bank account and transfer out any office money within 14 days of receipt.

This is only likely to be done where the person dealing with the money is uncertain as to its correct classification. This option allows the money to be banked promptly pending a decision as to how it should be treated.

(d) *Money received from the Legal Aid Board*

As mentioned at para. 5.9, Rule 21 contains special provision for legal aid practitioners.

Transfers between clients (Rule 30(2))

5.24 You are required to obtain the written authority of both clients in the case of private loans between clients. This does not apply to loans made by an institutional lender.

Record-keeping requirements (Rule 32)

5.25 You must keep records to show all dealings with client money, controlled trust money and office money relating to any client or controlled trust matter. The dealings must be recorded on a cash account (or record of inter-client transfers) and on a client ledger account. The current balance for each client must be shown or be readily ascertainable.

The records must show all dealings with client money and controlled trust money. It is, therefore, important to record any change in the person(s) for whom money is held.

74

For example, during or at the end of an administration beneficiaries will become entitled to funds. Normally there will be a cash payment to the beneficiaries which will be recorded as a cash payment from the client account on behalf of the personal representatives. However, the beneficiary may ask you to retain funds for them in the client account. In such a case you must record – on the client ledger accounts and also on the transfer record – that money is no longer held for the personal representatives but is now held for the beneficiary.

Two clients – one ledger account (Rule 32(6))

5.26   To regularise the practice of a solicitor opening one ledger account where he or she is acting for both lender and borrower in a conveyancing matter, Rule 32(6) permits the opening of only one ledger account, provided that the funds belonging to each client are clearly identifiable on the ledger. The permission does not extend to private loans.

Rule 32(6) is expressed to apply to mortgage advances. There is no mention of mortgage redemptions. If a solicitor holds money for a lender after completion of a sale, it will only be necessary to open a separate ledger account for the lender if you have been instructed by the lender to act in the redemption.

Regular bank reconciliations (Rule 32(7))

5.27   You are required to prepare bank reconciliations for all general and designated accounts containing client and controlled trust money at least every five weeks (in effect monthly). This is extended to at least every 14 weeks for controlled trust money held in passbook-operated separate designated client accounts.

Retention of paid cheques and bank statements (Rule 32(10))

5.28   Paid cheques must be retained for two years. You need not arrange for your bank to return paid cheques, if you arrange in writing that the bank keep paid cheques for two years. Other authorities for withdrawals from the client account must also be kept for two years.

Bank statements and all other records must be kept for six years (Rule 32(9)). These requirements extend not just to client accounts but to others such as non-client accounts where controlled trust money is held.

Authority for withdrawals from client account (Rule 23)

5.29   A withdrawal of funds from client account may be made without the bank which actually makes the transfer having to hold a written authority, for example, it can be done by telephone. However, before the transfer is made there must be in existence a specific authority in respect of the particular withdrawal, signed by one of the persons specified in Rule 23(1). Where this is done it is important that there are appropriate safeguards such as passwords. Note that in the case of a cheque, the signature on the cheque is a sufficient authority *but not if the cheque is blank*.

Who may authorise withdrawals from client account? (Rule 23)

5.30   Withdrawals from client account may be authorised by:

- a solicitor with a current practising certificate;

- a three-year FILEX employed by a solicitor;

- a licensed conveyancer employed by a solicitor where the office deals solely with conveyancing;

- a registered foreign lawyer who is a partner or director of the practice.

HOW DO THE 1998 RULES AFFECT PROBATE WORK?

5.31   When you are doing trust and/or probate work you will handle client money and controlled trust money. You will have to pay money into the appropriate bank accounts and follow the rules as to withdrawals. In particular, you will have to classify money correctly as client, controlled trust or office. The rules relating to client money and controlled trust money are much more similar than they used to be but there are still some differences.

Client money or controlled trust money?

5.32   Remember that this is the only choice. There is no longer a category of 'trust' money. Controlled trusts are trusts where a solicitor is the sole trustee or is a trustee with a partner or employee. As the notes to the Rules point out, this definition, which is statutory, gives rise to some anomalies. For example, an assistant solicitor who is a sole trustee is a controlled trustee; two assistant solicitors who are the only co-trustees are not; an assistant and a partner are controlled trustees. Where a trust is not controlled any money received for the trust is client money.

Which bank account?

5.33 Client money can go into the general client account or a separate designated client account. It can also be retained in cash or paid into a non-client account if the client so instructs.

Controlled trust money can go into the general client account or a separate designated client account which can be a current or deposit account. It can also be paid into a non-client account if the trustees' powers permit it or be retained in cash in the performance of the trustees' duties.

Reconciliation

5.34 Where money is paid into a general client account it will be subject to the requirement for reconciliations at least every five weeks.

The requirement will apply to controlled trust money in separate designated client accounts unless the account is passbook-operated in which case the requirement is at least every 14 weeks. Such a reconciliation is necessary even where the controlled trust money is held in a non-client account under Rule 18.

Records

5.35 The record-keeping requirements for controlled trust money have been extended to reflect more closely the record-keeping requirements for client money. However, where controlled trustees instruct an outside manager to run the business or property portfolio of an estate or trust, the manager may maintain, and must then produce, appropriate records for inspection by the Law Society.

Remember that if you are acting as a Court of Protection receiver, operating a joint account or operating the client's own account, you will be required to keep records and have them checked by the reporting accountant.

Interest

5.36 Remember that, if you pay controlled trust money into the general client account, you must be careful not to profit from your trust as outlined in para. 5.11 above.

In addition there are problems for solicitors in calculating how much interest is due to clients. You may have completed the administration and sent cheques to beneficiaries. If the beneficiaries fail to cash those cheques, you are likely to be under an obligation to pay the client interest unless the amount falls into one of the exceptions set out in Rule 24(3). The notes to the Rule say that whether or not a solicitor has to recalculate interest will depend on the circumstances of the case.

PART TWO

Probate, Wills and the Law

This Part includes guidance on certain legal aspects of probate work, and ends with a brief outline of the basics of succession law. The Handbook is not intended to be a legal textbook, however, and the Booklist (Chapter 29) includes relevant works.

Chapter 6

Liability for a client's fraud

By Steven Fennell, Solicitor, Dibb Lupton Alsop, Sheffield

This is a specially revised version of an article which originally appeared in the journal *Professional Negligence*. We are most grateful to Steven Fennell for revising the article, and to Tolley Publishing, for permission to reprint it. Because the law has grown increasingly complicated in recent years, the revision of this article considers only the position of solicitors (the original, published at [1991] *Professional Negligence* 151, took a wider approach).

INTRODUCTION

6.1 You may, in good faith, assist a client in a financial transaction which you imagine at the time to be perfectly proper, but which turns out to involve a fraud on a third party. You will then want answers to two questions – can you:

- be held liable in any way to the injured third party? and

- disclose details of the client's transaction to the third party once you discover (or more likely, suspect) the client's wrongdoing?

This chapter gives basic guidance on both of these issues:

- paras. 6.2–6.15 deal with the manner in which a professional may become liable for a client's fraud;

- paras. 6.17–6.19 deal with the problems of privilege and confidentiality addressed by the Court of Appeal in *Finers* v. *Miro* [1991] 1 All E.R. 182;

- paras. 6.20–6.23 suggest what action solicitors should take;

- para. 6.24 summarises the points made.

The Extent of Liability for a Client's Fraud

How liability can arise

6.2 The facts of *Agip (Africa) Ltd* v. *Jackson* [1991] Ch. 547, C.A., illustrate the sort of situations in which liability (in that case, for knowing assistance in a breach of trust: see para. 6.12) may be incurred.

The plaintiff company, Agip, was engaged in oil exploration in North Africa. Over a period of many years its chief accountant, a Mr Zdiri, had been defrauding it of substantial sums of money by substituting the names of dummy companies in the United Kingdom for the names of the rightful payees on the company's payment orders. The money was paid through Agip's bank account in Tunisia to the defendant accountants in the Isle of Man through a series of electronic transfers via New York and London. The defendant accountants set up the dummy companies and acted as directors, received the payments and passed them on, and finally put the companies into liquidation. The defendants did not take instructions directly from Mr Zdiri, and they did not appear to have known the precise nature of the fraud; rather they took instructions from a French lawyer who was acting as an intermediary.

When the fraud came to light, Agip sued the accountants over a payment of half a million dollars which had passed through one of the dummy companies. (By this point, only the accountants had enough money to satisfy a judgement in the plaintiff company's favour.) The accountants tried to excuse themselves by saying that they thought that they were merely involved in a scheme to circumvent Tunisian exchange controls.

The Court of Appeal held that the accountants were not liable at common law for money had and received, and neither were they liable in equity for knowing receipt and dealing, but that they were liable as constructive trustees for knowing assistance in a breach of trust. It is all too easy to imagine solicitors becoming involved by a client in a similar transaction.

6.3 Solicitors may incur liability for a client's fraud in the following ways.

For receiving the proceeds of the fraud – through:

(i) **unjust enrichment** and the common law of restitution (see para. 6.4), or

(ii) the tort of **conversion** (see para. 6.6); or

(iii) **a proprietary constructive trust** in equity (see para. 6.7).

For fault in assisting in the design – through:

(i)   personal liability under a **constructive trust** imposed for breach of trust, on the basis of:

    (a) *knowing receipt and dealing* (see para. 6.9); or

    (b) *dishonest assistance* (see para. 6.12);

(ii) breach of **contract** (see para. 6.14); or

(iii) the tort of **negligence** (see para. 6.14).

Each of these will be examined in turn.

A. Liability for receiving the proceeds of fraud

(i) Liability for unjust enrichment

6.4 The case of *Lipkin Gorman* v. *Karpnale* [1991] A.C. 548 shows how liability for unjust enrichment may be incurred. In that case, the House of Lords held that the doctrine of unjust enrichment is now a part of English law, having developed from the old action for the money had and received.

There are four tests for liability for unjust enrichment:

- the defendant must be enriched;

- the enrichment must be at the plaintiff's expense;

- it must be unjust, by which one means that there is a factor, such as a mistake of fact or duress, which renders the enrichment reversible, not simply that it is unfair; and

- there must be no defence.

Liability is strict: there is no need to show any degree of fault on the part of the defendant.

However, the application of these four tests to problem situations will normally lead to solicitors avoiding liability to make restitution.

6.5   Solicitors who are inadvertently involved in a dishonest transaction where unjust enrichment is an issue may receive their fees from the misappropriated funds, but in *Lipkin Gorman* the House of Lords recognised that bona fide purchase will be a defence to an action for restitution. Thus, provided that solicitors act in good faith, their services will amount to good consideration for the receipt of the fees, and they will not even be liable to return any fees received for themselves. (Liability to account for fees is considered again in para. 6.10 in the discussion on personal liability under a constructive trust.)

(ii) Liability for conversion

6.6   Solicitors must take far more care if they handle chattels on behalf of a client. The tort of conversion covers any dealings with a chattel inconsistent with the rights of the person entitled to immediate possession. The danger for solicitors is not that they will find themselves handling stolen goods, but that they may deal with stolen bills of exchange and other negotiable instruments, particularly cheques and banker's drafts. If a solicitor deals with a stolen cheque or banker's draft, he or she will be strictly liable for the face value of the instrument if there is anyone entitled to immediate possession *(Morrison* v. *London County and Westminster Bank* [1914] 3 K.B. 356; *International Factors Ltd* v. *Rodriguez* [1979] Q.B. 315; in *Lipkin Gorman* the House of Lords considered the problem of who is entitled to immediate possession). There is no defence of change of position to an action for conversion.

A detailed account of the complexities of the law relating to bills of exchange and the tort of conversion is not necessary here. While the Bills of Exchange Act 1882 provides defences in certain circumstances for those who have acted in good faith and given value, it is enough to warn solicitors that they should not handle endorsed cheques and banker's drafts from clients without being absolutely sure that the client had good title. Otherwise they could be liable for conversion.

(iii) Liability under a proprietary constructive trust

6.7   Liability can arise under this head where the defendants, other than a bona fide purchaser for a value without notice, are still in possession of all or part of the misappropriated funds. They will be liable to return what they still possess. The plaintiff's property must still be traced to the defendants, but the equitable tracing rules are more flexible than those of the common law, and can follow money through mixing with other funds provided that the relevant accounts have not been overdrawn *(Bishopsgate Investment Management Ltd* v. *Homar* [1995] 1 All E.R.

347). Thus in *Agip* the whole of the plaintiff's money could be traced in equity to the defendants, and it was not disputed that they were liable to return the relatively small amount of money which they still held.

The different sources of liability

6.8 Before considering the second way in which liability can arise (through 'fault' in assisting in the design), it is important to note that *liability under a proprietary constructive trust* must be distinguished from *personal liability as a constructive trustee* (see below). In a case of personal liability, the defendants are liable, not because they hold something which belongs in equity to the plaintiffs, but because they were wrongfully involved in a breach of trust. Consequently, the defendants will be liable for the total foreseeable loss suffered by the plaintiff as a result of the breach of trust in which they assisted, or the total amount knowingly received by them. This will be subject to an allowance for anything subsequently recovered. The plaintiff will not be able to claim anything in respect of losses which were not caused by the breach of trust in which the defendants assisted or as a result of which they received funds (*Target Holdings Ltd* v. *Redferns* [1995] 3 All E.R. 735).

B. Liability for 'fault' in assisting in the design

(i) Personal liability under a constructive trust

6.9 **Personal liability as a constructive trustee** arises in two ways – from:

(a) *knowing receipt and dealing*; and

(b) *dishonest assistance*.

(a) Liability for knowing receipt and dealing

To be liable for knowing receipt and dealing, the defendants must receive or apply the money for their own benefit. Consequently, in *Agip (Africa) Ltd* v. *Jackson* [1990] Ch. 265 Millett J. held that the defendant accountants could not be held liable under this head, and no appeal was made on this point. In most situations in which a solicitor handles trust property, the defence of 'ministerial receipt' will apply.

6.10 As in the case of liability at law for unjust enrichment (see para. 6.5), it seems that solicitors will not risk being held liable as constructive trustees in respect of fees paid out of misdirected funds, provided that they have acted honestly and in good faith, because the fees will be regarded as consideration for work done. The solicitor is in the position of a bona fide purchaser.

There has been a prolonged period of judicial uncertainty over the test for liability as a constructive trustee for receipt of misdirected funds. The courts have, on different occasions, favoured tests based on strict liability, constructive notice and dishonesty. However, in the four most recent cases:

- *Polly Peck International Ltd* v. *Nadir (No.2)* [1992] 4 All E.R. 769;

- *Polly Peck International Ltd* v. *Nadir (No.3), The Times*, 22 March 1993;

- *Eagle Trust plc* v. *SBC Securities Ltd* [1992] 4 All E.R. 488; and

- *Cowan de Groot Properties Ltd* v. *Eagle Trust plc* [1992] 4 All E.R. 700

the courts have favoured a test based on dishonesty or 'commercially unacceptable conduct' which takes account of the nature of the transaction and the individual's role in it. This follows the approach adopted in the earlier case of *Carl Zeiss Stiftung* v. *Herbert Smith and Co. (No.2)* [1969] 2 Ch. 276, one of the few cases to deal specifically with the issue of solicitors' fees. In that case the firm in question was paid for defending a claim that its corporate client held all its property on trust for a third party. The court held that as the firm had acted honestly and provided consideration for its fees, it could not be liable for knowingly receiving trust property. This outcome was approved (obiter) by the Privy Council in *Royal Brunei Airlines* v. *Tan* [1995] 2 A.C. 378, where Lord Nicholls characterised the situation as one of genuine doubt where the firm was not dishonest in accepting remuneration from one of two genuine claimants to the same fund.

While there is still some element of doubt, it appears that the courts are increasingly accepting the view that dishonesty is the appropriate test for liability. On this view, if the recipients of the misdirected funds are honest, they will only be liable to the injured party if they are found not to be bona fida purchasers, i.e. where the work done does not for some reason amount in law to good consideration.

6.11 Thus, if the recent cases are followed, solicitors who inadvertently become involved in fraudulent transactions will be able to keep their fees, even if the fees are the proceeds of a breach of trust, provided that they acted honestly. They will be regarded as bona fida purchasers. Moreover, even if a claim to the allegedly misdirected funds is made by the third party, an application to the court by the solicitors holding the funds may well result in permission being given for their legal fees to be paid from them. This happened in *Finers* v. *Miro* [1991] 1 All E.R. 182, where a firm of solicitors became aware that it was more likely than not that the money that they were holding on trust for their client had been acquired by fraud. While most of the case concerned the problem of confidentiality, the Court of Appeal did discuss the administration of the fund by the solicitors until its ownership could be established, and payment of legal fees was authorised.

(b) Dishonest assistance

6.12 Dishonest assistance in a breach of trust is the other form of personal liability in equity. Again, there was a long history of judicial uncertainty as to the appropriate test for liability for what was formerly referred to as 'knowing assistance', but the matter has now been definitively resolved by the Privy Council in *Royal Brunei Airlines* v. *Tan* [1995] A.C. 378. It is now clear that a person who dishonestly assists in any breach of trust will be liable to the injured party, even if the trustees themselves were honest. Lord Nicholls gave the example of trustees who innocently wish to deal with the trust funds in their care in such a way as to amount to a breach of trust, who instruct a solicitor to act for them. If the solicitor acts in the knowledge that a breach of trust is being committed, he or she will be liable to the beneficiaries.

The defendant must, of course, 'assist' in the breach of trust. A person who is peripherally involved in a transaction and who does not further the breach of trust in any way will not incur liability, even if he or she was aware of the breach (*Brinks Ltd* v. *Abu-Saleh and Others (No.3)* (1996) 60 Conv. 447).

6.13 Three further points need to be clarified in relation to the notion of dishonesty.

• *The meaning of the word itself*

The Privy Council took the view that the technical definitions of dishonesty which apply in the criminal law should not be used for civil claims. Instead, 'dishonesty' is defined as 'simply not acting as an honest person would in the circumstances', or 'conscious impropriety'. This will normally be a straightforward test. Difficulties arise when the defendant has taken a risk, or acted where he or she knows that there is an element of doubt, but again, a commonsense view is taken: 'The individual is expected to attain the standard which would be observed by an honest person placed in those circumstances. It is impossible to be more specific' ([1995] 2 A.C. 378, 390, *per* Lord Nicholls). Honest people may, for example, refuse to act, ask more questions, take advice or even advise of the risks and continue to act: it is all a question of fact.

However, the Privy Council went on to approve the case of *Cowan de Groot Properties* v. *Eagle Trust plc* [1992] 4 All E.R. 488, in which the High Court had adopted the test of 'commercially unacceptable conduct' in a corporate transaction. This emphasis on looking at the context of the transaction and the relationship of the parties means that the law continues to accept that some relationships, including those of solicitor and client, are based first and foremost on trust and confidence. There is no duty on solicitors to go to elaborate lengths to check the veracity of the client's account of the transaction: they need only ask questions when doubts start to arise as to the client's honesty.

- *The defendants will be dishonest even if they do not know the true nature of the fraud, provided that they know that something illegal is being planned.*

The cases suggest that the defendant's conduct must be examined to determine whether, in all the circumstances, a reasonable person would regard it as honest in the normal sense of the word. The conduct in question need not be a crime, although most forms of dishonesty will be criminal offences. The judge would have to take into account the prevailing attitude to the conduct in question among people doing the defendant's job. For example, one would have to ask whether or not a reasonable solicitor would have carried out the client's instructions without question, or would have asked the client to clarify the purpose of the transaction.

- *Duty to ask questions when suspicions are aroused*

It will be rare for dishonest clients to inform their solicitors of the nature of their plans. It is much more common for such clients to try to make up a more or less plausible excuse for what they want to do. In such a case, it will be no defence for a solicitor who does not question a dubious scheme to say that, had the solicitor asked questions, the client would have produced a satisfactory answer.

As Lord Nicholls explained in *Royal Brunei Airlines* v. *Tan,* an honest person does not deliberately close his eyes and ears, or deliberately not ask questions, lest he learn something he would rather not know, and then proceed regardless. The test of what an honest person would have done is largely a matter of common sense, depending to a large extent upon the nature and importance of the transaction and the individual's role within it.

(ii) Breach of contractual duties to take reasonable care and negligence

6.14   In *Royal Brunei Airlines* v. *Tan* [1995] 2 A.C. 378 Lord Nicholls considered the issue of professionals who act for trustees, who may owe duties of care in contract and tort. His Lordship commented that, in general, professionals will owe a contractual obligation to the trustees to perform their services properly, and that the rights flowing from this obligation form part of the trust property. Consequently, if the professional fails to comply with his duty to take reasonable care, the trustees can enforce that obligation for the benefit of the beneficiaries. To return to an example given above, if a solicitor fails to advise an honest but inexperienced trustee that his intended conduct will amount to a breach of trust, the solicitor will be liable to the trustee for any claim which the beneficiaries may make against him.

In the *Royal Brunei Airlines* case the Privy Council was clearly reluctant to create the possibility of indeterminate liability in negligence for third parties dealing with fiduciaries. Lord Nicholls commented that the standard of liability should normally be dishonesty: thus a solicitor acting for a company being defrauded by one of its executives will continue to owe a duty to that company to voice any concerns he may have. However, as beneficiaries cannot reasonably expect that all the world dealing with fiduciaries should owe them a duty of care to ensure that those fiduciaries are not behaving dishonestly, it will only be in extreme cases that a duty of care in negligence will give rise to liability on the part of an honest but careless third party.

Discharging duty of care

6.15   Even if a duty of care does exist, it will be easily discharged. The relationship of solicitor and client must be one of trust, and so the solicitor need only question his or her involvement in a transaction if a reasonable person in his or her position would have had suspicions. Asking the client for an explanation will often discharge the duty, provided that the client's explanation would satisfy a reasonable person. Solicitors should not feel under any compulsion to look for ulterior motives behind their clients' dealings.

FRAUD AND PRIVILEGE AND CONFIDENTIALITY

Fraud and confidentiality

6.16 A solicitor who fears that he or she may inadvertently have become involved in a fraudulent transaction is placed in a difficult position with respect to client confidentiality. If the solicitor has not been dishonest, there should be no liability in respect of past acts (assuming, of course, that the approach in the most recent cases continues to be followed). However, the solicitor may incur liability by continuing to act, and his or her assistance in the past may allow the client to continue to defraud innocent persons.

The leading case on the options available to an inadvertent participant in fraud is the decision of the Court of Appeal in *Finers* v. *Miro* [1991] 1 All E.R. 182. The facts were straightforward. The solicitors in question assisted the client to set up a complicated series of trusts so that the ownership of his considerable assets would be hard to detect. They honestly believed that the client wished to conceal his property because he feared that it would be nationalised by foreign states. They then discovered a report of a committee of the United States House of Representatives which contained detailed evidence to the effect that the client had defrauded a now-insolvent American insurance company of large sums of money. The solicitors believed that the client's assets may have been the proceeds of the alleged fraud. The result of the complex series of trusts and companies set up to conceal the ownership of the assets was that the solicitors were in effect holding the client's assets on a bare trust for him.

The solicitors applied to the court under R.S.C. Order 85 for directions for dealing with the trust fund. In particular, they wanted to know whether or not they would be free to notify the liquidator of the American company of the application. The Court of Appeal held that they were free to notify the liquidator of the fact that they held large sums on trust for the client.

The Court of Appeal's approach

6.17 The starting point for the Court of Appeal was that communications between a solicitor and client for the purpose of furthering the client's fraudulent transaction are not confidential. Committing a fraud is not part of the solicitor–client relationship and so the professional duties do not arise. They are regarded as never having arisen if solicitors discover in the course of acting that clients have been using them to further a fraud. Solicitors can therefore disclose evidence of a fraud in such a case without the client's consent. Fraud for this purpose has been held to cover all forms of dishonesty, provided that the conduct in question amounts to real dishonesty and not merely disreputable conduct or a failure to maintain good ethical standards (*Gamlen Chemical Co.* v. *Rochem* (1977) unreported, C.A. transcript, *per* Goff L.J. followed in *Finers* v. *Miro*). The Court of Appeal then followed the decision of the House of Lords in *O'Rourke* v. *Darbishire* [1920] A.C. 581, which held that privilege and confidentiality are not applicable where the client consults a solicitor in order to learn how to plan, execute or stifle a fraud. Therefore, disclosure is permitted when the fraud has already been committed and the solicitor has been unwittingly used by the client.

Limits on disclosure

6.18   It is important to note the limits on this right to disclose information which the client would want kept secret. The information is only free from confidentiality when the solicitor has been consulted with a view to his or her advice being used to commit or conceal a fraud. If the client informs the solicitor that the fraud is already complete, and then requires advice which does not further the fraud, disclosure will not be acceptable: the solicitor will be in breach of both the law and the rules of professional conduct if details are disclosed without a court order.

Privilege and confidentiality

6.19   The position of solicitors is complicated by the fact that information may be privileged as well as confidential. The two concepts are distinct: privilege is much narrower than confidentiality, as it only relates to the inadmissibility of solicitor–client proceedings as evidence in litigation. *O'Rourke* v. *Darbishire* is authority that as fraud is outside the solicitor–client relationship, information relating to the solicitor's furtherance of a fraud is not privileged.

It will be rare for solicitors to acquire conclusive proof that their services have been used in a dishonest manner. It is more likely that they will merely have strong suspicions, which the client is unable to allay. This is what happened in *Finers* v. *Miro*. The Court of Appeal held that disclosure to the liquidator was justified because, on the evidence available, there was proof on the balance of probabilities that the alleged fraud had been committed.

ACTION BY SOLICITORS INVOLVED BY CLIENTS IN DISHONEST TRANSACTIONS

6.20 Having outlined the basic legal position relating to fraud and confidentiality, the next issue is the question of the appropriate course of action for any solicitor who fears that a client has been using his or her services to defraud an innocent third party.

Professional rules

6.21 Starting with the rules of professional conduct, the guidance given in *The Guide to the Professional Conduct of Solicitors 1996* is brief. It is contained in the first paragraph of the commentary to Principle 16.02 which states that:

> 'The duty of confidentiality does not apply to information acquired by a solicitor where he or she is being used by the client to facilitate the commission of a crime or fraud, because that is not within the scope of a professional retainer. If the solicitor becomes suspicious about a client's activities the solicitor should normally assess the situation in the light of the client's explanations and the solicitor's professional judgement.'

In a borderline case, where the solicitor is, for example, not clear whether or not he accepts the client's account of the matter, the solicitor would be well advised to contact the Professional Ethics Division of the Law Society (address in Chapter 30). This would be treated in confidence.

Legal problems

6.22 The recommended approach to the legal problems of inadvertent involvement in fraud is as follows. If the solicitor has been honest throughout the transaction, he or she will only be liable for the client's fraudulent acts which have already been committed if the links between the client and the injured party are so close that the solicitor is found to have a duty of care in tort. If suspicions arise, the solicitor can avoid liability for dishonesty simply by refusing to act further.

Disclosure of the past fraud will not protect the solicitor from liability in equity but, if you have strong prima facie evidence, it may be in the public interest. In difficult cases, the advice of the Law Society and the Solicitors Indemnity Fund Ltd (SIF) may be sought, although neither can give legal advice, which would have to be obtained from specialist solicitors and/or counsel. The approach of the Court of Appeal in *Finers* v. *Miro* suggests that disclosure will be proper where the solicitor believes that, on the balance of probabilities, his or her services were used improperly. Disclosure will never be appropriate in such a case before the client has been asked for an explanation of the apparent dishonesty.

If the solicitor has been negligent, and there is a possibility that disclosure will allow the injured party to minimise his loss, *Finers* v. *Miro* suggests that disclosure will still only be acceptable if there is prima facia proof of fraud on the balance of probabilities. This illustrates the need to satisfy the relatively low standard of reasonable care in such a case.

The proceeds of fraud

6.23   The greatest problem arises when the solicitor cannot simply refuse to continue to act because he or she is in fact holding some of the proceeds of fraud. The solution, again when the client has failed to satisfy the solicitor of the honesty of the transaction, is to apply to the court under R.S.C. Order 85 for directions on how to apply the funds held on trust. This happened in *Finers* v. *Miro,* where the Court of Appeal held that the court has jurisdiction to give directions for the administration of a bare trust, even where the apparent beneficiary opposes the application and asks for the funds to be paid direct to him or her. An application under Order 85 would therefore be essential if the client were to tell a solicitor with suspicions to pass the money on to someone else.

SUMMARY

6.24   As this area of law is complicated, a brief summary of the general principles may be useful:

- The starting position is that, obviously, a solicitor will be liable if he or she *dishonestly receives* any money (including fees) for his or her own benefit.

- A solicitor may owe a duty of care to a person defrauded by his or her client, but such a duty is likely to arise only when there are very close links between the solicitor, client and third party.

- If a solicitor dishonestly assists in a fraudulent transaction, he or she is likely to be liable for the full extent of the injured party's loss in all cases.

- Solicitors who have doubts as to the honesty of a client's transactions should always ask the client for an explanation. If the explanation is satisfactory, they can continue to act: the law does not expect solicitors to distrust their clients and furtively look for evidence of misconduct; neither does it expect solicitors to refuse to act unless they are aware of every last detail of the transaction, provided that the transaction is prima facie lawful. (In this context, see the extensive advice on money laundering issued by the Law Society and the warning cards on property fraud and money laundering included in the Guide as Annex 25G and 16D.)

- If, however, you are asked to handle or accept an endorsed cheque or bank's draft, remember that, if it has been forged or stolen, the rightful owner could have a claim against you for damages.

- Solicitors who have prima facie proof that they have been inadvertently involved in the commission of a fraud can disclose this information to the injured party, and can apply to the court under R.S.C. Order 85 for directions on how to handle any money still held for the client. Fraud covers all forms of dishonesty, but not simply disreputable conduct or unethical behaviour.

- If, however, the solicitor only has suspicions which do not amount to prima facie evidence, it would be wrong to disclose the information but, as a matter of professional conduct (and self-interest) he or she should consider whether it would be appropriate to refuse to act further. In all but the most obvious cases of fraud, the solicitor would be wise to consult the Law Society and SIF (addresses in Chapter 30) before doing anything. *The Guide to the Professional Conduct of Solicitors 1996* gives advice about termination of retainers at Principle 12.17.

- Finally, it must be emphasised that the law in this area is subject to rapid change. This chapter sets out the general principles as they were understood in January 1998. Solicitors would be wise to ensure that they keep their knowledge up to date.

POSTSCRIPT FROM THE LAW SOCIETY

6.25   The Professional Ethics Division and the Policy Directorate add:

> 'The position is particularly difficult if solicitors are suspicious that a client is or may be about to do something fraudulent. Having asked for an explanation, keep full attendance notes throughout detailing your thinking processes and the actions you take and why. One of the risks in this area is being regarded as having been wilfully blind to a client's dishonesty. It is a small step from this to it being more credible that the solicitor was involved in the fraud than that he or she could have failed to recognise it. Keeping full attendance notes is evidence of your non-involvement in any fraud; and although in the end you may be regarded as having taken a wrong decision, a clear record of your thinking will show that you considered the issues and acted in good faith. A useful article on trustees' liability, by Robert Ham Q.C., appeared in [1995] *Trust Law International* Vol.9, No.1.'

6.26   Money laundering may also be an issue in these cases. The Law Society's warning card on it is included in the *Guide to the Professional Conduct of Solicitors 1996* at Annex 16D and more guidance on the Money Laundering Regulations, which have major implications for solicitors, can be found in the Guide.

Chapter 7

Appointing guardians of children

By Gillian E. Cockburn of Cockburns, Guildford and David Hodson of The Family Consortium, London.

This is a revised version of an article which first appeared in the *Gazette*. We are most grateful to the authors for updating it.

INTRODUCTION

7.1 A guardian of a child is someone who is appointed to take over responsibility for a child in the event of the death of the child's parent or other carer. The appointment is not only necessary if a child has property or money but also to provide day-to-day care for the child, as the guardian will have the right to decide on the child's upbringing, health care, religion and education. It is very important to ensure that the right person or persons are appointed as guardians in accordance with the law.

The law on the appointment of guardians changed radically as a result of the Children Act 1989 (the Act) which came into effect from 14 October 1991. It is essential for the will drafter and probate practitioner to understand the changes introduced by the Act and in particular the concepts of parental responsibility and residence orders. In some cases it may also be important to liaise with a family law practitioner to find out what court orders have been made concerning a child which may in turn affect the appointment of guardians under the will.

WHO MAY APPOINT A GUARDIAN?

7.2 This is governed by section 5 of the Act, which provides that guardians may be appointed by:

(a) a parent with parental responsibility for the child (section 5(3)); or

(b) an existing guardian of the child (section 5(4)); or

(c)   a court in family proceedings (section 5(1) and (2)).

Except as set out below, the appointment in (a) and (b) becomes effective when the person who makes the appointment dies. At that time the guardian will acquire parental responsibility for the child.

Parental responsibility

7.3   The Act defines parental responsibility for a child as all the rights, duties, powers, responsibilities and authority which by law a parent of a child has in relation to that child and his or her property (section 3(1)).

Who has parental responsibility?

7.4   If the child is legitimate (or has been legitimated, or is adopted), the parents (or adopting parents) will each have parental responsibility (section 2(1) and (3)) and both may appoint guardians for the child in the event of their respective deaths (section 5(3)).

If:

- the parents of a child were not married to each other at the time of the birth; and

- the child has not been legitimated by the parents' later marriage or adopted,

the mother alone has parental responsibility for that child (section 2(2) and (3)). The father does not have automatic parental responsibility and so will not be able to appoint a guardian of the child on his death. However, the father may *acquire* parental responsibility (and therefore be able to appoint a guardian) in the following ways:

- through a court order granting him parental responsibility (section 4(1)(a)); or

- by entering into a parental responsibility agreement with the child's mother (section 4(1)(b)); or

- by being appointed, either by the mother or by the court, to assume parental responsibility after the mother's death.

The agreement must be in accordance with the Parental Responsibility Agreement Regulations 1991 (S.I. 1991 no. 1478, reg. 2) as amended by the Parental Responsibility Agreement (Amendment) Regulations 1994

(S.I. 1994 no. 3157). The agreement must contain the names of the child's parents and of the child to whom the agreement is to relate, and must contain the signature of both parents and be witnessed. Both parents must have their signature witnessed at court by a J.P. or court official and provide evidence of their identity (including a photograph and signature). The mother must also provide the child's full birth certificate. The agreement will only take effect once it has been filed at the Principal Registry of the Family Division in London. The agreement may be brought to an end only by a court order (section 4(3)). It should be noted that a parental responsibility agreement can only be made with an unmarried father and not with any other family member.

Who can be a guardian?

7.5 Subject to para. 7.6, a parent with parental responsibility for a child, or a properly appointed guardian, may appoint another individual to act as guardian for the child on his or her death (section 5(3) and (4)). Although the Act refers to an individual in the singular, more than one individual may be appointed in accordance with the Interpretation Act 1978, s.6(c). In addition, the Act also contemplates the subsequent appointment of further guardians (section 6(1)). However the term 'individual' would not include a trust corporation, local authority or other non-individual.

What is a residence order?

7.6 A residence order is a court order settling the arrangements to be made about the person with whom a child is to live (section 8(1)). It also affects the testamentary appointment of guardians and so needs to be considered by the will drafter.

A residence order can be made jointly in favour of both parents, or a parent and another carer of the child (section 11(4)). It may be made in the context of divorce, judicial separation, or nullity proceedings. It can be made in free-standing applications under the Act, for example to unmarried parents, grandparents or others who are given leave of the court to apply (section 10). It is not an automatic replacement of the care and control orders made under the pre-Children Act law; in many respects it is wider and more flexible. Also, unlike parental responsibility which is bestowed by law on all parents except as set out in para. 7.4 above, residence orders can only be granted by a court.

However, residence orders are not automatically granted to, say, the parent post-divorce who has the child primarily living with him or her.

By section 1(5), the court shall not make any order in respect of the arrangements for a child unless it considers that doing so would be better for the child than making no order at all. In practice, many family law courts are not making residence orders and other child orders on divorce if the arrangements between the parents for the child are working well. Will drafters should therefore enquire of clients whether there is an existing residence order and not presume that there is one simply because a child is living with a particular parent following a divorce or other family law proceedings.

THE APPOINTMENT OF A GUARDIAN

7.7 If, on the death of the appointor (even if the parents are separated or divorced):

- there is a surviving parent with parental responsibility; and

- the deceased did not have a residence order in his favour,

the appointment of the guardian *does not take effect until the death of the surviving parent* (section 5(8)). Then effective appointments by both parents will take effect simultaneously: this can lead to conflicts between the two separately appointed guardians which the court may have to resolve.

This also represents a change from the previous law under which the parent of a child could appoint a guardian to act jointly with the surviving parent. Now such an arrangement would only take place if the deceased parent with parental responsibility had a residence order in his favour and in force at the date of his or her death (section 5(7)).

If either:

- on the death of the appointer the child has no surviving parent with parental responsibility; or

- immediately before the death of the appointor, a court residence order was in existence in the appointor's favour regarding the child

then the appointment of the guardian takes immediate effect on the death of the appointor (section 5(7)).

A properly appointed guardian of a child may also appoint another individual to take his or her place as the child's guardian on his or her death (section 5(4)). However, if there is a surviving parent with parental responsibility and the guardian does not have a residence order in his favour then the appointment by the guardian will only take effect on the death of the surviving parent (section 5(8)).

How is a guardian appointed?

7.8   Under the Act, the appointment by a parent or guardian will not be effective unless it is made in a written document and dated. It must also be signed by the person appointing the guardian, except in the case of a document signed at the appointor's direction, in which case it must be signed in the presence of two witnesses who each then attest to the execution of the document (section 5(5)). An appointment made by will (or other testamentary document) signed at the appointor's direction must be properly witnessed as required under the provisions of the Wills Act 1837, s.9.

The court can also appoint a guardian (on specific application or in general family proceedings) if either:

- a child has no parent with parental responsibility; or

- a residence order has been made in favour of a parent or guardian who has died whilst the order was still in force (section 5(1)).

The former applies to orphans, or to children of unmarried fathers without parental responsibility. The latter applies even though the child may have a surviving parent, albeit without a residence order. In practice, the court is only likely to appoint a non-parent as sole guardian when the deceased, having a residence order in his or her favour, did not make a lifetime appointment and a third party is likely to be better able to care for the child than the surviving parent. (The full circumstances in which courts appoint guardians is beyond the scope of this Handbook.)

Can the appointment be revoked or refused?

7.9   During the lifetime of the person who has made the appointment, he or she may revoke the appointment in the following ways:

- by a further appointment of a guardian which is clearly inconsistent with the continuation of the first appointment (section 6(1));

- by specifically revoking the appointment in writing, subject to the same conditions for the appointment of guardians as set out in para. 7.8 above (section 6(2));

- if the appointment is made other than in a will or codicil, by destroying the original written document which provided for the appointment of the guardian, with the intention of revoking the appointment (section 6(3)); or

- by revoking the will or codicil which contains the appointment (section 6(4)).

The court has power to revoke the appointment at any time under section 6(7).

In addition, the person who is appointed guardian may refuse the appointment by any document in writing signed by him made within a reasonable time of his first knowledge that the appointment has taken effect (section 6(5)).

It should be noted that the Law Reform (Succession) Act 1995, which came into effect from 1 January 1996, contains provisions amending Children Act 1989, s.6 to revoke, on divorce, any appointment of a former spouse as guardian in a will. If such a parent has parental responsibility, his or her right over any children would be unaffected. However, any appointment by will of a step-parent (without parental responsibility) as guardian is affected by any later divorce. The result is that, unless there is anything in the will to the contrary, the appointment of a step-parent as guardian in such circumstances would be revoked.

What about pre-Children Act orders?

7.10 As noted in para. 7.2 above, section 5(3) of the Act provides that a parent with parental responsibility may appoint a guardian. What is the position then, in respect of orders made under previous enactments?

Transitional provisions contained in Schedule 14, para. 4 to the Act specify that, in the case of an order in force made under Family Law Reform Act 1987, s.4 giving the father parental rights and duties in relation to a child, that order is deemed to be an order under Children Act 1989, s.4. giving the father parental responsibility for the child.

In addition, Schedule 14, para. 6 provides that where an order is in force, made under specified enactments (Domestic Proceedings and Magistrates' Courts Act 1978; Children Act 1975; Matrimonial Causes Act 1973; Guardianship of Minors Acts 1971 and 1973; Matrimonial Causes Act 1965; Matrimonial Proceedings (Magistrates' Courts) Act

1960) which determines custody and/or care and control of and/or access to a child or any matter regarding a child's education *and* the child's father and mother were married at the time of the child's birth, each parent is deemed to have parental responsibility in accordance with Children Act 1989, s.2. Where such an order is in force and the child is not legitimate, section 2 applies with the following modification: where the existing order gives the father custody or care and control of the child, the court is deemed to have made an order under section 4(1) giving him parental responsibility for the child.

The transitional provisions also cover the question of residence orders, specifying that, for any reference in section 5 of the Act to a residence order in favour of a parent or guardian, there is to be substituted a reference to any existing order by virtue of which the parent or guardian has care and control of the child.

How do the provisions of the Act affect the appointment of guardians by will or codicil?

7.11   An appointment of a guardian may still be made in a will or codicil as these documents are written instruments under section 5(5). Although an appointment may be made in any written document, there is an advantage in appointing in a testamentary document as such documents are likely, by their nature, to be preserved, easily identifiable and be considered by those dealing with the estate of the appointor on death. However, as substitute or additional guardians may also be appointed in other written documents, the probate practitioner cannot assume that the guardians appointed in the will are the only guardians and enquiries should be made as to any other appointments which might take effect either instead of, or in addition to, the appointment in the testamentary document.

Even if a guardian is appointed in the will or codicil, the appointment may be revoked in any written document in accordance with sections 5 and 6 of the Act. Thus a will may be valid, apart from the appointment of guardians, which may have been revoked in a later non-testamentary document. The converse situation could never arise, i.e., a revoked will but a valid appointment of guardians due to the provisions of section 6(4), so that if a will or codicil is revoked, the appointment of a guardian contained in the testamentary document will also be revoked.

It is advisable, when dealing with an estate involving minors, to check whether there are any other written documents which may have revoked an appointment of guardians in a will or codicil.

However, it is possible to have an invalid will (e.g. if the formalities for signing and witnessing the will have not been complied with) containing a valid appointment of guardians. The appointment will be valid provided that the invalid will qualifies as a document in writing, is signed by the appointor, and is dated.

It has been common in the past for both parents to appoint a guardian or guardians to take effect on the death of the second parent. In general, it is no longer necessary that such a specific condition should be included within a will because under the terms of the Act, where both parents have parental responsibility (and there is no residence order in force), the appointment will not take effect until the second death.

At any one time more than one person may have the right to appoint a guardian for a child but the appointment of guardians on death will not, in general, take effect until the child's last surviving guardian or parent with parental responsibility dies. The situation may then arise of two or more separately appointed guardians acting. This should be taken into account by the probate practitioner.

As will be noted from para. 7.7 above, the position will be further complicated if there are any residence orders in force with respect to the child. Will drafters and probate practitioners should also take this into account. If clients are at all unclear as to the existence of residence orders, the prudent will drafter should make enquiries of the court or of a family law practitioner to ascertain the correct position.

If the will drafter is acting for the mother of a non-marital minor child, enquiries should be made as to the existence of any parental responsibility agreement, as the father of the child may then be able to appoint testamentary guardians. As the significance of parental responsibility is of such importance for the appointment of guardians, and the requirements for parental responsibility agreements are strict, it may be prudent for the will drafter or probate practitioner, in appropriate cases, to check the existence of a valid agreement at the Principal Registry. Enquiries should be directed to the Children Section, First Avenue House, 42–49 High Holborn, London WC1V 6NP (tel. 0171 936 6980). A fee of £20 is payable for every 10 years searched. Cheques should be made payable to HM Paymaster General.

There is no provision in the Act for successive appointments by the original appointor, (i.e., 'I appoint Jane Smith as guardian of my minor children and when she dies then I appoint her husband William Smith as guardian'). However, there seems to be no prohibition on substitutional appointments taking effect if the first choice as guardian does not survive the appointor (i.e. 'I appoint Jane Smith as guardian of my minor children but if she has predeceased me then I appoint her husband William Smith as guardian').

There are often a number of clauses included in wills giving executors, trustees and appointed guardians certain rights and powers in relation to financial provision for minor beneficiaries under the will. If the will refers to provision for the child being made to the child's guardian, care should be taken by executors and trustees as well as those administering estates to ensure that the named guardian is properly and effectively appointed.

Chapter 8

Time for probate

This is a revised version of an article which first appeared in the *Gazette*. We are most grateful to Gillian Cockburn of Cockburns, Guildford for revising and updating it.

Time-limits are of crucial importance in probate and estate planning. This chapter considers, in brief, some of the more important time-limits that practitioners should bear in mind during the administration of an estate.

OBTAINING THE GRANT

8.1 In general, a grant of probate will not issue from the probate registry within seven days of the date of death and a grant of letters of administration will not issue within 14 days of the date of death. In exceptional cases, a district judge or probate registrar may give leave for the grant to issue earlier but the applicant will first have to explain the need for expedition by way of a letter accompanying the application. (Non-Contentious Probate Rules (NCPR) 1987, Rule 6(2) as amended by NCPR 1991).

Caveats

8.2 If a caveat is entered to prevent a grant of representation being issued in an estate it should be remembered that the caveat will only remain in force for a period of six months from the date of entry (NCPR 1987, Rule 44(3)(a)–(c)). It may be extended for further periods of six months but each application for extension must be made in the last month prior to the expiry of the caveat.

RECTIFICATION OF THE WILL

8.3 It is possible to correct errors in wills of testators dying on or after 1 January 1983 provided the court is satisfied that the will fails to express the testator's intentions as a result of either a clerical error or a failure by the drafter to understand the testator's intentions (Administration of Justice Act (AJA) 1982, s.20). An application for rectification of a will must be made within six months of the date that representation to the estate is first taken out. The court does have power to consider applications outside the six-month period but the applicant has to show that there was a very good reason why the application was not made within the time-limit. If there is a possibility of rectification the personal representatives should not distribute the estate within the six-month period referred to above. (See AJA 1982 regarding distributions once the six-month period has expired.)

FAMILY PROVISION CLAIMS

(See also Chapter 10)

8.4 Certain individuals have the right to apply for financial provision from the estate of a person who dies domiciled in England and Wales (Inheritance (Provision for Family and Dependants) Act 1975 (IPFDA), s.1). A claim must be made within six months of the date that representation to the estate is first taken out (IPFDA, s.4). If there is a possibility of a claim the personal representatives should not distribute the estate within this period. (See IPFDA, s.20 for more on distributions.) The court does have power to allow a claim to be made outside the six-month period but this power is rarely exercised.

INTEREST AND LEGACIES

(See also Chapter 15)

8.5 Personal representatives must administer the estate properly and should not unduly delay the payment of legacies. Personal representatives who delay payment without good reason may find themselves personally liable to pay interest to aggrieved beneficiaries. In certain cases, legatees have the right to interest at 6 per cent per annum (R.S.C. Order 44, Rule 10) on their legacies, if they are paid late as follows:

(a) **General pecuniary legacies** should be paid within one year (the executors' year) from the date of death. Where they are paid outside that period they must carry interest calculated from the first anniversary of the death (when the right to receive the legacy arose). Any interest paid will come from the residue of the estate (from monies which might otherwise have passed to the residuary beneficiaries).

(b) **Specific legacies** do not carry the right to interest but they do carry any income arising from the gift, subject to the wording of the will.

(c) **Immediate legacies** will carry interest from the date of death if it is clear from the will that the testator or testatrix intended that the payment should be made immediately on death. Legacies (whether immediate or contingent) provided for the maintenance of the testator's or the testatrix's children will also carry interest from the date of death.

(d) **Future or contingent legacies** will in general carry interest from the date the future event or contingency occurs.

(e) **Residuary gifts** do not carry interest in accordance with these provisions. However, residuary beneficiaries are entitled to a share in any income the estate generates after payment of estate liabilities and legacies.

ADVERTISING FOR CREDITORS

8.6 Personal representatives should consider advertising for creditors and potential beneficiaries before starting to distribute the estate (Trustee Act 1925, s.27). The point during the administration at which the advertisement is inserted will depend on a number of factors, varying with each estate. The advertisement gives notice of the personal representatives' intention to distribute to those who may have claims against the estate. A suitably worded advertisement should be inserted in the *London Gazette* and in a newspaper circulating in any area where the deceased owned land. In addition, the personal representatives should also consider advertising elsewhere if there are any special factors affecting the estate. The advertisements must give claimants at least two months to notify the personal representatives of their claim. After the advertisements have been inserted, and assuming that no claimants have come forward in the two-month period the personal representatives may distribute the estate with reference only to claims known to them at the time of distribution.

INTESTACY

8.7 Under the intestacy laws, the surviving spouse has the following rights, both of which should be exercised within 12 months of the date that representation to the estate is first taken out:

- to redeem the life interest and instead receive a capital sum (Administration of Estates Act 1925, s.47A as amended by AJA 1977); and/or

- to have the deceased's interest in the matrimonial home appropriated as part of the surviving spouse's interest in the estate (Intestates' Estates Act 1952, Sched.2).

INHERITANCE TAX ('IHT')

Payment of tax

8.8 The due date for payment of inheritance tax (IHT) on death is six months after the end of the month in which the death occurs (Inheritance Tax Act 1984, s.226). Late payment will result in interest charges under sections 233 and 234. However, when the application for the grant of representation is made, any IHT payable on the non-instalment option assets (e.g. money, chattels, quoted shares, etc.), must be paid at that time even if prior to the due date.

IHT on instalment option assets (as set out in IHTA 1984, s.227) may be paid by 10 equal yearly instalments if the personal representatives so elect. If this election is made, the first instalment is due six months after the end of the month in which the death took place and the remaining nine instalments on successive anniversaries of that six-month date. The election is usually made within the Inland Revenue account but it may also be made separately at a later date. In practice there does not appear to be any specific time-limit in which this election should be made.

Delivery of accounts

8.9 An account must be delivered to the Inland Revenue within 12 months of the end of the month in which the death occurs (IHTA 1984, s.216). Regulations may be made under section 256 dispensing with this requirement in certain cases, (e.g. excepted estates). Failure to deliver an account within the time-limit may render the personal representatives liable to penalties (IHTA 1984, s.245).

Reliefs and exemptions

8.10 If an estate includes a holding of qualifying investments (usually quoted shares) which are sold within 12 months of the date of death for less than the probate value, the personal representatives, or other person liable for the tax, may apply to have the lower sale price substituted for the probate value (IHTA 1984, ss.178 and 179). In addition if land or an interest in land is sold within four years of the date of death for less than the probate value, the personal representatives, or other person liable for the tax, may be able to substitute the lower sale price for the probate value (IHTA 1984, ss.190 and 191). In the case of deaths before 15 March 1990 the sales must be made within three years following the death.

Variations and disclaimers

8.11 It is possible to vary the terms of a will or the provisions applicable to an estate under the intestacy laws and to elect that the varied provisions shall take effect (for IHT and/or capital gains tax ('CGT') purposes) as if those provisions had been included in the deceased's last will (IHTA 1984, s.142 and Taxation of Chargeable Gains Act (TCGA) 1992, s.62(6) and (7)). A variation must be made in writing by the people who would otherwise benefit from the varied assets within a period of two years from the date of the death. Elections for IHT and/or CGT must be made within six months of the date of the deed of variation. The Revenue may allow longer than six months in which to make the election but it would be inadvisable to rely on the Revenue exercising this power.

A disclaimer of an interest under a will or under the intestacy laws must also be made in writing and within two years of the date of death. However, no elections are necessary for the disclaimer to be treated as though made by the deceased for IHT or CGT purposes.

Property settled by will

8.12 Capital distributions or appointments from a discretionary will trust within two years of the date of death (or any shorter period stated in the will) will be treated as having been made under the deceased's will and taking place at the date of death (IHTA 1984, s.144). This provision only applies if the capital distribution or appointment is an event which would otherwise have been chargeable to IHT. Thus a capital distribution or appointment from the property within the first three months after death would not qualify (IHTA 1984, s.65(4)).

Quick succession relief

8.13 If the deceased's estate was increased by a chargeable transfer within five years of the date of death then quick succession relief will be available to reduce the IHT payable on the death (IHTA 1984, s.141). The reduction is a percentage of part of the IHT paid on the earlier transfer. The percentage applicable will depend upon the period between the transfer and the date of death.

Overpayments of IHT

8.14 Claims for repayment of overpaid IHT (including interest) must be made within six years of the payment of the tax (IHTA 1984, s.241). However, if too much tax was paid as a result of a mistake of the Inland Revenue then a repayment can be claimed within 20 years.

Underpaid IHT

8.15 The Revenue will not bring any proceedings for underpaid tax once a period of six years has expired from the later of:

- the date when the payment of tax or the last instalment was made and accepted; and

- the due date for payment of the tax or last instalment (IHTA 1984, s.240).

This restriction on the Revenue will not apply if there is any fraud, wilful default or neglect on the part of the person liable for the tax.

Events prior to death

8.16 There are a number of important time-limits for probate practitioners in relation to pre-death events. For instance, chargeable transfers and potentially exempt transfers made within a period of up to seven years before death must be taken into account by the personal representatives in the calculation of the IHT due on the transferor's estate at death (IHTA 1984, s.7 and s.3A).

Gifts with reservation may also have to be taken into account when calculating the IHT due on death if the gifts are either still subject to the reserved interest at the date of death or alternatively the reservation was released within seven years before the date of death (Finance Act 1986, s.102 and Sched. 20).

There may also be a liability to IHT payable by the transferees of these different types of lifetime transfers following the death of the transferor within the seven-year period. Any additional IHT payable by a transferee as a result of the death will be due for payment six months from the end of the month in which the death occurs, but payment by instalments may be available in certain cases (IHTA 1984, s.226).

However, if the transferee does not pay within 12 months of the end of the month in which the death occurs the Revenue may look to the personal representatives for payment of the tax (IHTA 1984, ss.200, 204: see also Chapter 14 on personal representatives and IHT). It is important, therefore, for the personal representatives to make full enquiries to discover any lifetime transfers. If any are discovered, the estate should not be fully distributed until the tax due on these transfers has been settled and an appropriate certificate of clearance issued by the Capital Taxes Office.

Capital Gains Tax

8.17 Personal representatives are entitled to the individual's annual CGT exemption for the tax year of death and the following two tax years (TCGA 1992, s.3(7)). After that time an annual CGT allowance will not be available unless the personal representatives qualify in another capacity, e.g. as trustees. It should be noted that under the self-assessment regime (i.e. for 1996/97 onwards) the due date for payment of CGT is now 31 January following the end of the tax year in which the gain was made.

Income Tax

Appeals

8.18 An appeal against an income tax (or CGT) assessment or an appeal against an amendment to a self-assessment must be made in writing and lodged within 30 days of the issue of the assessment or notice of amendment (Taxes Management Act (TMA) 1970, s.31). *Inland Revenue v. Wilkinson* [1992] S.T.C. 454 demonstrates the importance of making a formal appeal against tax assessments. An application for postponement of payment of some or all of the tax assessed may be made at that time. The Revenue may allow appeals to be made outside the 30-day period but they are under no obligation to do so.

Returns

8.19   During the course of the administration it may be necessary to submit income tax returns. In order to avoid the possibility of automatic penalties and surcharges (see para. 8.20) always make enquiries of the Inland Revenue about the deceased's income tax affairs and do so as soon after the death as possible. To avoid interest and penalties under the self-assessment regime completed returns must be submitted to the Inland Revenue by 30 September following the end of the tax year (if the taxpayer wishes the Inland Revenue to calculate the tax due). If the taxpayer calculates the tax himself then the return should be submitted to the Inland Revenue by 31 January following the end of the tax year (or if the return is issued after the end of October, then within three months of the date of service of the return). Taxpayers who do not submit self-assessment returns by the due date will be subject to an automatic penalty of £100 (TMA 1970, s.93). A further penalty of £100 will be charged if the return is still outstanding after a further six months. In cases of more serious delay other penalties will be charged. It should be noted that, in general, a self-assessment return is not considered to have been submitted unless it is complete. Thus 'to be advised' figures are not acceptable (although best estimates may be).

Payment of tax

8.20   Under the self-assessment regime, tax must be paid in full by 31 January following the end of the tax year. In addition, payments on account in two equal instalment for the current tax year may be required to be paid by 31 January in the tax year and the following 31 July. A balancing payment may then be required on the following 31 January. Interest will be charged on overdue tax plus a 5 per cent surcharge if the balancing payment is outstanding more than 28 days after the due date (TMA 1970, s.59C). A further 5 per cent surcharge may be payable if the tax is still unpaid more than six months after the due date.

PREVENTING PROBLEMS

8.21 Missing just one time-limit could prove to be an expensive error involving an application for extension of the normal time-limit, interest charges, and even a claim for damages. It may also spoil a good solicitor–client relationship.

How can a practice guard against missing an important time-limit? It is clear that there are too many time-limits to rely on memory alone. The use of a central diary (whether handwritten or on computer) operated by a responsible member of the practice may be of considerable benefit. Fee earners could provide the diary keeper with a list of their important dates, perhaps by completing a pro forma list. The diary keeper would then be responsible for reminding each fee earner of the date well in advance of the time-limit concerned. If a fee earner was unexpectedly absent, his or her important dates would not be missed as the diary keeper would be able to bring the date to the attention of another member of the practice. Used in this (or a similar) way, a central diary system could prove to be invaluable in the running of an efficient and trouble-free probate practice.

Chapter 9

Probate and benefits

By David Thomas

This chapter is based on an article written by Jan Luba, 2 Garden Court, Middle Temple, London for the *Solicitors Journal* in 1992. David Thomas has revised and updated it. We are most grateful to Jan and the *Solicitors Journal* for permission to use this material and to David Thomas for updating it.

David is a solicitor in private practice in Chobham and a consultant to the Child Poverty Action Group.

INTRODUCTION

9.1   Traditionally only those on above-average incomes have sought a solicitor's advice following the death of a relative or friend. Those in low-income families have not – either because the deceased would rarely have left substantial capital assets or because they are deterred by the prospects of substantial costs. Now all that has started to change. Even in a family with a history of modest or low income, substantial capital assets may be left (usually a freehold or leasehold property which has been the deceased's home).

Clients in this situation will need advice on at least three matters:

- how to meet funeral costs;

- how to provide for surviving relatives; and

- the effect on family finances of the distribution of the estate.

THE SOCIAL SECURITY SYSTEM

9.2   The social security system is very complicated, and may change fundamentally under a Labour Government. There are at present a whole array of benefits. Some are means-tested (such as **income support** and

114

housing benefit), some are non-means tested (such as **disability living allowance/attendance allowance** and **retirement pension**), while the jobseeker's allowance can be either.

Some benefits are not themselves means-tested, but are nevertheless taken into account when assessing someone's entitlement to means-tested benefits (for example, **widow's benefits**). Similarly, some benefits 'overlap' with one another – i.e. it is not possible to get full payment of each. However, means-tested benefits are payable if a client's total income is below specified thresholds (and he or she does not have too much capital – usually £8,000 but sometimes £16,000).

A further classification is that some benefits (such as **incapacity benefit**) are contributory – in other words, there is normally no entitlement unless sufficient national insurance contributions have been paid – whereas others are non-contributory (such as the means-tested benefits and **disablement benefit**, which is payable following an industrial accident or disease).

In addition, some benefits are taxable (such as **retirement pension**) whereas others are not (such as **child benefit**).

Finally, claimants normally have an *entitlement* to a benefit if they satisfy the eligibility conditions. However, this is not so with the **discretionary social fund**, which makes grants or loans to the poorest.

It should not be overlooked that, in additional to social security benefits, your client may also be entitled to health service benefits (such as free prescriptions) or to help from the local authority (such as free school meals for any children, housing grants and 'care in the community'). However, this chapter concentrates on social security benefits.

Immediate assistance

9.3   If consulted very shortly after the death, you may be required to give basic advice on the necessary steps to be taken. For those on the lowest incomes, advice and assistance can be given under the Green Form Scheme. Clients, if distressed, may not be able to absorb much detail from an interview at this stage. However, you may wish to give them two free Benefits Agency leaflets, *Help When Someone Dies* (FB29) and *What To Do After a Death* (D49). These are obtainable from your local Benefits Agency office or, if you want to make a bulk order (five or more), from The Stationery Office, The Causeway, Oldham Broadway Business Park, Chadderton, Oldham OL9 9XD.

Paying for the funeral

9.4 Low-income clients cannot, of course, be expected to have readily available the substantial funds now required to pay for a funeral. You may need to offer advice about the availability of help from the social security system. The advice can, if appropriate, be given under the Green Form Scheme.

The rules for claiming a funeral payment are complicated and have recently been tightened. They are set out in the Social Fund Maternity and Funeral Expenses (General) Regulations 1987 (as amended) (S.I. 1987 no. 481). This is known as the **regulated social fund.** In essence, your client must comply with the following main conditions:

- He or she (or a partner) must be getting a qualifying benefit, i.e. **income support, income-based jobseeker's allowance, family credit, disability working allowance, housing benefit or council tax benefit.** 'Partner' includes someone with whom the client is living as husband or wife (Social Security Contributions and Benefits Act 1992 ('SSCBA'), s.137).

- He or she (or a partner) must have accepted responsibility for paying the costs of the funeral. If he or she was the deceased's partner, or had been looking after a child who has died, that is normally sufficient. However, there are more stringent conditions to satisfy if the claimant was a close relative, or close friend, of the deceased. For example, he or she will need to show that there is no 'immediate family member' who is not getting a qualifying benefit and that it was reasonable to assume responsibility for the funeral costs.

  Note that it does not necessarily matter that someone else actually arranged the funeral on your client's behalf, provided that that person can be said to have been acting as your client's agent (Social Security Commissioner's Decision CIS/975/97).

- The funeral must have taken place in the UK (or elsewhere in the European Union in the case of an EU national: *O'Flynn* v. *Adjudication Officer* [1996] All E.R. (EC) 541).

How much can be claimed?

9.5 A claimant is entitled to certain specified costs, such as the cost of burial or cremation and one return fare incurred either in arranging or attending the funeral, and up to £600 for any other expenses. However, one must then deduct various sums, including:

- any assets of the deceased which are available without a grant of probate or letters of administration;

- money from an insurance policy or occupational pension;

- a sum payable under a pre-paid funeral plan;

- any capital your client or his/her partner has over £500, or £1,000 if either are over 60.

The Benefits Agency can recover a funeral payment from the deceased's estate under Social Security Administration Act 1992, s.78(4) (it is a first charge) but not normally from the claimant.

The claim form (SF200) is available from the registrar's office or from the local Benefits Agency office. The claim must be made within three months of the funeral.

Income for the deceased's partner

9.6 Against a low-income background it is unlikely that the deceased will have left sufficient income-generating capital to provide fully for a spouse or cohabitee after death. The partner of the deceased may accordingly need advice about how best to secure state support.

Widows

9.7 You should be able to help the client identify and claim the special statement benefits for widows. These are paid under the national insurance system depending upon the contribution record of the late husband. He is treated as having satisfied the contribution conditions if death resulted from industrial injury or disease.

Widow's benefits are paid irrespective of the widow's income. There are no equivalent benefits for female cohabitees or ex-wives of the deceased. The range of available benefits (from which you can select the appropriate one for the client to claim) comprises:

- **widow's payment:** a tax-free lump sum of £1,000 if the widow was under 60 when her husband died, or if she was over 60 but her late husband was not claiming category A retirement pension when he died;

- **widowed mother's allowance:** a weekly benefit, currently worth at least £62.45 a week, if a woman is raising a child or is pregnant (by her late husband);

- **widow's pension:** a weekly benefit payable where the widow was over 45 but under 65 when her husband died or when widowed mother's allowance ceased. Payment ceases when the widow reaches 65. The rate varies from £18.74 to £62.45 a week, depending partly on the widow's age at the time of her husband's death (the older she was the higher the payment).

Claim forms are available from local Benefits Agency offices. The claim must be made within three months of death (with payment made retrospectively from death). You may need to advise that payment of either of the two weekly benefits will cease if your client remarries. (It is suspended during a period of cohabitation with a new partner.)

Many widows will have to top up these national insurance benefits by claiming means-tested benefits (such as **income support** or **income-based jobseeker's allowance**) in order to provide a minimum level of income. There are also special rules to help widows with other national insurance benefits and contributions, in particular **incapacity benefit** and **retirement pension.**

Benefits Agency leaflet NP45 *Widows' Benefits* contains a useful summary of the various rules.

Widowers

9.8   There is no widower's benefit (although this is currently being challenged under the European Convention on Human Rights). A husband or male cohabitee is expected to return to work immediately after the death and thus to obtain an income from employment. If not employed, there will probably be some entitlement to the normal range of welfare benefits but no special provision is made for the recent bereavement.

A widower who is over 65 might be advised to claim a **Category B retirement** pension for widowers (SSCBA, s.51) if not already receiving a full retirement pension based on his own national insurance contributions. To qualify his deceased spouse must have paid sufficient contributions and both must have been over pensionable age when she died.

A widower may also be eligible for any **deferred state pension increase** or **graduated retirement pension** earned by his late wife.

In addition, a widower who is under 65 and is incapable of work long term may also come within special rules governing incapacity benefit –

in essence, if he was incapable of work at the time of his wife's death, or became so soon afterwards, he is entitled to the benefit at the long-term rate after a year of incapacity , despite not having paid sufficient national insurance contributions. There are also special rules for terminally ill widowers claiming incapacity benefit.

Provision for the deceased's children

9.9   Again against a background of low income, the deceased may have left insufficient funds to provide a full income for surviving dependent children.

If the children are being raised by the surviving parent, that parent should be getting **child benefit**. From April 1998 the extra amount paid to lone parents was scrapped. The surviving parent should, however, notify the Inland Revenue of his/her entitlement to **additional personal tax allowance.** In addition to advising on the detail of statutory entitlement, you could usefully supply a copy of Benefits Agency leaflet FB27 *Bringing Up Children* (which describes the full range of benefits available).

If the children are being raised by a step-parent or another adult who is not the parent, that person should be advised to consider claiming **guardian's allowance** in addition to ordinary child benefit. The benefit is payable if, either both parents are dead, or one of them is dead and the other has either gone missing or has been sentenced to a term of imprisonment of at least five years.

Guardian's allowance is tax free and worth over £500 per annum. DSS leaflet NI14 contains the details.

Administering the estate

9.10   In administering the estate against a low-income background, you need to have special regard to the way in which the social security system may be of relevance.

You should consider the possible need for repayment of any overpaid means-tested benefits. The Benefits Agency from time to time discover that former benefit claimants who have died have left funds or assets which were undeclared and which would have reduced or eliminated benefit entitlement had they been declared. If the claimant misrepresented, or failed to disclose, a material fact, any resulting over-payment may well be recoverable from the estate of the deceased (see Social Security Administration Act 1992, s.71 and *Secretary of State for Social Services* v. *Solly* [1974] 3 All E.R. 922). Publication of the usual notices for potential creditors may well protect the estate from late Benefits Agency claims: *Secretary of State for Social Services* v. *Blackie* [1975] C.L.Y. 3126.

Similarly, you should check whether the Benefits Agency are still paying benefit into the deceased's bank account. They can usually recover such payment even if there was no misrepresentation or failure to disclose.

On the other hand, you will need to call into the estate any outstanding welfare benefits due to the deceased. It may well be that a variety of benefits were being paid from several different benefit payment offices. Your local office should be able to let you have the relevant addresses.

If the beneficiaries of the estate are themselves claimants of means-tested benefits (such as **income support, housing benefit** and **council tax benefit**) the distribution of the estate will have an impact on their own benefit entitlement if it results in their holding total capital in excess of £3,000. A beneficiary cannot avoid the rule by leaving the funds in the hands of the solicitor (*Thomas* v. *Chief Adjudication Officer*) (C.A.) reported as an appendix to Social Security Commissioner's Decision R(SB) 17/87 by The Stationery Office).

Conclusion

9.11   Benefit rules are very complicated. What is said in this chapter can only be a basic summary. As well as the very helpful Benefits Agency leaflets, practitioners may wish to obtain the comprehensive guides produced by Child Poverty Action Group, 1–5 Bath Street, London EC1V 9PY.

Postscript

9.12   In [1997] *New Law Journal,* 24 October, 1549 and 31 October, 1589, there was an interesting article by Helene Pines Richman, 11 Stone Buildings, Lincoln's Inn on enabling trusts for disabled beneficiaries. It covered both lifetime and will trusts and reviewed the state benefits available for the disabled.

Chapter 10

IPFDA claims

This chapter was specially written by Dawn Goodman, who heads Withers' specialist trust and probate litigation team. We are most grateful to her for doing so.

IPFDA AND WILLS

10.1 You cannot guarantee to exclude the possibility of a claim under the Inheritance (Provision for Family and Dependants) Act 1975 (IPFDA) but there are some simple steps you can take when drafting the will which may reduce the likelihood of a claim or, if one is made, reduce its chances of success.

Check background facts

10.2 Establish the extent of all your client's family and dependants. There is no point in skating round the issue of a client's secret relationships and non-marital children, only to find that claims are made against the estate after he or she is dead.

Ask questions

10.3 Your client may have dependants who are not immediately obvious to him or her as such. Examples are gratuitous payments to a niece or nephew, or accommodation provided for a mother-in-law, companion, or even an elderly nanny or other former member of staff.

Options

10.4 If your client has been providing for people who could claim against the estate as dependants, but who do not fall within any of the other categories of claimant under the IPFDA – spouse, former spouse who has not remarried, cohabitant, children (including adopted and non-marital children and those treated as children of the family; see para. 10.21) – the client should be advised that the chance of a claim could be reduced by:

- making provision by will or otherwise for them; or

- ceasing to maintain them.

If the second option is taken, you should also advise your client to make it clear to any dependants that he or she no longer assumes responsibility for their maintenance. A memorandum can be left with the client's will explaining that maintenance has ceased but it is preferable for the client to send a letter (keeping a copy) to each dependant explaining that maintenance (or the assumption of responsibility) is ceasing.

Spouses

10.5 Some clients will say they are making no or little provision for their wife or husband because she or he has adequate personal assets. This may reflect a misunderstanding on the client's part about what would be regarded for these purposes as adequate assets, so make further enquiries and ensure that your client understands the position.

Ex-spouses

10.6 A former spouse may make a claim if he/she is receiving maintenance at the time of the ex-spouse's death. It is best to try to forestall the claim by making some provision.

Leaving a memorandum

10.7 If your client fears a claim under the IPFDA but does not wish to make provision for the potential claimant, he or she should be encouraged to leave a memorandum with the will explaining why no provision was made, unless your client's reasons for making no provision are unreasonable, in which case the memorandum could do more harm than good.

There appears to be a trend in IPFDA actions towards the introduction of parallel claims – proprietary estoppel, declarations as to beneficial interests, mutual will obligations, claims based on a contractual relationship with the deceased – to bolster inheritance claims. Such claims are based on a combination of the deceased's intentions and of fact. The claim will only be made after the deceased's death. Often there are no independent witnesses so the surviving claimant is free to give their version of the deceased's intentions, unchallenged.

With this in mind, it may well be appropriate for a detailed attendance note of the initial instructions to be copied to the client with the draft will. The client should be asked to confirm the attendance note details are correct when confirming instructions to engross the will. The attendance note should be kept, as with any memorandum, with the will. At least then there is an accurate record of the testator's intention.

People with special needs

10.8   If your client has dependants with mental or physical disabilities, and is assuming that the state will support them, warn your client that the local social services department can make an application on behalf of the dependants for provision from the estate.

Cohabitees

10.9   If your client is living with someone as a cohabitee, your client should be advised that a will may be necessary to provide for his or her partner. Cohabitees cannot claim under the intestacy rules and will not be able to make a claim under the IPFDA, if:

- they were not living together for two years prior to the death;
- they were not dependent;
- they were a same sex couple.

They can be severely disadvantaged. This includes gay and lesbian couples and any others where marriage is never an option.

Section 3 of the Law Reform (Succession) Act 1995 includes new guidelines which the court should consider when applications are made by cohabitees. They are:

- the age of the applicant and the length of the period during which the applicant lived as the husband or wife of the deceased and in the same household as the deceased; and
- the contribution made by the applicant to the welfare of the family of the deceased including any contribution made by looking after the home or caring for the family.

Caveats

10.10   Sometimes a claimant lodges a caveat against the issue of the grant – this is wrong use of a caveat and you should be able to get it warned off.

What should be done

10.11 If a claim has been issued, PRs should be cautious about how they administer the estate. Broadly speaking, PRs faced with a claim should pay debts and funeral expenses and collect in the assets of the estate; but they should not distribute until the claim has been disposed of.

Small legacies or cases of hardship

10.12 If there are small legacies which are unlikely to be affected by the claim, or beneficiaries are experiencing hardship, PRs can seek agreement of the parties affected, including the claimant, to payment of legacies or a distribution to relieve hardship (*Re Ralphs, Ralphs* v. *District Bank* [1986] 1 W.L.R. 1522). If consent is not forthcoming, an application can be made to the court for directions (R.S.C. Order 85, Rule 2).

If the converse applies and it is the claimant who is suffering hardship, and the beneficiaries will not agree to a distribution, the claimant can apply under IPFDA, s.5 for an interim payment.

Time-limit

10.13 Claimants have six months from the issue of the grant to put in a claim, so PRs will not be liable if they distribute the estate more than six months after obtaining the grant if no IPFDA application has been issued.

A Trustee Act 1925, s.27 advertisement does not protect PRs who distribute after two months has expired from the date of advertisement but within six months from the grant of probate.

PRs as claimants

10.14 Obviously, as a solicitor for the PRs, you cannot act both for potential plaintiff and potential defendant(s) in the IPFDA claim. If a PR or proposed PR is, say, a widow who does not think that her late husband's will or the application of the intestacy rules provides for her adequately, then she must be independently advised by another firm on whether or not to claim.

A claimant who is one of the proposed PRs can have power reserved. It is not necessary to renounce if he or she is going to make a claim. A PR who has taken out a grant and proposes to claim need not be removed from office.

In this situation your firm can continue to act in the administration with the agreement of all PRs. The PR who is claiming as a plaintiff and the PRs who are defending the claim as beneficiaries should instruct two firms other than yours, i.e. there will be three firms involved. Any PRs who are not claimants or beneficiaries can be represented by you in the litigation. The PRs as a body should adopt a neutral role and not attempt to defeat the claim. Without this approach being seen to be followed, the administration of the estate is likely to grind to a halt while the claim is pending.

Sole PRs

10.15   If the intending claimant is the *sole* PR, he or she might prefer not to take out the grant (although power might be reserved). In such a case, the grant may have to be taken out by the person next entitled, or by a nominee of the intending claimant pursuant to Supreme Court Act 1981, s.116.

PRs as beneficiaries

10.16   The PRs are also often beneficiaries who are resisting a claim. Although PRs should adopt a neutral stance, leaving it to the claimant and the beneficiaries to fight the matter out, beneficiary PRs are not obliged to be neutral in their capacity as beneficiaries.

Difficulties arise where one or more PRs are professionals and another is a beneficiary who wishes to contest the claim. If all PRs are content to accept your advice, or counsel's, on how to handle the claim, and are not causing costs to be incurred unnecessarily (for example, by refusing to settle a meritorious claim), you should not have a conflict of interest in acting for all the PRs.

Nevertheless, it is much better to ensure that the PR with the beneficial interest is separately represented in his or her capacity as beneficiary.

How to handle a claim

10.17   If you learn about a claim which appears meritorious before proceedings are issued (and the would-be claimant is either in time or is likely to get an extension) consider asking the beneficiaries (if *sui juris*) if they are willing to enter into a deed of variation. You must advise them to obtain independent advice.

Once the claim is issued, the PRs should promptly provide the information required by R.S.C. Order 99 unless all parties agree to freeze the obligation to respond by affidavit in order to save costs.

PRs must comply with their obligations to bring to court matters within their knowledge which may be relevant to the court's exercise of its discretion. Equally, they should maintain a neutral position with regard to the merits of any claim and not usurp the function of the beneficiary defendants.

Although PRs have extensive common law and statutory powers (see Trustee Act 1925, s.15) to compromise claims against the estate, provided that they act in good faith, these powers do not extend to compromising an IPFDA claim because the claim, instead of being against the estate, is to become a beneficiary in the estate. The PRs ought to leave the claimant and the beneficiaries to negotiate a settlement but should indicate:

- their readiness to assist by providing up-to-date information on the composition and administration of the estate;

- their desire to be involved at the final stage of negotiations to ensure that the agreement reached between the parties is workable from the administrative point of view and that the PRs' own position on costs is protected.

Solicitor PRs should be concerned to ensure the part they play is as limited as possible. The estate should not be put to additional expense by unnecessary attendance.

It is usually appropriate for PRs to seek directions from the court that the beneficiaries' advocate represent them during proceedings.

Charitable beneficiaries and the IPFDA

10.18   (For more on charitable beneficiaries see Chapter 15.)

A charity can agree to a compromise of proceedings through its duly authorised officer.

The charity may need separate advice on whether to agree a compromise and if in doubt can seek an order from the Charity Commissioners or a letter of opinion or advice under Charities Act 1993, ss.26 and 29, but this is not normally necessary.

In some cases, charities may feel a moral obligation to renounce part of their entitlement and under Charities Act 1993, s.27 the Charity Commissioners have powers to authorise charity trustees to give effect to a perceived moral obligation. Charities cannot give effect to a moral obligation without such authority. The Charity Commission has produced a very useful booklet CC7 *Ex Gratia Payments by Charities*.

Costs

10.19 Unless the PRs have acted unreasonably (such as by adopting too proactive a stance) or for their own benefit rather than that of the estate, they are entitled to receive their costs out of the estate, on the indemnity basis (R.S.C. Order 62, Rule 6).

A successful claimant's costs are usually paid from the estate, commonly on the standard basis; conversely, an unsuccessful claimant's costs are not always borne by him or her. Frequently, an unsuccessful claimant is not ordered to pay the costs of the PRs or other defendants. PRs should be aware of the effect on the estate of costs orders in favour of a number of parties and it may be appropriate to bring this to the attention of the claimant and beneficiaries.

Wasted costs

10.20 Solicitors for the PRs should be aware that, if they have acted improperly and unreasonably or have been negligent, and in consequence any party to the proceedings has incurred additional costs, they can be disallowed their costs or asked to meet all or any wasted costs of another party (Supreme Court Act 1981, s.51(6) (as amended); R.S.C., Order 62, Rule 11). An example of causing wasted costs would be the negligent provision of incorrect information about the size and nature of the estate when preparing the PRs' affidavit under R.S.C., Order 99, Rule 5.

The case of *Ridehalgh* v. *Horsefield and Another* (No.2) [1994] 3 W.L.R. 462 considered the question of when a wasted costs order might be sought against the opposing solicitor or barrister. In *Wall* v. *Lefever, The Times* 1 August 1997 the Court of Appeal said that the wasted costs jurisdiction would only be used where the conduct of the professional advisers was clearly improper, unreasonable or negligent.

Chapter 11

Contentious probate

This chapter was specially written for us by Henry Frydenson of Paisner & Co. and we are most grateful to him for doing so.

INTRODUCTION

11.1   The proportion of contentious work in private client departments is growing rapidly. The growth is partly the result of an increasingly litigious society and partly the result of the fact that there is more wealth around for people to argue over.

Practitioners who find that more work of this type is coming their way may be interested in joining the newly formed Association of Contentious Trusts and Probate Specialists. The purposes of the Association include raising the standard of contentious work and developing a common approach. Members agree to endeavour to act in accordance with a voluntary Code of Conduct. Under this Code members agree where appropriate to try to use the full range of solutions, in particular alternative dispute resolution, and where possible to encourage the use of the same legal team where parties have common interests.

Application forms are available from Robert Hunter of Allen & Overy.

IDENTIFICATION OF ISSUES

11.2   When advising a client it is important to identify the points which are likely to be in issue.

If there is a will there will be two possible questions relating to the will:

- Is the will valid? This may require considering any of the following questions. Have the formal requirements for making a will been complied with? (See Wills Act 1837, s.9.) Did the testator have the capacity to make a will? Do claims of undue influence or lack of knowledge and approval arise?

- How is a particular provision in a will to be construed?

METHODS OF ATTACK

11.3   Where a person is unhappy with the terms of a deceased's will or the provisions which would arise on intestacy there are various grounds of possible attack. Before considering these grounds in detail you should always give thought to what the outcome of a successful attack would be. For example, the overthrow of a will *may* result in intestacy or in the provisions of an earlier will remaining in effect. There is absolutely no point in overthrowing the later will if your client will have no rights on intestacy or under the earlier will.

Consideration must also be given to the all-important question of costs which will be examined later.

Lack of testamentary capacity

11.4   It is interesting to note that the test of testamentary capacity still remains that established as long ago as 1870 in the case of *Banks* v. *Goodfellow* [1870] L.R. 5 Q.B. 549.

Mental states are presumed to continue so if a person is normally mentally capable it will be presumed, provided the will appears rational, that he had capacity when he made the will. However, this presumption is rebuttable by evidence.

The difficulty in bringing a case where lack of capacity is alleged is to gather together sufficiently convincing evidence. It is very important to try to get together the evidence before advising the client on the likelihood of success.

Lack of due execution of the will

11.5   The burden of proving that the will was executed in accordance with Wills Act 1837, s.9 (as substituted by the Administration of Justice Act 1982, s.17) is on the party seeking to establish the validity of the will.

It may be possible to challenge the will on the following grounds:

- The signature was not made by the testator in the presence of two witnesses present at the same time, but see *Couser* v. *Couser* [1996] 1 W.L.R. 1301.

- The two witnesses did not subscribe or acknowledge their signatures to the will in the presence of the testator.

- The signature of the testator was not intended to give effect to the will.

- The signature which appears on the will was not in fact made by the testator himself or for him, or in his presence, or by his direction.

Undue influence

11.6   This is one of the most difficult allegations to sustain, since the primary witness – the deceased – is unavailable to give evidence and so by definition not able to assist the court.

Where you allege fraud or undue influence and lose you will be particularly at risk of a costs order being made against your client.

It should be clearly understood that there is nothing inherently wrong with influence by itself; people who make wills are influenced by various factors when deciding on what they will include in their will. What the law will not allow is *undue* influence.

Beneficial interest under resulting or constructive trust

11.7   It may be possible to claim a beneficial interest under a resulting or constructive trust.

Lack of knowledge and approval

11.8   As mentioned above, proving undue influence in relation to a will is extremely difficult whereas sustaining an allegation of lack of knowledge and approval is somewhat easier.

However, you are not allowed to disguise what is in reality a plea of fraud or undue influence as a lesser plea of lack of knowledge (*Re Stott* [1980] 1 W.L.R. 246).

The burden of proving that a testator knew and approved the contents of his will, rests with the person seeking to prove that will.

Where a will has been prepared in circumstances which raise suspicions, the burden of proof is upon the person attempting to set up the will to remove any such suspicions and to prove positively that the testator knew and approved of the contents of the will. Accordingly, where a person seeks to prove a will he has prepared and under which he takes a benefit, he must provide clear proof that the testator knew and approved of that part of the will under which he takes a benefit.

Claim under the Inheritance (Provision for Family and Dependants) Act 1975

11.9   If your client falls within one of the categories set out in section 1 of the Act it may be possible to make a claim under the Act.

N.B. The Law Reform (Succession) Act 1995 introduced a new category of cohabitee into section 1 in respect of death occurring on or after 1 January 1996. See Chapter 10 for a more detailed discussion of Inheritance Act claims.

THE PRACTITIONER'S TOOLS

Law Society ruling September 1959 – *Larke* v. *Nugus* [1979] 123 S.J. 337, C.A.

11.10   There is often a need for information about the circumstances in which a will was made. Solicitors are under an obligation to provide information about wills which they have prepared.

In accordance with the Law Society Professional Purposes Committee Ruling of September 1959 there is an obligation on a solicitor who prepares testamentary instruments to state the circumstances relating to the preparation of these instruments. The Law Society's recommendation was considered in the 1979 case of *Larke* v. *Nugus* by the Court of Appeal in an appeal from the decision of Browne Wilkinson J.

Caveats

11.11   (See Non-Contentious Probate Rule 44.)

A caveat is a notice issued out of the Principal Probate Registry or a district registry or sub-registry preventing a grant from being issued. If a person does not wish to prevent the issue of a grant but wishes to be notified when a grant is made, a standing search is appropriate.

Citations

11.12   (See Non-Contentious Probate Rules 46 and 47.)

Where a probate dispute can be seen on the horizon, those named as executors may well have a natural reticence to do anything. In addition, very often if the validity of a last will is called into question, the executors may be unhappy to release earlier wills.

In all these cases it is necessary to seek the assistance of the Principal Probate Registry by way of a citation. A citation is a document issued out of the Principal Probate Registry or a district registry and can be issued for any one of the following reasons:

* *Citation to accept or refuse a grant*

   Where there is a delay in obtaining the grant and the person entitled does not renounce his entitlement to do so, a citation may be issued.

* *Citation to take probate*

   Where the executor has intermeddled in the estate and thereby accepted office but has not applied for a grant within six months of death, the citation is to take the grant. The citor may be any person with an interest in the estate. Non-Contentious Probate Rule 47 allows a grant to the citor as an alternative to an order directing the executor to take a grant within a specific time.

* *Citation to propound a will*

   Where the validity of a will is doubted, a person entitled on intestacy or under an earlier testamentary document may cite the executors and persons interested under the alleged will to propound it. It should be noted that a citation is not appropriate for executors appointed by a will doubting the validity of a codicil.

   The procedure with a citation is to lodge it in draft form with the district judge/district probate registrar so that he can settle it.

   There are alternatives to the citation procedure which may be more effective. Citations are often used to try to force someone who is being dilatory to do something. However, even if the citation is successful in the short term, future progress may still be slow.

Subpoena procedure

11.13 (See Non-Contentious Probate Rule 50.)

If the original will/codicil is in the possession of a person who will not release it and is thus preventing an application for a grant by the person entitled, an application may be made under Supreme Court Act 1981, s.123 for the issue of a subpoena by the district judge/registrar. The application is supported by an appropriate affidavit. The effect of the subpoena is to require the person in possession of the will to file it in the registry. The subpoena must be served personally and endorsed with the penal notice. Committal is not normally the result of disobedience. More usually the person is ordered to attend for examination as to possession of the testamentary document.

If a person is not in possession of the will but has knowledge of it, section 122 allows the court to require the attendance of such a person for examination. It is a contempt of court not to comply. This could apply to the witnesses to a will who have declined to swear an affidavit of due execution.

Supreme Court Act 1981, s.116

11.14 Where there are appropriate circumstances the court can pass over the persons entitled to a grant and appoint such person or persons as the court feels expedient. This form of application is particularly useful where those entitled to a grant cannot be traced or where it is desired to appoint some person who is not interested in the estate as beneficiary or creditor.

The application is made *ex parte* under Non-Contentious Probate Rule 52 to a district judge or probate registrar, supported by an affidavit. It is possible to pay a fee of £5 to have the affidavit approved by the registrar.

THE TYPES OF PROBATE ACTION

Probate action re validity of a testamentary document

11.15 The action is commenced by the executor or someone else with an interest under the document or someone opposing a grant. Persons entitled on intestacy may put an executor to proof of the will. The attesting witnesses may be called for examination or to swear an affidavit of due execution.

Action regarding interests

11.16 An interest action is one in which a person's interest in opposing a will or claiming the right to letters of administration is disputed. Such an action may involve proof of a person's entitlement, for example by production of a birth certificate. Such actions are often about validity of a marriage or legitimacy. The applicant in an interest action will ask the court for a declaration against the person who is claiming entitlement to a grant and instead to make an order in his favour. If the court can be persuaded to make an order, the person who was not entitled to the grant will have their right 'cleared off' and the grant will issue to the person who is properly entitled to administer the estate.

Actions regarding the revocation of a grant

11.17 Such an action would be appropriate where a grant has been improperly obtained by a person not entitled or where the will is invalid. On an intestacy the action may force a person who has obtained letters of administration to prove his entitlement. If a will is subsequently found the action will be to revoke the earlier grant and pronounce the will's validity. The court will be asked to pronounce against any earlier will and in favour of the later document which will in turn enable a correct application for a grant to then be made.

Where a grant has been obtained by mistake, e.g. a filing department has produced the wrong will which has then been proved, an application should be made by the person who obtained the grant with an affidavit specifying the error. The district judge/registrar will then make an order revoking the grant and a further correct application may then be made, see Non-Contentious Probate Rule 41.

In a revocation action the original grant should be filed within seven days of the writ of summons or within 14 days of service of the defendant as the original grant.

Action for the removal of the personal representative

11.18 This form of action was introduced by Administration of Justice Act

1985, s.50. If the application by summons does not request the appointment of a substituted personal representative, the court will not allow the estate to be unrepresented. The applicant will swear an affidavit giving reasons for the removal and as to the suitability of the replacement personal representative who must consent to act. An example of this would be where a partner in a firm is an executor and then leaves the firm. It would be appropriate for him to be removed and replaced with another partner.

Under Supreme Court Act 1981, s.116 as stated above the court has discretion to appoint as administrator any person it considers expedient even if the person entitled, for example on intestacy, would thereby be passed over.

Appointment of a judicial trustee

11.19 Applications are governed by the Judicial Trustees Act 1896 and the Judicial Trustees Rules 1983.

This can be a more expensive exercise than the appointment of a new personal representative under Administration of Justice Act 1985, s.50 but may be the more practical solution where, for example, the sole personal representative has a beneficial interest in the estate and there has been a substantial breakdown in confidence and/or communications between him and the other beneficiaries.

The judicial trustee has all the powers and discretions of a properly appointed personal representative but the court has wide powers to give directions as to the custody of the funds in the estate. Following the appointment of the judicial trustee the trustee or any beneficiary interested can apply to the court for further directions by letter.

Breach of trust or breach of fiduciary duty

11.20 Executors who, through negligence and default, have caused loss to an estate will clearly be open to an action by a beneficiary of the estate. Such neglect or default might consist of failures to carry out the provisions of the will; making distributions to persons not named in the will; a failure to maintain neutrality between the beneficiaries on the one hand and the claimants on the other; executors who derive a personal benefit from the estate; or failure to obtain sufficient information regarding the estate.

Administration actions: R.S.C., Order 85

11.21   Order 85, Rule 1 provides the definition of an administration action: 'an action for the administration under the direction of the court of the estate of a deceased person'. In certain cases the court will as a result of an administration action take on the administration of the estate. This will usually happen where the estate is actually insolvent, though such orders should not be sought where an application for other special forms of relief can be made.

R.S.C. Order 85, Rule 2 provides examples of matters which may be sanctioned by the court:

(a)   the determination of rights or interests of beneficiaries;

(b)   order for payment into court of funds held by the executors;

(c)   order for approval of any proposed transaction;

(d)   order for the production of estate accounts;

(e)   order directing a person to do or stop from doing anything in the administration of the estate.

Applications under this order may be brought by beneficiaries or the executors or other interested parties.

Summons to deliver an inventory and account

11.22   This is an extremely useful procedure. It is available in the probate registry and is therefore relatively cheap. Every deponent to an oath leading to a grant of administration swears 'to exhibit on oath . . . a full inventory of the estate and when so required render an account of the administration'. (See Administration of Estates Act 1925, s.25(6).)

This means that anyone with a beneficial interest in the estate can apply by summons at any time for an inventory and account.

The summons issues out of the registry from which the grant issued and should be supported by affidavit.

When you ask for an inventory it is a good idea to ask for an order for your costs. If you attend the summons with an idea of the costs incurred the registrar can assess costs there and then which avoids the 7½ per cent taxing fee which would otherwise be payable.

The probate registry's jurisdiction is limited to ordering an inventory and account. If you want an administration order you will have to go to the Chancery Division under Order 85.

Beddoes summonses

11.23 A problem often faced by executors is whether in the administration of an estate they should defend a claim brought against them, initiate an action on behalf of the estate or compromise a claim on behalf of the estate. One form of Order 85, Rule 2 application is a Beddoes Summons which derives its name from the case of *Re Beddoes* v. *Cottam* [1893] 1 Ch. 547. An executor who brings or defends a claim without obtaining leave of the court may find himself exposed to the costs that arise. The decision as to the granting of a Beddoe Order in the executor's favour is a matter which the court will decide in its absolute discretion in every particular case. A Beddoe Order is not given as of right by the court.

The case of *Singh* v. *Bhasin and Anor*, *The Times*, 21 August 1998, is a salutory illustration of the risks of not seeking an order.

In some cases it will also be prudent for executors to seek directions from the court under Order 85, Rule 2.

Rectification under AJA 1982, s.20

11.24 Under Administration of Justice Act 1982, s.20 the court may order that a will be rectified so as to give effect to the testator's intention. There are two grounds for such rectification:

- in consequence of a clerical error; or

- in consequence of a failure to understand the testator's instructions.

It is important to appreciate that section 20(1)(b) applies where the testator's instructions are not understood which is not the same as a failure to carry out those instructions. Thus, rectification will not be available where the testator or his solicitor does not understand the meaning and effect of words used, unless it is unclear what the testator's instructions were or he had failed to inform his solicitor.

Claims against solicitors

11.25 If rectification is not available due to an error by the solicitor who prepared the will, the disappointed beneficiary may have a claim against the solicitor.

COSTS

11.26 Supreme Court Act 1981, s.51 provides that in contentious probate actions all parties' costs are at the discretion of the court.

It is, however, true to say that a 'wind of change' has been blowing for some time in relation to the old 'rule of thumb' that, if the proceedings were reasonable, costs would usually come out of the estate. The issue of costs is now looked at very carefully, and the party who loses can often find himself saddled with *inter partes* standard costs (and on occasion with indemnity costs) particularly if it is found that he has instituted untenable or unreasonable proceedings. A prudent practitioner will therefore always keep the question of costs under review and where appropriate make without prejudice offers in accordance with the Calderbank principle.

Chapter 12

The law – a review

There are many excellent works covering the law relating to probate and succession already available (see Booklist, Chapter 29). This Handbook is not intended to be a legal textbook but a summary of the principal legal issues may be helpful generally, and also as a pointer to some of the grounds on which you may find the validity of a will, or parts of it, being challenged.

IS THE WILL VALID?

Check the following:

Age

12.1 Was the testator or testatrix over 18 (or on active service)?

Mental capacity

Requirements

12.2 Did the testator or testatrix understand:

- the nature of his or her act and its effects;
- the extent of his or her property; and
- the moral claims which ought to be considered?

For the classic statement of the test of testamentary capacity, see *Banks* v. *Goodfellow* (1870) L.R. 5 Q.B. 549.

Proof of capacity

12.3 Capacity is presumed unless the contrary is shown.

There is a presumption in favour of a duly executed will if it is rational on the face of it, i.e. those opposing it must prove lack of capacity.

If the testator or testatrix generally lacked mental capacity (e.g. he or she was mentally ill), lack of capacity is presumed; this can be rebutted.

N.B. The time for testing capacity is normally when the will is executed. However, if the testator or testatrix was competent when giving instructions, but not at actual execution, the will is nonetheless valid if he or she recalls giving the instructions and believes the will to accord with them: *Parker* v. *Felgate* (1883) 8 P.D. 171.

Intention

Requirements

12.4   The testator or testatrix must intend:

- to make a will; and

- to make the particular will executed. He or she must, therefore, know and approve its contents: *Guardhouse* v. *Blackburn* (1886) L.R. 1 P. & D. 109.

Attestation clause

Whilst an attestation clause is not required by Wills Act 1837, s.9, if such a clause is included and recites that the formalities of section 9 were observed, it will raise the presumption of due execution. Further, the inclusion of such a clause will normally avoid the necessity of providing the registrar with an affidavit of due execution.

Proof of intention

Knowledge and approval of the particular will are presumed from the fact that the testator or testatrix had capacity and executed the will, unless:

- he or she was blind or illiterate or the will has been signed by someone else on his or her behalf (e.g. in the case of someone totally paralysed). Here the registrar must be satisfied that the testator or testatrix had knowledge of the will's contents and execution;

- suspicious circumstances are present (e.g. the will substantially benefits the person who prepared it). Here, the greater the degree of suspicion, the stronger must be the affirmative proof to remove it: *Fulton* v. *Andrew* (1875) L.R. 7 H.L. 448, *Wintle* v. *Nye* [1959] 1 W.L.R. 284. If there is a question of suspicious circumstances, is there a careful and full record of events? In some cases the burden of proof may be so heavy as to be impossible to discharge, as in *Wintle* v. *Nye*.

Rebutting the presumption of knowledge and approval

If knowledge and approval are presumed, those opposing the will must prove that such knowledge and approval were absent by establishing that:

- the testator or testatrix was induced to make the will by force, fear or fraud; or

- he or she was subjected to undue influence and so did not make the will voluntarily. In the case of a will, undue influence must be tantamount to coercion, i.e. the testator or testatrix being driven to make the will against his or her wishes, e.g. by physical threats or actual violence; or incessant nagging may suffice: *Wingrove* v. *Wingrove* (1885) 11 P.D. 81. However, persuasion (appeals to sentiment, ties of kindred, etc.) is permissible.

Motives are irrelevant.

Mistake

12.5 Mistake will invalidate a will, or that part of it included by mistake, but only if the relevant words are present without the testator's or testatrix's knowledge: it will not save a disposition where the testator or testatrix was mistaken as to the effect or meaning of the words used. Thus, he or she is deemed to know and approve the technical language used by the person drafting the will: even though that person was mistaken as to its legal effects, such language must be admitted to probate, *Re Horrocks* [1939] P. 168.

Conversely, a mere clerical slip or error (such as a typing mistake) will generally be omitted from probate unless it has been brought to the testator's or testatrix's notice: *Re Morris* [1971] P. 62.

Formalities

12.6 Wills Act 1837, s.9 states:

'No will shall be valid unless:

(a) it is in writing and signed by the testator, or by some other person in his presence and by his direction; and

(b) it appears that the testator intended by his signature to give effect to the will; and

(c) the signature is made or acknowledged by the testator in the presence of two or more witnesses present at the same time; and

(d) each witness either:

  (i) attests and signs the will; or

  (ii) acknowledges his signature, in the presence of the testator (but not necessarily in the presence of any other witness). . . . '

Whereas previously the signature had to be at the foot or end of the will, the rule now is that in (b) above. The emphasis is on giving effect to the will as far as possible whilst not opening the door to fraud.

Signature is given a wide meaning: a mark, an initial, and even a thumb print have all been held to suffice

but not a seal. Even an incomplete signature will do: *Re Chalcraft* [1948] P. 222, *Re Cook* [1960] 1 All E.R. 689. See also the *Weatherhill* v. *Pearce* [1995] 1 W.L.R. 592. Presence is also given a wide meaning: see *Couser* v. *Couser* [1996] 1 W.L.R. 1301.

HAS A DOCUMENT BEEN INCORPORATED?

12.7 To be incorporated as part of a will an unexecuted document must be:

- in existence at the date of execution of the will;

- referred to in the will as already existing; and

- clearly identified in or identifiable from the will.

Care should be taken to avoid reference in a will to an existing document if incorporation is not intended. The registrar may require production of any such document, with evidence of possible incorporation.

The consequence of incorporation is that the document incorporated will be open to public scrutiny, as it will be admitted to probate with the will.

ARE TWO WILLS MUTUAL?

12.8 To be mutual, wills must be drawn up by two testators:

- in favour of agreed beneficiaries (not necessarily each other: *Re Dale* [1994] Ch 31);

- stating that the wills are not to be revoked without the consent of both parties - unless there is a clear written agreement to this effect the wills are not mutual: *Re Goodchild* [1997] 1 W.L.R. 1216.

Once one testator dies with a will in the agreed terms, the property of the survivor becomes subject to a trust. Thus, the property will pass to the agreed beneficiary even if the surviving testator makes a new will purporting to leave the property elsewhere.

When drafting it is better to avoid mutual wills, if at all possible. There are uncertainties with regard to the powers of the surviving testator to deal with the property in his or her own lifetime. Many people think that the surviving testator is free to deal with his or her property until death. If that is correct, the mutual will may provide little protection for the agreed beneficiary as there may be few assets left by the time the surviving testator dies.

The recent case of *Re Hobley Deceased, The Times* 16 July 1997 shows that there can be difficulties in deciding whether or not the first testator has died with a will in the agreed terms where there has been any kind of alteration to the agreed will.

There is a useful article on recent cases on mutual wills in [1997] *Trusts & Estates* November, 83.

TYPES OF LEGACY

Legacies may be categorised as follows.

Specific

12.9 This is a gift of property forming part of the testator's or testatrix's estate at death and distinguished in the will from other property of the same kind, e.g. 'my race horse Red Rum', 'my dwelling-house Blackacre, or such other dwelling-house in which I shall reside at the date of my death'.

Even a gift of money may be a specific legacy (*Re Wedmore* [1907] 2 Ch. 277) although this is relatively rare.

General

12.10 This is a gift of property not distinguished in the will from other property of the same kind, e.g. 'to X the sum of £5,000; to Y £5,000 shares in ICI'. Whilst most general legacies are of money, it is not essential that they be so – although clearly an attempt to give a general legacy of some types of property would create problems and might well be void for uncertainty (e.g. 'to X a horse'. How does one define a horse, what value, etc?).

Demonstrative

12.11 This is a general legacy payable out of a specific designated fund, e.g. '£1,000 payable out of my paid-up share account with X Building Society'. Here, in so far as the fund is still in existence at the testator's or testatrix's death, it will be treated as a specific legacy. In so far as it is not, it will be treated as a general legacy and abate accordingly should there be insufficient in the estate to discharge debts without recourse to the other general legacies.

N.B. The distinction between specific, demonstrative and general legacies is particularly important because:

- a specific legacy is subject to ademption; a general one is not, e.g. if Red Rum (see para. 12.9 has been sold, given away, or has died during the testator's or testatrix's lifetime, the legatee will get nothing unless there is a substitutional provision (as in the case of the gift of Blackacre (again, see para. 12.9));

- a general legacy must be applied for payment of debts before a specific one;

- a demonstrative legacy is only treated as a specific legacy in so far as the designated fund remains at the testator's or testatrix's death.

Pecuniary

12.12 This is a gift of money which may be specific, general or demonstrative. Administration of Estates Act 1925, s.55(i)(ix) defines a pecuniary legacy as including:

> 'an annuity, a general legacy, a demonstrative legacy, so far as . . . not discharged out of the designated property, and any other general direction by a testator for the payment of money, including all death duties free from which any devise, bequest or payment is made to take effect.'

Thus a legacy specified to be free of tax or free of expenses will be treated as a legacy conferring an extra benefit, the amount of which would be equivalent to the tax or expenses being paid out of the estate.

Residuary

12.13 This is what is left after all debts, liabilities, legacies and other expenses have been paid.

Where residue is left to be divided between an exempt and a non-exempt beneficiary (e.g. a charity and a member of the deceased's family) problems arise as to how the burden of tax should fall. See the discussion of *Re Benham* in paras. 15.30–36.

With regard to legacies to institutions (including charities) you need to know whether or not the institution is charitable, as the cy-près doctrine only applies to charities, and charities are not bound by the rule against perpetuities. This means that a charity can generally take an interest under a will no matter how distantly in the future it vests.

The Charity Commission (address in Chapter 30) may be able to advise if problems arise. More information on charitable beneficiaries is included at para. 15.27 onwards.

Is Interest Payable?

12.14 Legacies should be paid with due diligence and usually within the executors' year. Even where the will directs earlier payment, this cannot be compelled.

Interest (payable from residue) normally runs from the time when payment is due (or otherwise if so provided by the will, e.g. 'and I direct that the said legacy shall carry the interim income'). It appears that the rate of interest is 6 per cent p.a. as this is the rate which would apply if there were a judgment in the matter (R.S.C., Order 44, Rule 10; see also *Williams on Wills* (see Booklist, Chapter 29)).

Exceptionally, interest runs from death where the legacy is:

- charged on realty;
- in satisfaction of a debt charged on unconverted realty;
- to the testator's or testatrix's minor child(ren); and
- to any other minor if in respect of maintenance.

PROVISION ON INTESTACY

(N.B. The statutory legacies quoted are applicable for deaths on and after 1 December 1993.)

Deceased was married at death

12.15 The Family Law (Succession) Act 1995 introduced a survivorship period for spouses of 14 days in respect of deaths occurring on or after 1 January 1996:

(a) If the intestate leaves issue (e.g. children and/or grandchildren) the spouse takes:

 (i) personal chattels absolutely (as defined by Administration of Estates Act 1925, s.55(1)(x)); and

 (ii) £125,000 plus interest at the rate of 6 per cent from death until payment (free of tax, with costs and interest coming from the residue); and

 (iii) a life interest in half the residue, the remainder and the other half going to the children on the statutory trusts.

(b) If the intestate leaves no issue, but does leave a parent or brother or sister of the whole blood or their issue, the spouse takes:

 (i) the personal chattels absolutely; and

(ii) £200,000 plus interest as above; and

(iii) half the residue absolutely.

(c) If the intestate leaves no issue, no parents, no brothers or sisters of the whole blood or their issue, the spouse takes the whole estate absolutely.

Deceased was unmarried (or divorced or widowed)

12.16   The estate goes to the intestate's:

(a) issue on the statutory trusts; if none, to

(b) parents; if none, to

(c) brothers and sisters of the whole blood on the statutory trusts, failing whom to remoter relations and, if none, to the Crown or the Duchy of Cornwall. The Treasury Solicitor will deal with the estate in these cases (see para. 14.3). The Treasury Solicitor has a discretion to make payments from the estate to anyone unrelated but close to the deceased during his or her lifetime.

Personal chattels excludes any which are used for business purposes. It also excludes money or securities for money, but has been held to include, for example, valuable collections.

Under the statutory trusts (Administration of Estates Act 1925, s.47), a child of the intestate has a contingent interest in the estate. This is satisfied if the child reaches 18 or marries before that. A child dying under 18, unmarried, is treated as never having existed.

If a child of the intestate does not survive him or her, but leaves a child or children, then that child or those children will take his, her or their deceased parent's share (in equal shares if more than one), again contingently on attaining 18 or marrying before that.

Spouses: special rights

12.17   The surviving spouse may elect (generally within 12 months of the grant) to:

- redeem any life interest in the estate in return for a lump sum

(Administration of Estates Act 1925, s.47). If the spouse so elects for inheritance tax purposes, this does not count as a transfer of value by the spouse. He or she is treated as if, instead of being entitled to the life interest, he or she had been entitled to the lump sum from the outset;

- take the matrimonial home, or the deceased's share in it, in or towards satisfaction of any absolute or capitalised interest in the estate (Intestates Estates Act 1952, Sched. 2). The value of the house is taken at the date of appropriation, not of death: *Re Collins* [1925] 1 W.L.R. 309. To qualify, the surviving spouse must be living in the house concerned at the intestate's death.

Exceptions to the surviving spouse's right to take the matrimonial home include cases where the intestate's interest in the property was a tenancy expirable (by notice or otherwise) within two years of death and where the house forms part of a commercial unit, such as a farmhouse on a working farm or a flat in a family hotel.

If the value of the matrimonial home is more than the spouse's statutory legacy, the spouse may make up the shortfall.

The surviving spouse may *require* personal representatives to make this appropriation, in direct contrast to the position under Administration of Estates Act 1925, s.41, under which PRs may (whether the deceased died testate or intestate) appropriate his or her property in (or towards) satisfaction of interests in the estate, subject to the consent of the other beneficiaries, if the need for this has not been dispensed with in the will.

Hotchpot

12.18 The Law Reform (Succession) Act 1995 abolished the rules as to Hotchpot in their entirety for deaths occurring on or after 1 January 1996.

Intestates Estate Act 1952

12.19 If spouses die in circumstances where the order of death is uncertain, this Act excludes the rule in Law of Property Act 1925, s.184 where the older spouse dies wholly or partially intestate. In such a case, the property passing under the intestacy of the elder will, contrary to the general rule, devolve as though the younger did not survive. This provision effectively prevents the older deceased person's estate passing to his or her in-laws.

Law of Property (Miscellaneous Provisions) Act 1994

12.20 This Act came into effect on 1 July 1995. Helpful articles on this, by Philip Rossdale and Robin Towns, appeared in [1995] *Solicitors Journal*, 28 July and [1995] *New Law Journal*, Probate Supplement 29 September. The Act affects sales of land by PRs and also vests intestates' property pre-grant in the Public Trustee (instead of the President of the Family Division).

Trusts of Land and Appointment of Trustees Act 1996

12.21 This Act came into force on 1 January 1997. It abolished the trust for sale and strict settlement in respect of land and introduced the 'trust of land'. Trustees of land have all the powers of an absolute beneficial owner including the power of sale.

Property of an intestate is no longer held on a trust for sale.

Where a will creates a continuing trust section 11 imposes an obligation on trustees of land to consult beneficiaries of full age with an interest in possession when exercising any function in respect of land.

Section 12 gives a beneficiary with an interest in possession a right to occupy land in certain circumstances.

Section 13 allows trustees to regulate the respective rights of beneficiaries where more than one has an interest in possession.

These provisions can be varied by the will.

Helpful articles appear in [1996] *Solicitors' Journal*, 1154 on the will drafting implications of the Act, in [1996] *Family Law*, December,736 on the provisions of the Act relating to joint ownership, expansion of trustees' powers and beneficiaries' right of occupation and in [1997] *Conveyancing*, July/August, 263 on drafting to restrict trustees' powers.

Appointment and Removal of Trustees and Personal Representatives

Retirement

12.22 There is no power for a personal representative who has taken a grant simply to retire from the office of executor in favour of another person. However, where a will appoints a person to act as executor *and* trustee, it will be possible for that person to retire from the office of trustee.

When does a personal representative become a trustee?

This can be a difficult question. Once the personal representative has ascertained the amount of residue available to the residuary beneficiary and, if appropriate, obtained approval of the estate accounts it is likely that the personal representative then holds the remaining assets as trustee. If, however, other assets or liabilities were discovered, the personal representative would have to deal with these assets or liabilities as personal representative since that office is never lost.

In what circumstances can a trustee retire and/or appoint new trustees?

The circumstances may be covered by the will. If not, the provisions of Trustee Act 1925, ss.36 and 39 will apply. These sections allow a trustee to retire provided this does not result in there being a sole remaining trustee and provided the continuing trustees consent. Continuing trustees can appoint replacement or additional trustees. The personal representatives of a sole trustee who has died can appoint replacements.

Removal of personal representatives by the court

12.23 Under Administration of Justice Act (AJA) 1985, s.50 the court has a discretion to appoint a new personal representative or representatives in the place of existing personal representatives or any of them, or to terminate the appointment of one but not all the personal representatives (unless appointing at least one substituted personal representative).

The court's jurisdiction under section 50 is not limited to cases of conflict between personal representatives. It can be used where a personal representative wishes to retire.

Where the court has ordered the administration of the estate under R.S.C. Order 85, Rule 1 (a comparatively rare event) it has power to appoint personal representative(s).

The court has power to remove personal representatives and appoint new ones under Trustee Act 1925, s.41 where without an order it is 'inexpedient, difficult or impracticable' to appoint a new trustee or new trustees (including personal representatives). Such appointees may be 'in substitution for or in addition to any existing trustee or trustees'. The wording of section 41 is sufficiently wide to enable the court to remove personal representatives and trustees from the office for other than the common causes - residing permanently abroad, becoming mentally disordered, becoming bankrupt or being convicted of serious crime. In *Probate Disputes and Remedies* (Sweet & Maxwell) Dawn Goodman and Brendan Hall state that:

> 'The court will not exercise this jurisdiction lightly and will generally do so only:
>
> (a) when there has been a breach of duty and the court thinks that the estate will not be safe, or will not be administered in accordance with the will or the intestacy rules;
>
> (b) where it is in the interests of the beneficiaries that the personal representatives be removed; or
>
> (c) where there is considerable friction between the personal representatives.
>
> In *Letterstedt* v. *Broers* (1884) 9 App. Cas. 371 the court was at pains to point out that there are no hard and fast rules and that the main guide in these cases must be the welfare of the beneficiaries. In the majority of cases an application is made under the AJA 1985, s.50 rather than under the Trustee Act 1925, s.41.'

There is power under Judicial Trustees Act 1896, s.1 for the court to appoint a judicial trustee but this is rarely used.

N.B. The Law Society has power under the Solicitors Act to apply to court for the appointment of a new trustee in substitution for a solicitor who is a controlled trustee. This would be a step of last resort.

Trusts of Land and Appointment of Trustees Act 1996, s.19

12.24 It is worth noting that under section 19 of this Act beneficiaries who are of full age and capacity and between them entitled to the whole beneficial interest can compel the retirement of the existing trustees and the appointment of trustees of their choice.

In the past beneficiaries who were at odds with their trustees could not simply change the trustees (*Re Brockbank* [1948] Ch. 206). In such circumstances they had to bring the trust to an end and then resettle the property with trustees of their choice but this would frequently have had adverse CGT consequences. The new provision is subject to contrary intention in the will or trust instrument. However, for most people the CGT advantage will outweigh the concern over arbitrary replacement of trustees so only rarely will it be appropriate to exclude the section 19 power.

It is important to note that because of the requirement for full age and capacity and absolute entitlement to the whole beneficial interest there will be comparatively few occasions where section 19 will be relevant.

POWERS AND DUTIES OF EXECUTORS AND TRUSTEES: A SUMMARY

Powers

12.25 Unless executors' powers are extended or varied by the will, these are limited to the powers given to them by statute. The main statutory powers are in:

- **Trustee Investments Act 1961**: a power to invest, which is relatively restricted. A power to buy a house for a beneficiary to live in is not included in a power to invest in land, and must be expressly given. (N.B. Minor amendments were made by the Investment Opportunities Act 1994.) The Act was to have been varied by the Trustee (Investment Division of Trust Fund) Order 1996. This would have enabled up to 75 per cent of the trust fund to be invested in wide range investments. However, the Order was lost as a result of the 1997 General Election.

- **Administration of Estates Act 1925, s.39**: gives PRs all the powers of trustees of land (generally the powers of an absolute owner).

- **Administration of Estates Act 1925, s.41:** gives power to appropriate assets.

- **Administration of Estates Act 1925, s.42**: enables payment of a minor's gift to be made to a trust corporation or at least two trustees, if the minor is absolutely entitled.

- **Trustee Act 1925, s.23:** gives powers of delegation: agents, bankers, solicitors, stockbrokers, etc., may be employed to carry out executors' functions: *Re Vickery* [1931] 1 Ch. 572. Trustee Act 1925, s.25 as amended by Powers of Attorney Act 1971, s.9 authorises delegation of any trustee's functions by power of attorney for a period not exceeding 12 months.

  Note that in the absence of express authority there is no power to use nominee companies to hold trust investments. This can be very awkward for trustees. Application can be made to the court under Trustee Act 1925, s.57. Also see Chapter 24.

- **Trustee Act 1925, s.31**: gives power of maintenance: relates to income.

- **Trustee Act 1925, s.32**: gives power of advancement: relates to capital.

Exercise of powers

12.26   These powers are fiduciary. A sole, or sole surviving, executor or executrix may act alone in all cases. Where there is more than one executor or executrix, authority is joint for land (i.e. all must execute any deed) and joint and several for some personalty (i.e. just one may deliver an asset (e.g. jewellery) to a beneficiary and get a good receipt and discharge).

The Law of Property (Miscellaneous Provisions) Act 1994 covers aspects of sales of land by PRs, including the contract for sale: see para. 14.19.

Duties

12.27   The executors must safeguard the estate and with due diligence:

(a)   collect and realise the assets;

(b)   pay the debts and legacies;

(c)   distribute the residue of the estate among the beneficiaries.

The future

12.28   Both the Law Commission and the Trust Law Committee are reviewing trustees' powers and duties with a view to wholesale reform. However, this will inevitably be some way in the future.

FOREIGN ASSETS AND DOMICILES

Foreign assets

12.29   If the deceased died domiciled in England and Wales, but with assets in another country, a foreign will may have been made. A lawyer of that country may have to be instructed. Usually it is necessary to extract the grant in England and Wales first and then send it accompanied by a sealed and certified copy of the will to a local practitioner. This does not apply in a country where the Colonial Probates Acts apply, or in Scotland or Northern Ireland.

More information on foreign property is included in paras. 13.27 and 27.7.

Foreign domiciles

12.30   If the deceased died domiciled outside England and Wales, but left assets in England and Wales (unless the Colonial Probates Acts apply, or the deceased was domiciled in Scotland or Northern Ireland) it will be necessary to obtain a grant in England and Wales - see NCPR 1987, Rule 30. (See also para. 27.7.)

PART THREE

Practical Probate

This Part deals with some of the practical aspects of probate work which have caused difficulty in the past. It starts by covering inheritance tax, then deals with problem-solving, preparation of the accounts and some of the issues arising from distribution, and it ends with a series of checklists which take you from the beginning of the administration right through to the closing of the file.

Chapter 13

Inheritance tax

Contacting the CTO

13.1   The Capital Taxes Office (CTO)'s address is:

Ferrers House   Tel: 0115 974 2400
PO Box 38   Fax: 0115 974 2432
Castle Meadow Road
Nottingham NG3 1BB

DX: 701201 Nottingham 4

General enquiries about inheritance tax: Tel: 0115 974 2400
Shares Valuation Division (SVD)
enquiries: Tel: 0115 974 2222
Customer services: Tel: 0115 974 2424
Stationery: Tel: 0115 974 3040

Inheritance Tax Rates 1998–99

(For transfers to non-exempt beneficiaries)

Transfers on deaths occurring on or after 6 April 1998 and lifetime transfers taking place within three years of death

13.2   *Value of property passing*   *Rate*

Up to	£223,000	Nil
Exceeding	£223,000	40%

Lifetime transfers taking place between three and seven years of death

13.3   There is a tapering relief available on such gifts but it takes the form of a reduction in the tax which would otherwise be payable. Thus, it only becomes effective if the total of the lifetime transfers made between three and seven years of death exceeds the limit of the nil rate band.

Years before death in which transfer made	Percentage of death rate tax payable
3–4	80%
4–5	60%
5–6	40%
6–7	20%

N.B. Gifts made between seven and 14 years before the death, although themselves not liable to tax, may affect the rate of IHT applicable to gifts within the seven-year period.

Annual exemption

13.4   £3,000 (plus £3,000 for the previous tax year if unused).

Reliefs

Business property relief/agricultural property relief

13.5   Each at 100 per cent or 50 per cent of the value of the property transferred, depending on the nature of the assets and subject to minimum ownership requirements.

Woodlands relief

13.6   The value of trees or underwood growing in non-agricultural woodlands can be left out of account by election and the tax deferred until disposal of the timber.

National Heritage property

13.7   Exempt from inheritance tax if so designated by the Revenue and undertakings regarding the property are given and complied with.

This Practice Note has been issued by the CTO:

'Inheritance Tax "Heritage" Property. IHTA 1984, s.30

The Capital Taxes Office (CTO) no longer requires to see, at the pre-grant stage, Inland Revenue accounts in which a claim for conditional exemption is made.

Inheritance tax is essentially a self-assessed tax and legal personal representatives should be able to justify their claim during the post-grant examination of the account. It will assist the CTO if the following question is answered when the account is completed. (It will be incorporated in the accounts when they are revised.)

Did the deceased own or have an interest in possession in any "heritage" property which was given exemption from Capital Taxes on an earlier chargeable occasion for IHT/CTT/ED/CGT? If so, please provide full details and the CTO reference if known.

The register is available on the Internet at www.cto.eds.co.uk'

Quick succession relief

13.8 Available on a sliding scale when a transfer on death takes place within five years of an earlier transfer on which tax was paid, the point on the scale depending on date of the second death.

THE INLAND REVENUE ACCOUNT

Is one necessary? Excepted estates

13.9 The following unedited notes are taken from the Revenue's leaflet IHT 12 and are reproduced with their permission.

WHEN IS AN EXCEPTED ESTATE GRANT APPROPRIATE?

Background

This leaflet is for practitioners. It explains when you can take out an excepted estate grant. It also explains when you cannot. **It relates only to deaths in England, Wales and Northern Ireland**. Please read the leaflet carefully and use the flowcharts to help you decide whether you can take out an excepted estate grant.

1. Introduction

Inheritance Tax Act 1984 (IHTA 1984), s.256 permits the Revenue to make regulations dispensing with the requirements to deliver an account for inheritance tax. The Revenue has made regulations under this section. This means that in certain, non taxpaying estates, an account does not have to be delivered. If an estate fulfils the criteria in the regulations, it is an 'excepted estate'. If the estate is 'excepted', you do not have to deliver an account of the estate to obtain a grant of representation.

The Revenue amends the regulations from time to time to update the financial limits. They were amended in 1991, 1995, 1996 and again in **1998.**

This leaflet explains the regulations applying to deaths on or after **1 April 1991.**

2. Which estates are excepted?

a. Value of estate

The **gross** value of the whole estate must not exceed **'the limit'.** 'The limit' depends on when the death occurred.

To decide whether the estate exceeds the limit, you must include:

- property which has passed under the deceased's will or intestacy;

- nominated property;

- the value of the deceased's beneficial interest in any **joint assets,** including assets passing by survivorship **even if they are exempt; and**

- property which is exempt from tax or entitled to 100 per cent relief.

Date of death	*The limit*
After 31 March 1991 and before 6 April 1995	£125,000
After 5 April 1995 and before 6 April 1996	£145,000
After 5 April 1996 and before 6 April 1998	£180,000

For deaths after 5 April 1998, the limit is **£200,000.** But to test whether the limit is exceeded, you must add the value of **'specified transfers'** to the **gross** estate. ('Specified transfers' are chargeable transfers of cash, **quoted** shares or securities made in the seven years before the death.)

b.   *Domicile*

An estate is not excepted if the deceased died domiciled outside the United Kingdom. (The Channel Islands and the Isle of Man are **outside** the United Kingdom.)

c.   *Settled property*

An estate **is not excepted** if the deceased had an interest in possession in the settled property. Even if the value of the settled property, together with the value of the property passing under the deceased's will or intestacy, is less than the limit, you must deliver an Inland Revenue account of the deceased's own estate before you can get the grant.

d.   *Foreign property*

An estate **is not excepted** if more than £30,000 (or £15,000 if the death was before 6 April 1996) of the gross value of the estate consists of property situated outside the United Kingdom.

e.   *Lifetime gifts*

An estate **is not excepted** if the deceased made chargeable or potentially exempt transfers (PETs) within seven years before the death, **unless the death was after April 1996 and the transfers were 'specified transfers' which total not more than £50,000.**

You need not take account of exempt transfers, such as:

- gifts or other transfers of value made to the deceased's spouse unless, at the time of the gift, the deceased was domiciled in the United Kingdom and the spouse was not. (The **'spouse exemption'**);

- gifts of money, or of quoted shares or securities, where these together with any other non-exempt gifts do not total more than £3,000 in any one year to 5 April. (The **'annual exemption'**);

- outright gifts to any individual of not more than £250 in any one year to 5 April. (The **'small gifts' exemption);**

- **wedding gifts** of not more than £5,000 to either party to the marriage of the deceased's children (including step-children and adopted children), £2,500 (grandchildren) or £1,000 to anyone else;

- gifts of money if the executors or intending administrators are satisfied that they are wholly exempt as **normal gifts out of income.**

  For a transfer to be exempt as a normal gift out of income you must be able to show that:

  - it was part of the normal expenditure of the deceased, i.e. habitual or part of a pattern;

  - it was made out of income (taking one year with another);

  - the deceased had enough income left to maintain his or her usual standard of living.

  [This exemption may not be available for renewal premiums on a policy of insurance where the deceased had purchased an annuity at any time.]

f.   *Gifts with reservation*

An estate is not excepted if the deceased made a gift with reservation of benefit which continued until death. [If a reservation ceased within seven years before the death, there is a chargeable transfer.]

3.   When can the Revenue insist on delivery of an account?

If you have taken out an excepted grant, the Revenue can still insist on delivery of an Inland Revenue account. We will do so in a sample of estates. If we require delivery of an account, we must give notice in writing within 35 days of the issue of the grant of representation. **The Regulations require that we give this notice to the legal personal representatives rather than any solicitor acting for them.**

4.   What if I find out after taking out the grant that the estate is not excepted?

If you have taken out an excepted estate grant and then find out that the estate did not fulfil the criteria, you must tell the CTO. (For example, you might discover that there was settled property.) If this happens the CTO may insist on delivery of an account even though the 35-day period has elapsed.

5. What happens if an account is not required

If the Revenue do not give notice that they require an account within 35 days of the grant, all persons are discharged from any claim for tax on the deceased's death. However, this does not discharge any person from tax if there is fraud or failure to disclose material facts. Nor does it stop the collection of tax if further property is found later.

6. Estates that are not excepted

If an estate is not excepted, you must deliver an Inland Revenue account to obtain a grant of representation. We describe the forms of account below.

IHT 202

You can use this form if the deceased:

- died after 18 March 1986;

- was domiciled in the United Kingdom;

- had no property outside the United Kingdom;

- made no lifetime gifts;

- had no interest in settled property;

- the total net value of the estate **after** any exemptions and reliefs is not more than the inheritance tax threshold at the date of death; **and**

- the total **gross** value of the estate **before** deducting exemptions and reliefs is not more than twice the threshold at the date of death.

IHT 201

You must use this form if the deceased died after 18 March 1986 **and** was domiciled outside the United Kingdom.

IHT 200

You should use this form in all other cases if the deceased died after 18 March 1986.

In Northern Ireland, the equivalent account forms are IHT 202N, IHT 201N respectively.

If you need a grant for a death before 18 March 1986 or if you need details of the excepted estate regulations for deaths before 1 April 1991, you should contact the CTO Enquiries Section. (Telephone 0114 974 2400, or in Northern Ireland 01232 315556 ext. 2337.)

If you need to write to the CTO, the addresses are:

Capital Taxes Office, Ferrers House, PO Box 38, Castle Meadow Road, Nottingham NG2 1BB or DX 701201 Nottingham 4;

Capital Taxes Office, Level 3, Dorchester House 52–58 Great Victoria Street, Belfast BT2 7QL or DX 2001 NR Belfast 2.

N.B. This leaflet is for guidance only. It reflects the tax position at the time of writing. It is not binding by law, and in a particular case there may be special circumstances which need to be taken into account.

13.10 New forms were introduced early in 1993. A most helpful booklet (IHT 210) *Guidance Notes on the Completion of Inland Revenue Accounts* was produced in March 1996.

The most common ones are:

- **IHT 200**: see paras. 13.11, 13.27 and 13.30;

- **IHT 202**: shorter but restricted to use when:

    (a) the deceased died domiciled in the UK; and

    (b) all the assets in the estate are situated in the UK; and

    (c) the deceased made no lifetime transfers chargeable to CTT or IHT within seven years of death; and

    (d) the total net value of the estate - after deducting exemptions and reliefs - does not exceed the inheritance tax threshold at death (currently £223,000 for deaths on or after 6 April 1998); and

    (e) the estate comprises only property in the UK and passing under a will or intestacy, or by nomination, or beneficially by survivorship (N.B. Regardless of the value of the estate, if it includes settled property, form 200 must be used); and

(f) the total gross value of the estate, before exemption and reliefs, does not exceed twice the IHT threshold at death.

Excepted Estates Flow Chart for deaths after 5 April 1996

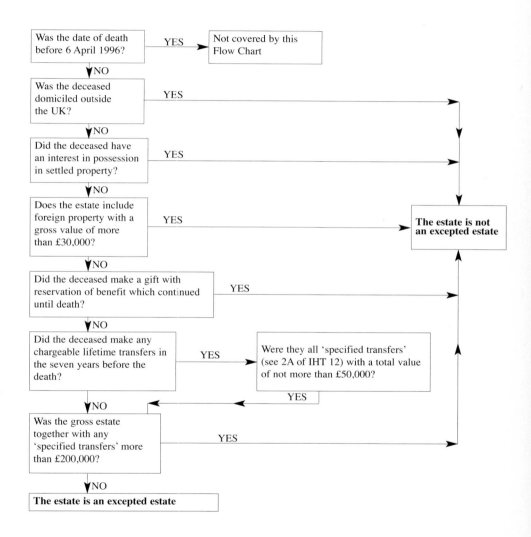

- **IHT 200:** use for application for a first grant of representation when the deceased dies domiciled in England and Wales, Scotland or Northern Ireland and IHT 202 cannot be used;

- **D-3:** corrective account - appropriate where further assets are discovered or errors were made in the first Inland Revenue account (IRA), e.g. valuations or estimates were inaccurate. Minor discrepancies may be dealt with in correspondence if the Capital Taxes Office agrees;

- **IHT 201:** use if the deceased was domiciled outside the UK at death. (This must be accompanied by IHT 26, giving a short history of the deceased's life, with relevant dates.)

You may obtain copies of these forms, preferably by faxing your request, from:

Capital Taxes Office
Stationery Section
Fax: 0115 974 3030.

COMPLETING FORM IHT 200

13.11   The Inland Revenue booklet IHT 210 mentioned above is excellent, but the following pointers may also be helpful.

General information (page 1)

13.12
- Having decided on the appropriate registry, complete the IRA accordingly. If a district registry is used, the IRA should read, e.g. 'The Manchester District Registry'.

- Always include basic details such as your reference, telephone number, postcode and DX code.

- The format required for birth and death dates is as follows: 20 Dec 1943.

- Tick the appropriate boxes re marital status, surviving relatives and domicile.

- Remember to include the deceased's income tax district and reference number, if known.

- Give the executors' or intending administrators' correct names and addresses. You can alter the order from that in the will if you wish.

Section 1: Lifetime gifts or transfers of value (page 2)

13.13   The aim of these questions is to ascertain the deceased's liability to IHT, by establishing the cumulative total at death and setting out information regarding other assets included in the estate for IHT purposes:

- Tick the appropriate box 'yes' and 'no'. Transfers of value listed on page 4 in booklet IHT 210 should not be included (e.g. to spouse, annual exemption, etc.).

- List all transfers of value and, if several have been made in the relevant period, attach a separate schedule giving the details required. If the PRs claim that no IHT is payable on reported transfers, reasons must be given and the relevant exemption(s) or relief(s) claimed.

- The benefit of exemptions and reliefs must be claimed. Evidence to show eligibility must be submitted if required by the Inland Revenue (e.g. if the deceased was a working farmer and agricultural property relief is claimed, evidence of his or her length of ownership and of a practical involvement in the day-to-day running of the farm may be required). The burden is always on the taxpayer to claim the benefit of exemptions and reliefs, and to adduce evidence to substantiate the claim(s).

- Failure to claim an appropriate exemption or relief could lead to an action in negligence against the adviser concerned.

Section 2: Nominated and joint property (page 3)

13.14 • This refers to statutory nominations, e.g. savings certificates. It does not relate to insurance policies where the benefit has been assigned to third parties by the deceased during life, nor to so-called 'nominations' of discretionary payments under employees' pension funds. (The latter are not in any event part of the deceased's estate at all, as the deceased had no vested right to them).

- Section 2A or 2B should be completed as appropriate. (See notes on Section 3 below.)

- Give details of jointly owned property, e.g. house, bank accounts, etc. This should be done on a separate sheet. Evidence may be needed of the circumstances of any purported joint ownership, for example, the extent to which each co-owner contributed originally.

- Jointly owned property will also be relevant to partners and cohabitees. The test whether cohabitees' contributions can lead to ownership is whether the contribution was of a capital (usually substantial) rather than an income (usually smaller) nature. Thus, labour and/or money expended on building an extension to a home may be seen as falling into the first category, whereas buying weekly food out of a salary or wage tends to be regarded as the second. However, the courts are taking an increasingly flexible view - after all, the contribution to food and other household expenses by one party relieves the resources of the other.

  Whilst things may be much simpler if such contributions are well documented, in reality, evidence may be hard to find. Receipts, bank statements, etc., may well help.

  Property owned jointly by spouses is exempt from IHT because it is passing between spouses, not because it is passing by survivorship. Thus, such property should always be included in the IRA as above and any exemption claimed on page 9 as appropriate.

- Remember that business partnership property will, subject to the usual ownership period and other conditions, qualify for IHT business property relief and the instalment option facility. Such property should be included in Section 3B on page 6 and not here.

Section 3: Free estate in the UK (pages 4 to 6)

13.15 Section 3A relates to property without the instalment option, while Section 3B relates to property with the instalment option. The format in each case is a list of assets, first giving a gross value, and then a list of the liabilities deducted from the gross value, to give a net value.

Section 3A: Property without the instalment option (pages 4 and 5)

13.16 Pages 4 and 5 comprise a schedule of the deceased's assets in the UK, excluding property subject to a general power of appointment which should be included in Section 5 along with property gifted, subject to a reservation. The items on the schedule are generally self-explanatory, but:

- The list on page 4 is not exhaustive - do not be afraid to amend or add to it, e.g. under 'Any other income . . .' (seventh item from the foot of page 4). If the deceased was entitled to pension arrears, insert 'pension' after '. . . as statement annexed'.

- Only stocks and shares not eligible for the instalment option should be listed here. Check whether the shareholding is sufficient to give the necessary control, to decide whether the instalment option applies. List all such holdings on Form IHT 40. In large estates it will save time to have a professional valuation schedule prepared (the cost of which can be added to the base cost of the securities for capital gains tax purposes – *Richards Executors* (1971) 46 T.C. 626).

- Money in the bank and interest accrued should be itemised separately.

- Detailed separate statements relating to bank accounts, mortgages, etc., should be attached to the IRA.

- The necessary apportionments, e.g. in respect of pension and other income, should be calculated and detailed in separate statements and attached.

- Refunds, e.g. council tax, will be assets in the estate, as will income and other tax refunds and arrears to state benefits up to the date of death. All should be detailed as such.

- Income accrued due: this relates to unpaid income due to the deceased as life tenant – if relevant, apportionment to date of death is necessary.

- Salary, etc.; due to date of death is included under 'Any other income . . .'.

- Policies of insurance and bonuses: those written in trust for a third party under this head should be excluded – but details should be given on page 2 (above).

- Income tax refund: include details if relevant.

- Personal chattels: include actual amount if sold; estimated value if not. Personal chattels can be sold pre-grant – but this is unwise as any such dealing with the deceased's property can constitute inter-meddling. A sole, or one of joint, personal representative(s) can pass title in such property by delivery.

- Interest in expectancy: include details here of any reversionary interest to which the deceased was entitled, but only if the reversionary interest does not qualify as excluded property. See the notes on the form and Inheritance Tax Act 1984, s.48.

- Other personal property: include here lump sum pension funds to which the deceased was entitled (i.e. not those payable at the discretion of the trustees and not ex-gratia payments, e.g. in relation to fatal and all other accidents.) Monies from mortgage protection policies, etc., should be included under 'Any other income . . . '.

- Total gross property in the box half way down page 5.

- List deceased's general liabilities, e.g. credit card, electricity account, etc. Do not include mortgages secured on land forming part of the free estate.

- Itemise funeral expenses separately: these must be reasonable and by concession, can include reasonable expenses for mourning and for a tombstone.

- Insert net value at the foot of page 5.

Section 3B: Property with instalment option (page 6)

13.17 Section 3B applies to instalment option property. If such property is included in the estate, PRs should always elect to pay by instalments at this stage, i.e. on submission of the form. If it is, in fact, subsequently decided to pay outstanding instalments in one lump sum, the Inland Revenue will not object. Electing to pay by instalments keeps options open and gives greater flexibility.

IHT is normally due six months after the end of the month when the transfer, i.e. the death, takes place (e.g. when the death occurs on 15 April, the due date is 31 October).

For property in respect of which the instalment option is available, the first instalment will be due on the normal due date, and remaining instalments on each anniversary of that date after that. The kinds of property on which tax can be paid by instalments are land, some holdings of unquoted shares and securities, businesses and timber. As soon as the property is sold, all the tax is payable. In the case of non-agricultural land not comprised in a business, interest accrues on the outstanding balance of the tax. In other cases interest accrues on instalments paid late.

It is possible for the Inland Revenue to register a charge in the Land Registry against the PRs in respect of any outstanding IHT.

In order to avoid the unnecessary payment of interest, payments should be made when due and diarised accordingly and/or arrangements made with the PRs' bank. Interest which becomes payable as a result of late payment, or which accrues on the unpaid portion of the tax, is not deductible for income tax purposes.

Page 6 follows the same format as Section 3A:

- List all assets carrying the instalment option and passing into the deceased's estate; include gross values. Appropriate reliefs are claimed on page 9.

- Joint property passes outside the estate and therefore is not mentioned here but is detailed in Section 2, page 3.

- If there are several properties, include the total value on page 6 then list them in detail on form IHT 37.

- Total all instalment option property in the box half way down page 6.

- List liabilities, e.g. mortgages, charges, etc.

- Insert net value at foot of page 6.

Section 4: Foreign property (page 7)

13.18   Section 4A deals with non-instalment option property, Section 4B with instalment option property. As for Section 3, list assets first, liabilities second.

Remember to enter net values of property in both Sections 4A and 4B.

Section 5: Settled property and gifts with reservations (page 8)

13.19 • Here details of the deceased's interest in trust property (e.g. a life interest) must be given. You should answer the question at the top of the page even if there is no settled property.

171

- Any property qualifying for the instalment option should be accounted for in Section 5B. All other properties should be shown in Section 5A.

- In both Sections 5A and 5B there are two boxes, distinguishing property on which tax is being paid on delivery of account, from all other property.

- Liabilities should again be deducted from the gross values in both Sections 5A and 5B.

Section 6: Summary of exemptions and reliefs (page 9)

13.20 • Claim exemptions and reliefs, e.g. spouse, business property relief, charity, etc., here and not on earlier pages where the assets are listed, although a brief note (e.g. on an exemption in relation to a joint share in the matrimonial home) may have been made earlier.

• Only quick succession relief and double taxation relief are claimed elsewhere (on page 10).

• Enter claims for exemptions, etc., in the appropriate box, according to whether the property itself was listed under Section 3A, 3B, 4 or 5 (e.g. personal chattels under Section 3A passing to spouse - value (transferred from 3A) £50,000 then relief £50,000).

Section 7: Declaration of liability (page 9)

13.21 In essence, PRs must state whether any debts or liabilities claimed are liabilities (e.g. mortgage, income tax liability) or 'artificial debts'. Finance Act 1986, s.102 provides that 'artificial debts' are not deductible (e.g. Ann gave her son a picture in 1988, 'bought it back' in 1989, but did not pay the purchase price).

Assessment of IHT (pages 10 and 11)

13.22 All the totals from the preceding sections are carried forward to this page.

Probate summary

13.23 • Transfer the appropriate figures from the earlier parts of the form. (See para. 13.29.)

• Once this is completed it will be possible to indicate to the residuary beneficiaries the approximate likely extent of their inheritances.

Declaration (page 12)

13.24 • Insert the type of grant applied for, e.g. probate of the will, letters of administration or letters of administration with will annexed.

• Delete 'I/we/our' as appropriate.

• Do not alter the third box down the page, if the PRs have been unable to value any particular asset(s), e.g. something so rare that only one or two experts in the world can give an opinion and neither is available at the time. (Such an instance could, of course, give rise to the necessity to complete form D–3.) Otherwise delete this section.

• Each PR must sign and date the form.

REVENUE LEAFLETS

13.25 The Revenue have produced leaflets, following discussions with practitioners on information it would be helpful to send with accounts. A summary of leaflet IHT 9 on completing Inland Revenue accounts 200, 201 and 202 is given in para. 13.26.

IHT 1 has been replaced by five separate booklets: IHT 14 on the responsibilities of personal representatives; IHT 15 on how to calculate liability; IHT 16 on settled property; IHT 17 on businesses, farms and woodlands; and IHT 18 on foreign aspects. IHT 10 covers foreign property and a note about it is included at para. 13.27. IHT 11 gives details about paying inheritance tax from National Savings.

It is well worth obtaining the originals from the CTO (address at the beginning of this chapter).

The CTO stresses that, in making their comments, they 'do not wish to impede the application for a grant of representation'. They say, however, that if you have, when you apply for the grant, the information mentioned, it will help to focus their enquiries if you send it to the CTO with the account.

13.26 Summary of the CTO's leaflet IHT 9 – 'Information We Suggest You Provide with an Inland Revenue Account'

Section 1

If you have answered 'yes' to the second question, about insurance policies not included on p.4, keep a copy of the policy itself before surrendering the original, as the CTO may wish to see it. Also send copies of documents relating to policies held in trust.

Section 3

The CTO would find additional information helpful in these cases:

- PEPs – give a breakdown of shares and cash held.

- Loans – if a loan is shown as an asset in the estate, at less than the amount of the loan, explain how you have calculated the discount and why.

- Insurance policies and bonuses - again, send copies of correspondence with the company if this confirms the value.

- Furniture valuations - again, send a copy of the valuation; if none has been obtained, give brief details of the effects, showing who valued the items and on what basis, if sales are planned. [See para. 13.32.]

- Unadministered estates - if the deceased had an interest, give the official reference for the estate if you know it, or the name and date of death. The CTO will want a list of assets of the earlier estate unless the second deceased's interest was a pecuniary legacy or specific bequest only.

Liabilities

- Cheques not cleared - you are asked to show to whom these were issued and why.

- Professional fees - confirm these relate wholly to services rendered before death (services after death are not of course IHT-deductible).

Funeral expenses, memorials, etc.

- If the sum involved substantially exceeds 'what might be expected', give an itemised breakdown and explain the circumstances.

Section 3b

- Mortgage protection policies - say whether there was one, and give details.

- Equitable interests in property - say who is claiming this and how the interest arose.

- Partnerships and businesses - show the nature, how long the deceased had owned an interest, how that interest and the value of goodwill was calculated, and send the relevant valuation accounts. For partnerships, send a copy of the deed but if there is none, say when the partnership started, by whom and in what shares the capital was provided and the proportions in which profits and losses were divided.

Exemptions and reliefs

- Small charities – unless the charity is a household name, it will help the CTO if you give the charity number.

- Agricultural and business property relief - in leaflet IHT 9, the CTO give the full text of questions 3 and 4 from the standard enquiry forms which they issue when these reliefs have been claimed. They suggest including answers to these questions with the account as this may enable them to instruct the District Valuer sooner.

Deeds of variation

- If a deed is executed before the grant, include clauses in the recital naming the proposed PRs and stating their intention to apply for a grant and at which probate registry. The CTO go on to say that you can then self-assess the account on the basis of the varied will or intestacy provided either:

  - notice of election has been included in the instrument itself; or

  - the parties have signed a separate notice of election.

- Send these documents with the account.

- If you know an estate is to be varied when you are preparing the account, the CTO advise that you mention this in a covering letter with it. Their leaflet IHT 8 gives more information.

175

IHT 10: Inheritance tax and foreign property

13.27   IHT 10 details the kind of information the CTO would find helpful to have early on, and gives guidelines for property in the USA, South Africa, Republic of Ireland, France, the Netherlands, Sweden, Italy and Switzerland. When the deceased was domiciled in the UK *and* there is property outside the UK in the estate, if the foreign property is valued at more than £30,000 (£15,000 if the death was before 6 April 1996), regardless of the *total* value of the estate, IHT 200 is the right form. If the foreign property is taxable abroad, UK relief may be available (but not on interest or penalties). IHT 18 on foreign aspects is also useful.

POINTS FROM THE INLAND REVENUE

Notes from the CTO

13.28   These notes are written by Diane Veale, who is Customer Service Manager at the Capital Taxes Office. They outline points from recent meetings the CTO held with the Law Society and with the British Bankers Association. Practitioners' main concerns are summarised, with the CTO response. These notes are being circulated (in an appropriately amended version) within the CTO.

Practitioners' concerns and how the CTO can help

Practitioners' questions/topics	*CTO replies*
• Payable orders made to personal representatives: Has there been a change of policy?	No. The CTO has always made them out to the legal personal representatives *unless* it has a valid mandate which states otherwise. Staff have been reminded to check whether a mandate has been completed. CTO will consider including a mandate on the IHT 200 and application for clearance when these are revised.
• Practitioners would like to provide less detailed information where the charity relief or spouse exemption covers the whole estate.	No action. Revenue needs the information (but estimated values for individual items can be used if stated as such).

Practitioners' questions/topics	*CTO replies*
• CTO staff are being too 'pernickety': for example, asking for D–3s for every amendment.	Staff have been reminded about their instructions and to take a commonsense approach.
• Does CTO really need a letter from National Savings as evidence of amount saved (in certificates or otherwise)?	No. Staff should use their common sense.
• Delays in receipt of confirmation that there is no tax to pay on trust funds which are wholly exempt or relieved.	Staff have been reminded that there is no need to delay in these cases. (Changes to the free estate cannot affect the trust if it is wholly exempt or relieved.)
• In which circumstances are penalties imposed? There is a feeling that sometimes these are unreasonable.	The CTO has prepared a leaflet dated February 1996 which sets out guidelines on charging penalties. The Public Accounts Committee expressed concern about the low level of penalties for inheritance tax. The CTO has set up a Compliance Team headed by an Inspector of Taxes to ensure their approach is consistent with that of the rest of the Revenue.
• Electronic delivery of accounts.	To be considered by CTO computer group when current projects 'bedded in'.
• Feeling that CTO is asking for professional valuation of chattels too often – this increases costs.	See last bullet point below.

CTO's concerns and how practitioners can help

CTO concerns	*Practitioners are asked to:*
• Difficulty in tracing references, particularly in death of life tenant cases.	State the CTO reference if known and state the full name and date of death of life tenant *in the heading* on correspondence.

CTO concerns	*Practitioners are asked to:*
• Omission of information from accounts (can lead to investigation for penalties).	Indicate when values are estimates and explain at the beginning any problem areas which may give rise to changes later.
	Read leaflet IHT 9 *Information We Suggest You Provide with an Inland Revenue Account.* [See paras 13.20 and 13.26.]
• Delay when we need to see copies of life policies (e.g. if policy is written in trust).	Keep copies of policies before returning them to the insurance company.
• Unnecessary work in pre-grant section.	Make sure correct signatures are on accounts for estates (i.e. personal representatives'). Send IHT 200 straight to cashiers if tax already calculated. Send IHT 202 straight to the Probate Section.
• Confusion over when expected estate grant can be taken out.	Read leaflet IHT 12 *When is an Excepted Estate Grant Appropriate?* and follow the flowchart [see para. 13.9].
• Concern about whether estimates for household and personal goods are realistic. These seem to have remained static for years.	Find out whether any specific items are insured and encourage valuers to make realistic estimates and family members to list the main items.

Additional reminders

13.29 *Calculation of the tax and interest*

- Personal representatives have a duty to complete their Inland Revenue account form properly. They have a legal responsibility to pay the full amount of tax for which they are liable, before they send the account to the probate registry with their application for a grant of representation. Practitioners acting as, or on behalf of, personal representatives are expected themselves to calculate the correct amount of tax due.

- Remember when you calculate the tax payable on the free, unsettled estate that you must enter on page 11 of form IHT 200 a figure for each of the following:

  - the value of any settled property;

  - the cumulative total value of any chargeable lifetime transfers;

  - the value of any gifts with reservation.

  Failure to do this may result in a substantial underpayment of tax pre-grant.

- Practitioners should supply the CTO with as much information as possible with the account to enable more focused enquiries to be raised after the grant has been issued. A classic example is 'Cohabitees' contributions – can they lead to ownership?' Both the CTO and practitioners want to provide a good speedy service to their respective customers. It will save time if the IRA contains a statement of the basis of an ownership claim rather than waiting for the CTO to raise enquiries.

- You may now apply to the probate registry for Grant de Bonis Non Administratis without first sending CAP A5–C to the CTO.

DEATH OF A LIFE TENANT: CTO APPROVED STANDARD LETTER

13.30   The CTO approve the letter below to notify them of a life tenant's death. They add that applications for clearance on CAP 30 should not be made until these can be issued. There is no point in submitting the CAP 30 with, for example, the IHT 100.

> The Director
> Capital Taxes Office
> DX 701201 Nottingham 4   [Date]

Dear Sir

The Trust of Mr Fred Bloggs (Settlement 1948/Will dated 10/4/50)
Date of Death: 1/5/53
Your Reference: F/123456/53
Life Tenant: **Mrs Freda Payne**
Date of Death: 25/10/98

The Life Tenant of this Trust has died. We enclose a copy of the Trust Instrument.

We also enclose a completed form IHT 100 with supporting schedules. Please acknowledge receipt.

The Life Tenant's Estate will be dealt with by:

Morse & Co, Solicitors, Lewis House, 22 Burt St, Oxford OX1 20X

*[We have not yet been able to ascertain the value of the Life Tenant's free estate.]

OR

*[We understand that the value of the deceased's free estate is about £200,000.]

We look forward to receiving an assessment or, in due course, confirmation that we may lodge form CAP 30.

Yours faithfully

(Jaguar & Co)

* Include as necessary: this will help the CTO decide whether to issue a provisional assessment immediately. They can only do this if they know the value of the free estate.

PRODUCING YOUR OWN INLAND REVENUE FORMS

13.31   The CTO have provided information for firms wanting to generate IHT account forms using their own computers. (See Inland Revenue booklet 11/96 *Guidelines for Producing Substitute Inheritance Tax Forms*.) The following edited extracts may be of interest.

Legislative context

- Inheritance Tax Act 1984, s.257(i) says that all accounts and other documents required for the purposes of the Act shall be in such form and shall contain such particulars as the Board may prescribe. The Board of Inland Revenue will accept an accurate facsimile of the prescribed form. You will need to obtain official approval for each different type of IHT form you intend to use. The CTO will give an approval reference which you must include on the bottom right hand corner of each form you complete (e.g. CTO approval ref. A197). You must also show the correct identifier on the bottom left hand corner of the first page.

What will be considered an accurate facsimile?

- Substitute forms must accurately reproduce the words and layout of the official form, but should not be colour printed. In other words, apart from the colour, they must be virtually indistinguishable from the originals.

- The facsimile must also be readily recognisable as an inheritance tax form when it is received at the CTO; and (presumably for ease of processing by them) the entries must be distinguishable from the background text. Taxpayers' reference should always be transferred from originals to copies, where appropriate.

- Applications for approval (the Revenue will readily discuss a printed sample, rather than a photocopy, in advance) and requests for further information should be made to: Forms Adviser, Inland Revenue, Capital Taxes Office, Ferrers House, P.O. Box 38, Castle Meadow Road, Nottingham NG2 1BB. DX: 701201 Nottingham 4.

Design notes

1. *Colour*

Your substitute should not be colour-printed. Also, you do not need to print it onto coloured paper.

Where the original form has different tints of colour, you should use differing degrees of monochrome shading.

2. *Logo*

You *must not* reproduce the Inland Revenue logo on any substitute that you produce. You should, however, include the text part of the header (i.e. the 'Inland Revenue Capital Taxes Office' part).

3. *Paper*

You should use the same size paper as the original (A4).

You should print on paper of a reasonable standard as the forms will need to survive for many years. You may print either single or double-sided.

4. *Text*

You *must* reproduce *all* of the text that appears on the original. Your text must also follow the same patterns of bold and italic as on the original.

The CTO standard font for its forms is UNIVERS (W1). You should use either this font or a similar sans-serif alternative, such as HELVETICA.

You should use all the same font sizes as the original and any other special styles (e.g. IHT 200 uses some white text on a dark background in its headings).

5. *Page content*

Each page on your substitute must contain the same information in the same order as the original. You should show page numbers clearly in the same place the originals show them.

6. *Lines and boxes*

You should try to achieve the same size and positioning of boxes as on the original.

It is important that your version keeps to the same proportional layout as those on the original. You should try to make sure that any boxes and lines are the same length and thickness.

7. *I am happy with my form, what happens next?*

You should print out two blank copies of your form and send them to the CTO at the address shown [above].

The Forms Adviser will tell you about changes you must make. When you reach the required standard, the Forms Adviser will give you a unique reference. You must show the reference on each form that you send to the CTO.

What forms are appropriate for substitutes?

Suitable accounts and forms are:

Accounts and inventories	Other forms
IHT 100	Cap D3
IHT 101	IHT 26
IHT 200	IHT 30 (formerly Cap 30)
IHT 201	IHT 35 (formerly Sect 5)
IHT 202	IHT 37
Cap Form A–3	IHT 38 (formerly Cap 38)
Cap Form B–3	IHT 40
Cap Form B–4	Mis 1G

N.B. If you want to use computerised forms but do not want to prepare the forms yourself, ask the CTO Forms Adviser to send you a list of the software firms who operate under licence. You can contact them yourself and choose the most suitable package.

VALUATION OF UPHOLSTERED FURNITURE NOT MEETING THE 1988 SAFETY REGULATIONS

13.32 The Incorporated Society of Valuers and Auctioneers (ISVA) and CTO have drawn up the following guidelines for the valuation for probate of items which cannot be sold at auction, or in the course of business generally, to realise capital.

This has been a particular problem following the introduction on 1 March 1993 of the ban on the sale of upholstered furniture which does not comply with the Furniture and Furnishing (Fire) (Safety) Regulations 1988 ('the Regulations'). The guidelines cover all goods for which Safety Regulations have been made under the Consumer Protection Act, although in practice it is likely they will mainly be applied to furniture.

The CTO do not intend to challenge valuations carried out in accordance with these guidelines:

1.   Items of low value which do not comply with the Regulations and which cannot therefore be sold 'in the course of business' can be given a nil value.

  Example: a divan bed which would normally be valued at £20 but which does not comply with the Regulations can be valued at nil.

2.   Where items of substantial value do not comply with the Regulations, consideration should be given to the possibility and

cost of rendering them compliant. If this is feasible the valuation should reflect the cost involved and be adjusted downwards to make allowance for this.

Example: a set of six good reproduction dining chairs which would normally be valued at £600 is rendered unsaleable because the upholstery does not comply with the Regulations. A value should be placed on them taking into account the cost of re-upholstering at say £40 a chair and the valuation adjusted by £240 to £360.

3. Where the item to be valued does not comply with the Regulations and the cost of compliance would be uneconomical then a nil value can be applied:

Example: a three-piece lounge suite normally valued at £150 which does not comply with the Regulations and which would cost £500 to re-upholster can be given a nil value.

Paying Pre-Grant IHT

Interest on loans

13.33 The interest payable on qualifying loans taken out by the PRs to pay IHT pre-grant is deductible for income tax purposes from income in the PRs' hands in respect of a period of one year from the making of the loan.

Sources of funding

13.34 It is common to look to the deceased's bank for a loan to finance the payment of IHT, but other alternatives – such as encashing National Savings certificates (no grant being needed for this), or investments in nominee names, approaching the deceased's building society or asking family members – may be worth considering. However, the process is not quick and can slow down the obtaining of a grant quite substantially. The Revenue's booklet IHT 11 gives guidance on paying IHT from National Savings.

Below are two specimen letters which solicitors in private practice may adapt or adopt for the purpose set out on page iv but not for any other purpose. The first letter is to a bank seeking a global loan facility; the second letter is to a building society seeking the early release of funds.

'Global' loans facility – letter to bank

13.35 This is an edited version of a letter used by one practice to obtain special favourable facilities. If such an arrangement is established, consider in each case whether there are any issues which would make it advisable to suggest that clients seek separate independent advice on the arrangements for the loan on to them: for example, is this the cheapest arrangement currently available? Also, explain the details the bank will want and obtain the client's consent to passing on the information shown in item 6 of the specimen letter.

The Manager	Your Ref [ ]
[ ] Bank [etc.]	Our Ref [ ]
	Date [ ]

Dear

GLOBAL PROBATE LOANS FACILITY

I should like to discuss a new facility to enable us to arrange short-term bridging loans for clients to meet inheritance tax and probate registry fees.

As you will be aware, personal representatives have to pay inheritance tax and probate registry fees when they apply for a grant of representation (whether of probate or letters of administration) to a deceased's estate. In a typical situation, no funds will be available from the estate until the grant has been issued, which means a loan has to be arranged, usually from the deceased's bank.

The personal representatives may well not be familiar with the deceased's bank, and may therefore instruct us to make the necessary arrangements. In such cases, it would save my firm time and paperwork if we were able to arrange the necessary loan through your bank on an agreed basis.

I would estimate that, on average, the loans would be repaid after approximately six to eight weeks, or nine to 11 weeks if quoted securities have to be sold, allowing for the settlement period and registration with the company registrars.

May I suggest that the basis on which your bank may agree the provision of this facility might be along the following lines:

1. **'In principle' agreement.** I accept that the bank will need to treat the provision of this facility as being an 'in principle' agreement because each loan, for reasons including taxation, branch monitoring and the liabilities of the borrowers, will be set up separately but taken within the 'umbrella' limit. I would hope that the advantage of having this agreement in place would be that the setting up of such accounts could be negotiated with you locally on an immediate basis, rather than suffering delays while negotiating and setting up relevant arrangements with the deceased's bank in each instance.

2. **Global limit.** Having regard to the normal volume of estate administration conducted by this firm, I would suggest that this should be £[100,000].

3. **Availability.** I anticipate that the bank would wish the facility to be expressed to be available for 12 months and that it will be described by you as being technically 'repayable on demand'. If this be the case, I should appreciate your confirmation that the only likely circumstances under which such a demand might be made would be if for some reason the lending had become 'unsatisfactory'.

4. **To whom available.** The facility would be available to the personal representatives of deceased persons where this firm is acting for them.

5. **Purpose.** To enable the personal representatives to deal with the estate's liability to inheritance tax and probate registry fees.

6. **Account arrangements.** I anticipate that you will wish the firm to complete the bank's form of application to open an account on each occasion and it would be helpful if we could be supplied with a stock of these. If you wish, having obtained the agreement of the personal representatives, the firm can provide the bank with the application form, the appropriate Inland Revenue forms (IHT 200, IHT 201, IHT 202) confirming the amount due by way of inheritance tax and the details of the estate assets.

7. **Drawdown.** Each facility will be drawn as a separate loan, although partial drawings against that loan would need to be permitted.

8. **Interest.** I suggest that the rate of interest payable on the amount of

each facility outstanding from time to time might be [2 per cent] per annum above the bank's base rate from time to time in force. Presumably interest will be calculated on a daily basis and charged at quarterly intervals to each separate loan facility.

Please confirm that it will be possible, on request, for the bank to apportion the interest between the amount of loan drawn for payment of inheritance tax (on which tax relief can be claimed) and any part of the loan taken up for other outgoings such as the Probate Registry fees - which do not attract income tax relief.

9. **Arrangement fee.** I would hope that in view of this firm's connection with your bank no arrangement fee will be charged in respect either of the setting up of this facility or the taking up of each individual loan within it.

10. **Repayment and security.** Repayment would normally be made either from liquid assets, e.g. cash accounts, building society accounts, stocks and shares, etc., or from the sale proceeds of assets of the estate. As regards security, if each account is opened in the name of the firm and designated with the name of the estate, the firm will be responsible to the bank for the payment of each loan facility. We will, of course, secure our own position with the personal representatives in the context of this liability.

11. **Discretionary arrangements.** There will be occasions when the size of the estate is such that the amount required by way of loan would be too large to take under the global 'umbrella' facility. In such circumstances I would expect that we would approach you on behalf of the personal representatives to negotiate terms for a similar facility for the estate and which might involve a discounted rate of interest. I appreciate that you would not necessarily be able to provide as quick a response in this case.

If this facility is provided, my firm will be able to offer an improved service to its clients and the bank will derive benefit as well. I hope that I have covered everything which is relevant in this letter but please let me know if there is any further information you require.

Yours sincerely [etc.]

Release of funds – specimen letter to building society

13.36   The Manager   Your Ref [   ]
       [   ] Building Society [etc.]   Our Ref [   ]
                                       Date   [   ]

Dear

THE LATE MRS VICTORIA JONES

Mrs Jones' personal representatives would like to arrange for a withdrawal from her account[s] no[s] _____ [to pay] [the funeral expenses] [the inheritance tax] [Probate Court fees] [so the grant of representation can be obtained].

The payments needed are:

[Funeral expenses: £____, payable to _____]

[Inheritance tax: £ ____, payable to Inland Revenue.]

[Probate Court fee: £____, payable to HM Paymaster-General.]

We hope that you will be able to agree the personal representatives' requests. If so please send the forms they must sign.

We will register the grant with you when we have it.

Yours faithfully [etc.]

CGT – Costs of Establishing Title

13.37   The relevant Statement of Practice is SP8/94 set out below. When allowing deductions for the costs of establishing title, the Board of Inland Revenue will accept computations based either on the scale set out in the Statement of Practice or on the *actual* allowable expenditure incurred.

The revised scale takes effect where death occurred after 5 April 1993.

Gross value of estate	*Allowable expenditure*
A. Up to £40,000	1.75% of the probate value of the assets sold by the personal representatives.
B. Between £40,001 and £70,000	A fixed amount of £700, to be divided between all the assets of the estate in proportion to the probate values and allowed in those proportions on assets sold by the personal representatives.
C. Between £70,001 and £300,000	1% of the probate value of the assets sold.
D. Between £300,001 and £400,000	A fixed amount of £3,000, to be divided as at B above.
E. Between £400,001 and £750,000	0.75% of the probate value of the assets sold.

The scale does not extend to gross estates exceeding £750,000 where the allowable expenditure is to be negotiated according to the facts of the particular case by the inspector and the taxpayer.

Expenses incurred by corporate trustees

Following discussion with representative bodies, the Inland Revenue have agreed the following scale of allowable expenditure under Taxation of Chargeable Gains Act 1992, ss. 38 and 64(1)(b), for expenses incurred by corporate trustees in the administration of estates and trusts. The Board of Inland Revenue will accept computations based either on this scale or on the *actual* allowable expenditure incurred.

This scale is as follows:

(a) *Transfers of assets to beneficiaries, etc.*

    (i) Quoted stocks and shares

(A) One beneficiary	£20.00 per holding
(B) More than one beneficiary between whom a holding must be divided	As (A), to be divided in equal shares between the beneficiaries.

| (ii) Unquoted shares | As (i) above, with the addition of any exceptional expenditure. |
| (iii) Other assets | As (i) above, with the addition of any exceptional expenditure. |

(b) *Actual disposals and acquisitions*

(i) Quoted stocks and shares	The investment fee as charged by the trustee.
(ii) Unquoted shares	As (i) above, plus actual valuation costs.
(iii) Other assets	The investment fee as charged by the trustee, subject to a maximum of £60, plus actual valuation costs.

Where a comprehensive annual management fee is charged, covering both the cost of administering the trust and the expenses of actual disposals and acquisitions, the investment fee for the purpose of (i), (ii) and (iii) above will be taken to be £0.25 per £100 on the sale or purchase moneys.

(c) *Deemed disposals by trustees*

(i) Quoted stocks and shares	£6 per holding.
(ii) Unquoted shares	Actual valuation costs.
(iii) Other assets	Actual valuation costs.

This scale takes effect for acquisitions and disposals, or deemed disposals, by corporate trustees after 5 April 1993.

REVENUE'S NEWSLETTER

13.38 The CTO has introduced a quarterly newsletter for its customers. If you want to comment you can write to Diane Veale about this at the address given in para. 13.1.

POSTSCRIPT

13.39 The Capital Taxes Office is introducing a new Inland Revenue account which will replace the existing forms 200, 202 and 201.

The new form will be similar to the existing income tax self-assessment form. There will be a basic section to be completed for all estates. There will then be additional sections to be completed as appropriate. For example, where an estate includes business property you would complete the relevant section answering questions to establish whether or not the property qualifies for relief.

The existing IHT 40, IHT 37 and MIS IG (which asks additional questions where agricultural property is involved) will be incorporated into the body of the form.

It will be necessary to provide more information when applying for the grant which may slow down the obtaining of the grant. However, there should be less delay between obtaining the grant and obtaining clearance.

The CTO will pilot the new form from April 1999 and hopes to launch it in October 1999.

Chapter 14

Probate problems

Missing Beneficiaries

14.1   If beneficiaries cannot be traced there are a number of ways to deal with the problem:

- Genealogists may be instructed to trace the beneficiaries. The Society's Wills and Equity Committee has reviewed this and considers that it is permissible for solicitors to use firms which charge a fee to beneficiaries if traced, provided this is appropriate in the context of the size and overall circumstances of the estate.

- It may be possible for the DSS to forward a letter to the beneficiary. Address it to him or her, care of DSS Head Office in Newcastle (address in Chapter 30).

- The court's assistance may be sought. A Benjamin Order may be obtained which would allow the estate to be distributed on the basis of certain assumptions, e.g. that a particular person died without issue.

- Trustee Act 1925, s. 27 advertisements and searches should be made as early as possible in case they reveal helpful information.

If beneficiaries cannot be traced, indemnities may be taken from the other beneficiaries (but how good will these really be?) or consider if R.S.C. Order 43, Rule 8 (which permits the court to allow payment without reservation to meet costs) would be appropriate. Insurance may be taken out against beneficiaries eventually being found, or the entitlements may be paid into court under Trustee Act 1925, s.63 if appropriate: see Underhill and Hayton *The Law relating to Trusts and Trustees* (details in Booklist, Chapter 29).

Unclaimed Client Account Money

14.2   If money has been unclaimed for a long time, the Professional Ethics Division (address in Chapter 30) can advise.

Deceased with no Relatives

14.3   Practitioners should contact the Treasury Solicitor, Bona Vacantia Section (address in Chapter 30) immediately if approached about the administration of an estate in which there are apparently no living relatives. Time should not be spent on searches, nor costs expended, as the Treasury Solicitor is responsible for searching for kin, and may not be able to pay solicitors who have incurred expenditure (for example, employing genealogists) without his instructions. If the Treasury Solicitor traces kin, they may be unwilling to reimburse costs in respect of extensive work done before they were found. Therefore, if it appears that no relations survive, make contact with the Treasury Solicitor for advice as soon as you can.

Clients and Beneficiaries Lacking Mental Capacity

14.4   The Guide, Principle 24.04 and Commentary 1–3 cover the position if a client lacks capacity.

See also *Assessment of Mental Capacity – Guidance for Doctors and Lawyers* (Law Society publication).

If a beneficiary is mentally incapacitated (and cannot therefore give a good receipt) it may be appropriate to consider the appointment of a receiver through the Court of Protection, or payment into court under Trustee Act 1925, s.63.

On very difficult points, guidance may be obtained from the Practice Advice Service and the Professional Ethics Division (addresses in Chapter 30). *The Elderly Client Handbook* by Gordon Ashton (published by the Law Society) may also assist (see Booklist, Chapter 29).

PRS and Personal Liability

PRs' liability for unpaid IHT on PETs

14.5   To clarify the position, the following edited note was published in [1989] *Gazette,* 22 November.

'Personal representatives are liable for:

- the inheritance tax payable on potentially exempt transfers where the transferor dies within seven years of the transfer, if the tax has remained unpaid by the transferee for 12 months after the end of the month in which the death of the transferor occurs (Inheritance Tax Act 1984, s.199(2)); and

- any additional tax on inter vivos chargeable transfers payable as a result of the death.

A similar problem for personal representatives exists where property is treated as part of the death estate by virtue of the reservation of benefit rules. Such property will be treated as part of the donor's estate on death (Finance Act 1986, s.102(3)).

The Solicitors Indemnity Fund Ltd (SIF) confirm that where a solicitor incurs a civil liability in the course of his or her private practice then, subject to the provisions of the indemnity rules currently in force, this liability will be indemnified by the Indemnity Fund but only to the extent that otherwise funds are unavailable.

Further enquiries should be referred to SIF [address in Chapter 30].'

Subsequently, following representations from the Law Society, the Inland Revenue confirmed a letter of 11 February 1991 that, without prejudice to the application in an appropriate case of Inheritance Tax Act 1984, s.199(2):

'The Capital Taxes Office will not usually pursue for inheritance tax personal representatives who:

- after making the fullest inquiries that are reasonably practicable in the circumstances to discover lifetime transfers; and so

- having done all in their power to make full disclosure of them to the Board of Inland Revenue

have obtained a certificate of discharge and distributed the estate before a chargeable lifetime transfer comes to light.'

PRs' liabilities for unpaid tax on the death estate

14.6   Personal representatives are liable for IHT on the deceased's death estate (excluding settled property). Liability is limited to the extent of assets which the personal representatives have received or should have received.

However, they do remain liable to the extent of assets which they received and handed on to the beneficiaries. The case of *Howarth's Executors* v. *CIR* [1997] S.T.I. 640 (and discussed in [1997] *Trusts and Estates,* June, 71) illustrates graphically the danger to executors. An employee of a firm of solicitors acted as co-executor in an estate. One of the assets of the estate was land on which the instalment option was exercised. The land was transferred to one of the beneficiaries on the undertaking that he would be responsible for the payment of the instalments. Before the end of the 10-year period, the beneficiary became bankrupt leaving tax unpaid. The land was sold and, as the Revenue had not registered the charge over the land, the purchaser took free of the charge. The solicitors' employee was held personally liable.

The moral is clear: be very careful about distributing assets where there is an outstanding tax liability.

PRs' liability to creditors

14.7   Personal representatives are always in danger of a claim from unsatisfied creditors arising after assets have been distributed to beneficiaries. They can protect themselves from unknown claims by advertising for claimants under Trustee Act 1925, s.27. However, sometimes they may know that a possible liability exists but be uncertain as to the amount. Section 27 is then of no help since it protects PRs only against unknown claims.

Unquantifiable liabilities may arise perhaps under leases where the deceased was a tenant or as a result of the deceased being a member of Lloyd's. Limited protection is available in respect of leases under Trustee Act 1925, s.26.

In many cases the only solution may be to apply to the courts for guidance. This is obviously an expensive option and PRs may wonder if the cost can be justified. In the recent case of *Stone* v. *Chatway* [1997] *The Times,* 11 August Lindsay J. gave guidance on this subject. He stated that as only a court order could give complete protection it could not be wrong for executors of Lloyd's Names to insist upon the protection of a court order. For a fuller discussion see [1997] *Trusts and Estates,* 92 and also in the same issue at p.94 a discussion of possible liability for trustees arising from the ownership of leasehold property.

BANKRUPTCY

14.8   More and more firms are handling insolvent estates, which were once a rarity. An estate is only insolvent if the debts and liabilities cannot be paid, and is not insolvent if these can be settled, even if none of the legacies can be paid.

Sources of information

14.9   The legislation governing the administration of an estate which is insolvent is the Administration of Insolvent Estates of Deceased Persons Order 1986 (S.I. 1986 no. 1999). Berry, Bailey and Schaw-Miller's *Personal Insolvency – Law and Practice* deals with this issue. A useful outline of the law can be found in *Williams, Mortimer and Sunnucks on Executors, Administrators and Probate*. Briefer outlines of practice can be found in Philip Rossdale's *Probate and the Administration of Estates* and Roland D'Costa's *Executorship and Administration* (see Booklist in Chapter 29 for full details on all of these).

Practical issues

14.10   Philip Rossdale points out that if the PRs administer an insolvent estate ('a thankless task', he warns) a provision in the will authorising remuneration for the PRs will fail since this is of course a testamentary gift. Court authorised remuneration, he says, is different – see Supreme Court Act 1981, s.19. However, if the option of administering the estate under an insolvency administration order is taken, the administrator would have to be an insolvency practitioner and remuneration would then be a matter for the creditors.

While it is prudent, if there is a chance that an estate will be insolvent, to try and make an assessment of the extent of the problem before undertaking extensive work, you may not find out that an estate is insolvent until a substantial amount of time has been committed. What remains in the estate may be too small to cover the legal fees alone, even though funeral and testamentary and administration expenses have priority. Therefore, if potential PRs complete, as early as possible, a client questionnaire such as that designed by the Law Society and available from the Law Society (see Booklist, Chapter 29; address in Chapter 30), this can be helpful in assessing the situation. Solicitor–executors, and indeed, other executors, may wish early on to consider renouncing and should beware of intermeddling in an estate which may be insolvent.

Terms of business letters (see Chapter 3 on Client Care) may incorporate a clause governing the position in relation to costs incurred if the estate turns out to be insolvent, say the Professional Ethics Division. Even though they are entitled to an indemnity from the estate, PRs are personally liable for the solicitor's costs. *(Cordery on Solicitors,* 9th edition – see Booklist, Chapter 29 – has a useful discussion on the position.)

Joint property

14.11   A Court of Appeal decision *(Re Palmer (dec'd) (a debtor)* [1994] 3 W.L.R. 420, C.A.) has clarified the position about jointly held property. Whether or not the estate is dealt with under the Administration of Insolvent Estates of Deceased Persons Order 1986, jointly held property passes to the co-owner on death as usual and is not available to the administrator of the estate.

Bankrupt beneficiaries

14.12   Advice was given in [1993] *Gazette,* 24 February about what PRs should do if one of the beneficiaries has had a bankruptcy order made against him or her. Broadly, the risk is of personal liability for a PR who pays a legacy direct to a bankrupt beneficiary rather than the trustee in bankruptcy. Bankrupts must tell their trustees in bankruptcy about acquisition of property and it seems PRs could safely hand over money to a bankrupt beneficiary on proof that the bankrupt has complied with his or her duties under the Insolvency Act 1986, in particular sections 307 and 312, to inform the trustee in bankruptcy of everything affecting the bankrupt's property.

The article goes on to warn that PRs should be alert to potential problems if a bankrupt beneficiary suggests that the money should be paid over in a way which is at all unusual. As a last resort, Trustee Act 1925, s.63 allows money to be paid into court. The assistance of the court may also be sought under RSC, Order 85.

What steps, if any, should PRs take to find out whether beneficiaries are bankrupt? It is not usual to enquire about their financial status, but it is a different matter if PRs have notice that there may be a query about a particular beneficiary. A bankruptcy-only search under the Land Charges Act could be made (against any name a beneficiary might use) or the PRs could contact the Insolvency Service, Bankruptcy Search Room, Commercial Union House, 22 Martineau Square, Birmingham B2 4UZ (0121 233 4808).

Makers of wills are reminded in the article that they can revoke legacies to actually or potentially bankrupt beneficiaries, substituting discretionary trusts.

Rooney v. *Cardoona, The Times*, 4 March 1999 was an interesting case on bankruptcy and life policies under MWPA 1882, s.11.

PERSONAL REPRESENTATIVES SEPARATELY REPRESENTED – COUNSEL'S OPINION

14.13 The following unedited extract from *An Approach to Non-Contentious Costs* may be of assistance if one PR wishes to seek separate advice from the other(s). The opinion was originally published in the [1986] *Gazette*, 3 September, 2561–2562.

Costs: Personal representatives separately represented

The following notes are issued by the Law Society's Non-Contentious Business Committee. Since the Joint Agreed Case was reported in [1985] *Gazette*, 24 October, 2987, the number of enquiries which the Society has received from practitioners indicates a need to publish more detailed guidelines. The following guidelines have been settled by counsel but practitioners should note that the Society has no power to determine matters of law, and that matters of dispute may ultimately fall to be determined by the court:

1. The basic principle is that a personal representative is entitled to an indemnity from the estate in respect of costs and expenses properly incurred in the course of his office. Trustee Act 1925, s.23 expressly empowers personal representatives to employ and pay a solicitor to transact any business or to do any act required to be transacted or done in the administration of the estate.

2.   The indemnity will not, however, be available (where there is more than one personal representative) to each personal representative who chooses to instruct his own separate solicitor, as the right to instruct a solicitor is limited by the overriding principle that personal representatives must act properly in exercising their rights and powers. In particular they must not make, or cause there to be made, any wasteful or unnecessary payments out of the estate.

3.   Thus it is considered that in a normal case it is incumbent upon personal representatives to agree upon the joint instructions of solicitors.

4.   In certain cases it may be proper for more than one firm to be instructed, where, for example, in the case of a large landed estate, different skills are required; in such a case it is unlikely that more costs would be incurred than if one firm dealt with all the work.

5.   It is, of course, always open to a personal representative to seek independent legal advice separately from the advice given by the firm instructed on behalf of all the personal representatives, but in such circumstances he will normally not be entitled to an indemnity from the estate for the cost of doing so, and will have to pay such costs personally.

6.   Mere personal animosity between personal representatives does not justify the appointment of a separate firm so as to increase the costs payable by the estate.

7.   Exceptional circumstances justifying the instruction of a separate solicitor at the expense of the estate might include a case where a personal representative became aware of a devastavit or breach of trust by his fellow personal representative and required independent legal advice as to his position; or when the instructed solicitor refused or failed properly to carry out his instructions, thus necessitating the instruction of another firm (although here, strictly, no additional costs should be incurred, as the defaulting solicitor would not be entitled to recover his costs).

8.   It is also open to personal representatives to agree that they should be separately represented provided that the estate does not thereby bear any additional costs. As the instruction of two firms in respect of the same work will inevitably involve extra work, it will avoid subsequent dispute if the personal representatives also agree in advance to bear personally the extra costs involved (and agree the proportions in which they will do so).

9. Any personal liability incurred by personal representatives may, of course, be charged to the estate with the concurrence of all the beneficiaries, provided that they are all *sui juris* and are properly advised.

10. Where a personal representative instructs a practitioner in circumstances where he knows that another firm is already acting for the estate he should be made aware of the likelihood that he will be personally responsible for his costs.

11. A distinction may need to be made between the fees charged to the personal representatives by the appointed firm of solicitors on the one hand and fees charged by a solicitor–executor on the other hand. Provided that the 'professional charging clause' expressly so provided a professional executor may properly charge for his time and trouble in acting as an executor, as distinct from his firm's charges for legal work transacted. More than one professional person may be appointed executor and may be entitled so to charge, but such charges will in both cases be of a different nature from the fees of the firm jointly instructed by the personal representatives to do legal work.

12. Beneficiaries who take legal advice in connection with the administration of an estate will rarely be entitled to recover from the estate their costs so incurred, but they may be entitled to recover such costs from a defaulting personal representative who will not in such circumstances be entitled to recover them from the estate.

13. The Society is also asked from time to time to advise as to how the legal fees should be calculated in cases where more than one firm is involved in the administration of an estate. Opinions published in the Society's Digest in the past indicated a split of two-thirds/one-third; these were however published at a time when solicitors' fees were charged on a straight percentage of the value of the estate. Since the Solicitors' Remuneration Order 1972* this element is only one of the factors to be taken into account in assessing what is fair and reasonable in each case; the two-thirds/one-third split is therefore no longer appropriate. The value element does still have to be taken into account, and will be recognised in the fair and reasonable charges of the respective firms, bearing in mind the amount of work carried out by each firm, the degree of responsibility involved and other factors set out in Article 2 of the Solicitors' Remuneration Order 1972*. This is subject to the overriding principle expressed in para. 8 above that the estate itself

should not normally bear the additional expense occasioned by the employment of more than one firm.

[*Now overtaken by the Solicitors' Remuneration Order 1994 – see Chapter 2.]

Unsuitable PRs

14.14 Personal representatives may be passed over under Supreme Court Act 1981, s.116: an application to the High Court may be made if it appears that the person apparently entitled to take the grant is unsuitable. The person next entitled to the grant will not necessarily be appointed.

An application for the removal of a personal representative may be made under Administration of Justice Act 1985, s.50. This section also gives the High Court power to appoint someone else to act. (See also paras 12.22–12.24.)

Problems from Clients

Distressed clients

14.15 Clients coming for help and advice on probate may be suffering from grief and distress. Bereavement can generate many and conflicting emotions, which are not always expressed as one might expect. Sometimes clients' feelings spill over, so that the conduct of the administration is affected, for example by a family quarrel.

Helping bereaved clients, and coping with clients' feelings and emotions, can be difficult for practitioners. This is an added (and often un-recognised) source of stress for many practitioners, who may feel ambivalent about how to respond to the client and how to deal with their feelings.

Christopher Clulow, Director of the Tavistock Institute for Marital Studies in London, considered some of these issues in a number of short articles in the series 'Only Connect' in the journal *Family Law* during 1992 and 1993. Although directed mainly to solicitors working with divorce, the articles would be of great value and interest to all private client practitioners.

The Australian leaflet 'Coping with a Major Personal Crisis' (para. 23.3) is also useful reading. It may be worthwhile ensuring that your office holds an up-to-date list of local voluntary and other sources of help and support for distressed and bereaved clients.

You may be approached by a client involved in a major tragedy. The Law Society's Multi-Party Action Co-ordination Service exists to link the solicitors' firms instructed by those involved and their families and friends (see para. 23.2). The Red Cross has produced an excellent information pack for local authorities to use to establish a Disaster Appeal Fund. Relevant addresses are in Chapter 30.

Difficult clients

14.16   Sometimes clients are hard to please. It may just have to be accepted, but in a proportion of cases there may be some misunderstanding which could be discussed and perhaps removed. Asking such a client what the problem is, if appropriate, may be worthwhile, or a colleague may be able to assist. Prompt action may help to avert a complaint.

Are you being misled?

14.17   Not all clients are honest. If you suspect a client is misleading you or others involved, you need to discuss those concerns with the client, no matter how difficult this seems. There may be a completely reasonable explanation. The risks of involvement in another's dishonesty are analysed by Steven Fennell in Chapter 6. The Professional Ethics Division may be able to help (address in Chapter 30). See also the Green Card warning on property fraud and the Blue Card warning on money laundering (both in *The Guide to the Professional Conduct of Solicitors 1996* at Annex 25G and 16D).

REQUESTS FROM CLIENTS

That you renounce

14.18   Following a death, if a solicitor has been appointed executor or executrix, the family may request that he or she renounce probate. This tends to happen especially when the family live in a different part of the country from the solicitor, or they consider the estate to be small and uncomplicated. The advice given by the Office for Supervision of Solicitors (OSS) in these circumstances is that solicitors are not under any duty to renounce and may indeed be in possession of information imparted to them by the testator or testatrix which makes renunciation inappropriate; but that solicitors are free to agree to such a request and to renounce – the basic principle is the client's best interests.

For another firm to handle the work involved

14.19   This request is a variation on the request to renounce. If you have refused to renounce, there may be a request that the beneficiaries' chosen firm undertake the actual work instead of yours. This may be on a variety of grounds but cost (the other firm is cheaper), convenience (the other firm is nearer) or familiarity (the other firm is the residuary beneficiary's own solicitors) are the most common.

The OSS suggests that the presumption would be that you, having been appointed executor or executrix by the deceased, would undertake the winding up of the estate. You are free to agree differently. If you do so, you will need to consider what, if anything, the charging clause in the will allows you (see para. 14.13). If you wish to insist on handling the administration, bear in mind you may be storing up a great deal of difficulty and ill-will for the future.

No Charging Clause

14.20   If a will does not contain a charging clause, professional executors may not charge for their time without the approval of the beneficiaries. To give such approval all must be adult and *sui juris*. According to Barlow, King and King, *Wills Administration and Taxation, A Practical Guide* (see Booklist, Chapter 29), it is possible for a solicitor appointed executor or executrix to employ and pay individual partners in the firm, provided there is an express agreement that the solicitor–PR shall not participate in the profits nor derive any benefit from the charges: *Re Gates* [1933] Ch. 913. However, it is better practice in such a situation to inform clients that this problem has arisen and seek their consent to a charge being made. If legal advice is to be taken by lay PRs, they will incur costs in any event.

Solicitor–Executor/Executrix Witnesses the Will

14.21 If a solicitor–executor or –executrix witnesses a will containing a charging clause, entitlement to charge is lost, since a charging clause is treated as a legacy. Barlow, King and King (see para. 14.20) also state that if someone, having witnessed a will, later becomes a partner in the firm, this does not result in the loss of the benefit of the charging clause.

Charging Clause in Invalid Will

14.22 If a will proves to be invalid (for example, as a result of faulty execution) all legacies fail and naturally a solicitors' charging clause (being analogous to a legacy) also fails.

In *Gray* v. *Richards Butler* [1996] *Gazette*, 2 August, 29; [1996] *Solicitors Journal* 194 solicitors who had paid themselves under a charging clause contained in a will which proved to be invalid for want of due execution had to repay the residuary beneficiary of an earlier will. The court did exercise its inherent jurisdiction to order reasonable remuneration for work done by the firm which could have been undertaken for the earlier valid will.

Two-Year Discretionary Trusts and the Three-Month Trap

14.23 Most practitioners are aware of the dangers of making appointments within three months of the testator's death. This was highlighted in the case of *Frankland* v. *IRC* [1996] S.T.C. 735 and discussed in articles in the *Solicitors Journal* by Julie Evans (4 October 1996) and Catherine Sanders (25 October 1996).

Dealing with Mistakes

14.24 See *The Guide to the Professional Conduct of Solicitors 1996*, Chapter 29.

How one handles mistakes depends on the nature and significance of the error, and the applicability of the relevant principles in the Guide, but the following comments may also be of interest.

According to the Office for Supervision of Solicitors (OSS), relatively minor errors are usually best dealt with promptly by being frank with the client. Most clients will appreciate openness at an early stage and an explanation. It seems that clients find a lack of frankness (or an impression of it, from an absence of explanation, or failure to answer questions or reply to letters, etc.) more irritating, and more likely to found a complaint, than a prompt apology and explanation of the problem.

More serious mistakes create different issues. First these should be discussed with the Solicitors Indemnity Fund Ltd (SIF) (see the Guide, Principle 29.07 and commentaries). SIF's address is given in Chapter 30. You have a discretion whether to inform SIF of circumstances which you believe may result in a claim, and a duty to notify them of claims which have been made against you or which you learn will be made, in both cases if the amount is over £500: see Rules 19.1 and 19.2 of the Solicitors' Indemnity Rules. Secondly, clients may have to be advised to obtain independent advice (see Principle 29.08 and commentaries).

In either case, the Professional Ethics Division and the Practice Advice Service (addresses in Chapter 30) may be able to assist.

If solicitors acting for the other side have made an error which they refuse to deal with, or they do not reply to correspondence, it is open to you and/or your client to use the Rule 15 complaints procedure. If this does not resolve the matter, either you or your client may consider making a complaint to the OSS. Only the client, however, can ask for the complaint to be conciliated. Conciliation can be an effective means of resolving less serious disputes – more information from the OSS (address in Chapter 30).

SOURCES OF HELP

The court

14.25 The court can assist in a number of ways: an application under R.S.C., Order 85 may be made for help on a particular point, or for the court's assistance in the administration generally; a PR may be removed by the court under Administration of Justice Act 1985, s.50; and Trustee Act 1925, s.63, provides for payment into court, in appropriate circumstances, if trustees are unable otherwise to obtain good discharge. The court can also assist if it is impossible to trace missing beneficiaries (see para. 14.1) and Administration of Justice Act 1985, s.49 allows the court to pronounce on the validity of wills if the consent of the beneficiaries has been obtained. Clearly, the cost of such an application means that approaching the court is not one's first recourse, but there may be in the end no other alternative. Personal representatives' costs would usually be met from the estate (but see para. 14.13 for the counsel's opinion on the costs of PRs separately represented). An excellent series of articles by Dawn Goodman of Withers appeared in the *Solicitors Journal* in August and September 1994 on how to avoid problems and how the court can help. See also *Alsop Wilkinson (A Firm) v. Neary* [1994] *The Times*, 4 November, on trustees and litigation.

Treasury Solicitor

14.26 If it appears that the deceased left no family, the Treasury Solicitor is responsible for kin searches and dealing with the administration of the estate if none is found. (See para. 14.3 and Chapter 30 for the address), and an article in [1992] *Gazette,* 11 November, 32.

Official Solicitor

14.27 The Official Solicitor (address in Chapter 30) deals with personal injury work for children and adults without mental capacity, and also acts for children in other cases, as next friend or guardian ad litem where appropriate. The Official Solicitor also acts as trustee, obtains grants of representation for the use and benefit of those without mental capacity, and is asked to administer estates of certain intestates to allow IPFDA claims to be made. A most helpful article on the work of the Official Solicitor can be found in [1990] *Family Law* 53.

Court of Protection

14.28 The financial affairs of people lacking mental capacity to handle these personally are the responsibility of the Court of Protection. The Court publishes useful booklets for receivers and enduring attorneys (address in Chapter 30).

Probate registries

14.29 The Principal Registry is encouraging registrars to make contact with practices in their catchment areas, for example by meeting local law societies, which were asked to appoint a liaison officer to further this link.

The Probate Registry offers a very reasonably priced oath-settling service in cases of difficulty.

The Law Society

(Addresses in Chapter 30.)

14.30 The **Probate Section** caters for solicitors who have an interest in wills and trusts, tax planning, investment advice as part of financial planning, Court of Protection, care planning for elderly clients and estate administration. For more information see Chapter 28.

The **Practice Advice Service** answers solicitors' questions on legal practice problems in all areas of law. You can write or phone, asking for the Practice Advice Service.

The Professional Ethics Division offers confidential advice on the application and interpretation of the rules and principles of professional conduct. This advice encompasses such issues as how the rules affect your plans to develop your practice, or your relationship with clients, the court and others with whom you have dealings. You can write or phone during office hours.

The **Solicitors' Assistance Scheme** helps solicitors who find themselves in difficulties or potential difficulties and for one reason or another prefer not to consult the Law Society. It is administered by the Professional Ethics Division and is therefore separate from the Office for Supervision of Solicitors. Members are volunteers, some on recommendation from local law societies, and they form a nationwide network of solicitors available for consultation by fellow solicitors in need of guidance and advice.

Many solicitors find that being able to talk about their problems to an understanding and objective listener, rather than seeking specific advice, can often help them reach decisions more easily. Consultation can vary from a telephone call to a series of interviews. Often solicitors in trouble prefer to contact a scheme member outside their own area of practice.

When appointing scheme members, local law societies are asked to consider those who are not officers of the local society. If scheme members take office after being nominated, they are asked to resign from the scheme until the end of their term of office.

The scheme is operated on a completely confidential solicitor–client basis. No charge is normally made for an initial interview, but thereafter it is open to the individual scheme member (or his or her firm) to make a formal arrangement with the solicitor concerned. The Society does not give any guidance as to charges, or at what stage these should be made, but prefers to leave the matter to the discretion of scheme members themselves, according to circumstances.

Solicitors Indemnity Fund Ltd (SIF)

14.31 Problems which may involve a claim against you need to be referred to SIF (address in Chapter 30). You have a discretion whether to inform SIF of circumstances which you believe may result in a claim, and a duty to notify them of claims which have been made against you or which you learn will be made in both cases if the amount is over £500. See paras 1.6 and 14.24 and also see Rules 19.1 and 19.2 of the Solicitors Indemnity Rules.

Specialist solicitors and counsel

14.32 Counsel's opinion may be necessary on a variety of matters. If the question is one of construction, Administration of Justice Act 1985, s.48 allows a barrister of 10 years' standing to give an opinion to the PRs on which the court may, without hearing argument, allow them to act.

Rather than approaching counsel, some practitioners may like to consider consulting another firm of solicitors. This is a practice which is becoming established in certain specialist fields such as pensions and contentious probate.

It may be particularly useful to approach a professional colleague if a difficulty also raises conduct or practice issues, since another solicitor will be more aware than counsel of the impact of the Practice Rules and issues relating to practice as a solicitor.

Within the office

14.33   We all, from time to time, have files we get bogged down with or which are a constant headache. Try making a deal with a colleague to exchange headache files once a month. You may be able to skip through something which has stalled a colleague for days – and vice versa.

Personal

14.34   Stress is a major cause of illness. Many solicitors face huge pressures and a heavy burden of others' expectations and responsibility at work. There are now numerous books on stress in paperback in general bookshops, which help to identify symptoms and suggest solutions.

PARTING COMPANY

14.35   Sometimes, solicitors and clients have to part company. Clients may terminate retainers on any grounds they wish. Solicitors may terminate retainers in more limited circumstances. These are set out in Principle 12.10 and commentaries of the Guide. They include a client's supervening incapacity and the breakdown of trust and confidence.

Lay and professional executors, or two or more lay executors, may disagree about a number of issues. Where executors cannot agree, one may seek independent advice. An opinion given by counsel in 1986 on costs issues arising out of such a step is included at para. 14.13. It is clear from this opinion that a PR seeking independent advice may not in every case find that his or her costs would be paid from the estate.

Other problems arise where it is clear, or feared, that a client intends to act dishonestly, for example, by saying outstanding tax is to remain unpaid. In certain cases, solicitors may decline to act. It is rare, but does sometimes arise, that a third party should be informed. Principle 16.07 of the Guide refers to such problems and in difficult cases the assistance of the Professional Ethics Division (address in Chapter 30) is always available. Steven Fennell's article in Chapter 6 considers some of the issues. You should also be aware of the warnings given by the Society in relation to mortgage fraud and money laundering.

Chapter 15

Accounting and distributing

INTRODUCTION

15.1 Paragraphs 15.2–15.4, the specimen accounts for Victoria Thomas (paras. 15.6–15.14) and the explanatory notes which follow (paras 15.15–15.20) are based on materials prepared by the College of Law for trainee solicitors. We are most grateful to the College for their help in allowing us to reproduce these edited sections.

An increasing number of firms are turning to computerised packages to produce their accounts (see Chapter 17). Even so, we have set out the essential elements of the accounts in this chapter.

ESTATE ACCOUNTS

The duty to account

15.2 PRs are reminded of their obligation to keep accounts by the wording of all the oaths leading to grants of representation (giving effect to Administration of Estates Act 1925 (AEA), s.25).

The accounts should give a clear and accurate statement of the estate property and income, and contain full details of all receipts and payments (for which the appropriate corresponding documentation should be available).

Solicitor PRs are subject to the Accounts Rules (see Chapter 5) as well as the general law.

Form of accounts

15.3 The form of estate accounts varies. Some firms use the traditional 'side-by-side' format showing income and outgoings. Others, as here, a 'vertical' layout. The aim is always to give the PRs and residuary beneficiaries an explanation of the administration of the estate in an easily understandable form.

There is no prescribed layout or form for estate accounts, so you can use whatever format best suits the estate in hand, but the simpler and easier accounts are the better. They must, of course, give enough detail to allow a proper appreciation of all the transactions which have taken place.

The following elements are standard.

1. *Introduction.* This is a narrative setting out:

*   the date of death, the date and place of issue of the grant of representation, and the PRs' names;

*   if there was a will, a summary of the gifts made; otherwise, an outline of the effect in the estate of the intestacy rules;

*   the value of the gross and net estates and the amount of any IHT paid;

*   details of any joint property passing by survivorship, variations made, elections under IHTA 1984, s.142, funds held back in respect of future tax liability and other relevant information.

2. *Balance sheet.* You can group connected items under headings (such as 'legacies') for simplicity.

3. *Estate capital account.* This shows the value of the estate at death, the transactions effected during the administration period and the balance remaining.

*   If the estate is complicated, this account can be drawn up in two parts – (1) the estate at death (based on the IHT account and any corrective account) and (2) the transactions taking place during the administration. The first part would show the gross and net estates at death, as agreed for probate and IHT purposes. The second part would record transactions which took place during the administration affecting the assets in Part 1.

*   The probate valuation figures are used in accounts for ease of comparison and because they give an acquisition cost (for CGT purposes) for the beneficiaries' future disposals of the assets.

*   Sometimes there will be differences between the IHT account(s) and the estate capital account, arising from the different tax treatment and legal nature of certain kinds of property (for example,

reversionary interests, being 'excluded property', are left out of IHT accounts but appear, as assets, in the estate accounts; conversely, the deceased's share of jointly owned property passing by survivorship will be included in the IHT account but, as far as the estate accounts are concerned, will only be mentioned for information in the introductory narrative).

4. *Estate income account.* This shows all the income received during the administration period. When tax is deducted at source (for example, company dividends) only the net amounts of income received need to be shown; otherwise put in gross receipts, with an entry showing the basic rate tax which the PRs have paid.

• If equitable apportionments have been made, or if any income is apportioned to capital under the Apportionment Act 1870, show the full amount of the income the PRs receive, with the amount apportioned to capital being shown as an appropriation of part of the total.

• This account should also show individually any interim payments of income to beneficiaries so that they can check these against the annual certificates of deduction of income tax you have given them (forms R185E).

• Show any interest paid on general legacies, and any income produced by property which was given specifically in the will, as deductions from the total income received. You can deal similarly with expenses attributable to income.

• This account can be made up to each 5 April.

5. *Beneficiaries' or distribution accounts.* These are usually only made available to residuary beneficiaries, and show how each one's share is derived.

6. *Schedules or annexes.* More detailed information can conveniently be put here, to keep the main accounts uncluttered. Schedules may cover:

• debts at death;

• dividends received during the administration;

• investments owned at death – this will usually be in two parts: (1) showing investments retained and appropriated to, or divided between, the beneficiaries, and (2) showing the investments which were sold, along with gains and losses.

7. *Notes.* These may be helpful to draw attention to any aspects of the accounts which might otherwise be overlooked or unclear.

Planning for the end of the administration period

15.4 You should consider early on in the administration the discharge the PRs will eventually seek from the beneficiaries and whether any special arrangements need to be made, e.g. if any beneficiary lacks capacity. A discharge from residuary beneficiaries will only be valid if there has been full disclosure of the estate assets, the dealings with them and of the balances available for distribution. You should also anticipate the end of the administration period by, for example, settling all tax liabilities and arranging to withdraw funds from banks and building societies in good time.

PRs will want approval of the accounts from the residuary beneficiaries and may consider withholding some of the assets until this is forthcoming. Receipts for cheques or assets should be obtained and filed with the estate papers. (See para. 15.25 for guidance on obtaining receipts.) Minors cannot give a good receipt: if there is no authority for a parent to do so instead, AEA 1925, s.42 allows PRs to hand minors' entitlements over to trustees and so obtain a good discharge (but only where the minor is absolutely entitled).

SPECIMEN ACCOUNTS

15.5 The following specimen accounts for Victoria Thomas deceased illustrate the points made above, and are followed by notes, beginning at para. 15.15, explaining how these accounts were made up.

Victoria Thomas deceased

15.6 Miss Thomas died on 3 May 199–. Lowe Snow & Co. of Hixley held her will which was dated 15 August 1988 and (in summary) provided:

- Revocation clause

- Executors: (1) Miss Emily Thomas and (2) Miss Amy Thomas both of 'Hillview', Hixley, Cheshire.

- Charitable legacies: (all registered charities):
  - (1) £1,000 Cheshire Home of Rest for Horses
  - (2) £250 Hixley Dogs Home
  - (3) £250 Cheshire Donkey Sanctuary

- Receipts clause

- Residue, after debts, legacies, testamentary expenses – 'to such of them my said sisters Emily Thomas and Amy Thomas as shall survive me and if both equally between them'. (Gift over to RSPCA in event of both sisters predeceasing.) Both survived.

- Clause dispensing with consents to appropriation.

It was duly executed and attested.

Victoria Thomas – estate for probate and IHT purposes

15.7   £

Spring Cottage		198,000.00
Investments		39,512.00
Halifax Building Society		4,099.86
Cash in house		21.50
National Westminster Bank		5,827.92
Arrears of retirement pension		42.00
Contents – sold gross	500	
– others: estimated value	2,000	2,500.00
GROSS ESTATE		250,003.28
Less		
Electricity	£31.45	
Gas	£52.26	
Income Tax	£294.70	
Funeral	£525.00	903.41
NET ESTATE FOR PROBATE		249,099.87
Less		
Charitable legacies (exempt)		1,500.00
ESTATE FOR IHT PURPOSES		247,599.87
IHT PAYABLE		
on first 223,000		NIL

on £24,599 at 40 per cent		9,839.60
•	on delivery of account – on £49,599	1,971.07
•	on Spring Cottage – on £198,000	7,868.53
		9,839.60

15.8 A covering letter was sent with the accounts by the solicitors to the two PRs:

Dear Miss Thomas

YOUR LATE SISTER'S ESTATE

I enclose the estate accounts which include an outline of your sister's will, and the amount of the estate and of tax and other payments paid and so on.

May I remind you that, in relation to the £150 you have received from this firm by way of interest allowed, tax has not been deducted. £150 should therefore be included in your tax return for the tax year 199–/–.

Yours sincerely [etc.]

These are the accounts which were sent.

Accounts: Estate of Miss Victoria Thomas deceased

15.9 Included in these accounts are the following:

1. Introduction
2. Capital account
3. Estate income account
4. Beneficiary's account – Miss Emily Thomas
5. Beneficiary's account – Miss Amy Thomas
6. Schedule of investments showing probate values.

1. Introduction

Miss Victoria Thomas, late of Spring Cottage, Tottenhall Road, Hixley, Cheshire died on 3 May 199–, aged 82. Probate of her will dated 15 June 199– was granted on _____ to Miss Emily Thomas and Miss Amy

215

Thomas, the executors named in the will.

In her will Miss Thomas left these charitable legacies:

1. £1,000 to the Cheshire Home of Rest for Horses
2. £250 to the Hixley Dogs Home
3. £250 to the Cheshire Donkey Sanctuary.

The estate remaining after payment of these legacies, and after payment of Miss Thomas's debts and funeral and testamentary expenses, was given to Miss Emily Thomas and Miss Amy Thomas equally.

The net estate for probate purposes amounted to £249,099.87. For inheritance tax (IHT) purposes the taxable estate amounted to £247,599.87, the legacies to the charities being exempt. IHT amounted to £9,839.60. This has been paid and a certificate of discharge obtained.

The residue has been divided between the beneficiaries (Miss Emily and Miss Amy Thomas) and this is shown in the accounts. Miss Thomas's investments have been divided equally between the beneficiaries. The values stated in the beneficiaries' accounts form the acquisition value for the purposes of capital gains tax.

Part of the contents of Spring Cottage was divided between the Misses Thomas as they agreed, and the remainder was sold. Spring Cottage was sold at the agreed probate value. The estate's liability to income tax was met by deduction of tax at source.

Lowe, Snow & Co.

2. Capital account

15.10

ASSETS	£	£
Spring Cottage, Hixley		
Probate value	£198,000	
Net proceeds of sale		194,000.25
Investments per Schedule		
at probate value		39,512.00

Halifax Building Society

Share A/c – Capital	4,040.50	
– Interest to date of death	59.36	4,099.86

Cash –

In house		21.50

Bank A/c – NatWest, Hixley

Current A/c	721.42	
Deposit A/c	5,000.00	
– interest to date of death	106.50	
	5,106.50	5,827.92
Arrears of retirement pension		42.00

Contents of house and personal effects

Distribution in *specie* (estimated value)	2,000.00	
Proceeds of sale of rest	442.50	
		2,442.50
GROSS ESTATE		245,946.03

LESS

Debts due at death

M.A.N.W.E.B. – electricity a/c	31.45	
British Gas – gas a/c	52.26	
Inland Revenue – income tax due at death	294.70	

Funeral expenses

G. Smith & Co.	525.00	

Administration expenses

Commissioner's fees	9.00	
Probate Court fees	312.00	
Stockbroker Co. – valuation fees	17.25	

Lowe, Snow & Co. – charges for administering the estate	1,650.00	
VAT	288.75	
Inheritance tax	9,839.60	
		13,020.01
NET ESTATE		232,926.02
Less –		
LEGACIES		
Cheshire Home of Rest for Horses	1,000.00	
Hixley Dogs Home	250.00	
Cheshire Donkey Sanctuary	250.00	
		1,500.00
		231,426.02
RESIDUE		
Divisible –		
Miss Emily Thomas – one half	115,713.01	
Miss Amy Thomas – one half	115,713.01	
		231,426.02

15.11 3. Estate income account

Income Tax Year 199– to 199–	£	£
Dividends received		
1.8.199–		255.00
Interest received		
Halifax Building Society		
Interest to close a/c on 26.6.199–		76.02
NatWest Bank, Hixley		
Interest to close deposit a/c 30.6.199–		45.60
Refund of income tax		
Loan interest		15.55
		392.17

Less

NatWest Bank, Hixley

Interest on loan to pay IHT		62.20
		329.97

Divisible

Miss Emily Thomas – one half	164.98	
Miss Amy Thomas – one half	164.99	
		329.97

15.12 4. Beneficiary's account

MISS EMILY THOMAS

	£	£
Share of residue due to you per Capital Account		115,713.01
Share of income due to you per Income Account		164.98
Total due to you		115,877.99

Represented by –

Transferred to you

Shares at probate value

1,650 Marks & Spencer Ord. Shares	3,795.00	
900 Tesco Stores Ord. Shares	1,620.00	
640 Shell T & T Ord. Reg. Shares	8,316.00	
400 Lonrho Ord. Shares	1,175.00	
600 Tate & Lyle £1 Shares	4,850.00	
		19,756.00

Retained by you

Share of furniture at agreed value		1,000.00

Interim payments to you

10.7.199–	12,250.00	

13.11.199–	65,000.00	
		77,250.00
BALANCE now due to you		17,871.99
		115,877.99

15.13   5.   Beneficiary's account

MISS AMY THOMAS

	£	£
Share of residue due to you per Capital Account		115,713.01
Share of income due to you per Income Account		164.99
Total due to you		115,878.00
Represented by –		
Transferred to you		
Shares at probate value		
1,650 Marks & Spencer Ord. Shares	3,795.00	
900 Tesco Stores Ord. Shares	1,620.00	
640 Shell T & T Ord. Reg. Shares	8,316.00	
400 Lonrho Ord. Shares	1,175.00	
600 Tate & Lyle £1 Shares	4,850.00	
		19,756.00
Retained by you		
Share of furniture at agreed value		1,000.00
Interim payments to you		
10.7.199–	12,250.00	
13.11.199–	65,000.00	
		77,250.00
BALANCE now due to you		17,872.00
		115,878.00

15.14 6. Schedule of investments

PROBATE VALUES

Amount	Stock	Probate value	Miss Emily Thomas		Miss Amy Thomas	
			No.	Value	No.	Value
		£		£		£
3,300	Marks & Spencer Ord. Shares	7,590.00	1,650	3,795	1,650	3,795
1,800	Tesco Stores (Hldings) Ord. Shares	3,240.00	900	1,620	900	1,620
1,280	Shell Transport & Trading Ord. Shares	16,632.00	640	8,316	640	8,316
800	Lonrho Ord. Shares	2,350.00	400	1,175	400	1,175
1,200	Tate & Lyle Shares	9,700.00	600	4,850	600	4,850
		39,512.00		19,756		19,756

Notes on the specimen estate accounts

15.15 The accounts start with the narrative Introduction (para. 15.9), giving details of the grant and explaining the distribution of the estate.

In this estate, apart from three pecuniary legacies, the entire net estate was divided between two beneficiaries. So all that is required is a **capital account** (para. 15.10), showing assets and liabilities and the net residue, an **income account** showing income received during the administration (para. 15.11), and **beneficiaries' accounts** (paras 15.12 and 15.13) showing the division of their entitlements and how these were met between the beneficiaries, and a **schedule** showing details of the investments (para. 15.14).

Capital account

15.16 In preparing the capital account there is a choice: the account can be produced in two parts or in one:

- If the account is in two parts, *the first part* will mirror exactly the estate as disclosed in the Inland Revenue account (amended by any corrective account). The probate value of all assets, whether or not sold, will be listed together with deductions permitted for IHT purposes, e.g. debts due at death, funeral expenses. The figure produced will therefore be the same as that agreed with the Revenue, but of course it will not be the amount available for distribution to the beneficiaries: for example, administration costs may have been incurred which cannot be deducted for IHT purposes (e.g. IHT itself, solicitors' costs, probate court fees, etc.). These costs will have to be deducted in the *second* part of a two-part capital account, to produce a sum which *does* represent the net estate available for the beneficiaries.

- If the account is in one part (as here) it shows the net estate available for the beneficiaries. This method produces a different sum from the one shown in the Inland Revenue account, and shows the amount the beneficiaries are actually receiving after tax and administration expenses. It may be that most beneficiaries would find this more interesting and understandable than a two-stage capital account.

A one-part account is used in this example. Accordingly, for any items sold, e.g. Spring Cottage, the net proceeds of sale are used.

15.17   Some or all of the **investments** may have been sold. If so, the probate value of all the holdings will be included, plus or minus the gain or loss on sale as appropriate. (Details of the transactions would be shown in the schedule of investments.)

In this estate, and others where the investments are divided equally between the beneficiaries, the value included in the accounts is the probate value, i.e. value at the deceased's death. This is unlikely to be the same as the market value at the point when the shares are vested in the beneficiaries. However, any increase or decrease in value will be shared equally between the beneficiaries, so this produces no unfairness. The probate value is also the beneficiaries' acquisition value for CGT purposes.

All the assets, then, are listed at the probate value or actual realised value.

In relation to **bank and building society accounts**, etc., the probate value includes interest accrued to the date of death. For IHT purposes, this interest forms part of the deceased's estate and so is shown in the capital account. (Interest earned after death and before the closing of the account will be shown in the estate income account.) For income tax purposes, however, the accrued interest before death, and any interest received between death and the closing of the account are regarded as income of the PRs and should be included by them in their income tax return. Accordingly, the income shown in the income account is not the amount of income on which PRs actually pay income tax.

The **contents of the house** have been valued at an estimated £2,500. Some items have been sold and turned into cash. The actual amount received, i.e. the net proceeds of sale, is shown.

Once the gross estate is established, all the **debts and liabilities** are then deducted from the gross estate figure, including debts not permitted as deductions for IHT purposes.

A sum representing the net estate results. In this estate, of course, there are legacies to be paid before the net estate is distributed between the residuary beneficiaries. So, **non-residuary gifts** are deducted from the net estate figure, and then the **division of residue** is shown. These figures are transferred to the individual beneficiaries' accounts.

Income account

15.18 This deals with income received during the administration of the estate. In this estate, all the income is received in one tax year. If the administration straddled more than one tax year, two or more separate sets of figures would be shown.

If income is received net of tax, show the net figure. If income is received gross, the PRs will have to pay income tax at basic rate. This payment will be shown as a deduction from income. Also deducted here will be any payments out of income, such as interest on loans, interest on IHT, any solicitors' or accountants' charges related to post-death tax returns.

In this estate, income and capital are received by the same beneficiaries, and no such distinction has been made in the solicitors' charges. If different beneficiaries were entitled to income and capital, e.g. in a life interest, a proportion of the solicitors' charges, referable to income, would be deducted here.

Again, the net entitlement to income is shown, and the balances are taken to the beneficiaries' accounts.

Beneficiaries' accounts

15.19   The entitlements have been brought forward and listed. In this estate the beneficiaries are due capital and income.

Once the total due to a beneficiary has been ascertained, the account shows how this has been satisfied. There may be, as with Miss Emily Thomas, three elements:

- **Assets transferred 'in specie'.** Here, the shares were divided equally. As these were entered in the capital account at probate value, again probate values are used. Some furniture was also transferred 'in specie' at values agreed between the beneficiaries.

- **Assets which were retained by the beneficiaries.** This is regarded as an 'advance' of part of their respective entitlements, and brought into account.

- **Payments of cash on account, or interim distributions.**

Balancing the books

The balance after these calculations represents the amount due to the beneficiary and all together should add up to the amount left in the client ledger, after costs and disbursements.

If these figures do not agree, something has gone wrong. It can sometimes be a horribly trying process to find the mistake, but it must be found.

N.B. It could happen that a balance appears to be due *from* a beneficiary *to* the estate. This will usually mean that interim distributions were too big – these payments should only be made after considering all future liabilities, such as tax and costs. A situation like this often causes great difficulty, as the beneficiary will, at the very least, be disappointed.

Schedule of investments

15.20   Rather than include on the capital account details of the investments, these can be listed in a schedule or annex. As no items have been sold this schedule is simple, giving capital values and showing the division of the shares between the beneficiaries. If numerous dividends had been received these could also have been recorded in a schedule.

If items had been sold, the sale price and any gain or loss could be shown. This information would be included in the capital account.

CAPITAL GAINS TAX

15.21 PRs are chargeable to CGT in respect of gains realised on or after 6 April 1998 at the new uniform trusts rate of 34 per cent.

As with individuals an indexation allowance will be given for periods up to 6 April 1998 but not thereafter.

So, for assets held at 6 April 1998 and disposed of after that date an indexation allowance will be calculated for the period from acquisition to 6 April 1998. For assets acquired after that date no indexation allowance will be available.

Taper relief will be available to PRs and trustees who hold assets for an appropriate period.

PRs continue to receive the same annual exemption as an individual for the tax year of death and the two subsequent tax years.

PRs will be able to treat as allowable acquisition costs a proportion of the costs of obtaining the grant – details are set out in Inland Revenue Statement of Practice SP8/94. Costs of transferring the asset to the beneficiaries are also allowable (see Taxation of Chargeable Gains Act 1992 (TCGA), s.6(1)).

It is advisable to give a specific legatee a note of the value of the asset at the date of the death so that the legatee can calculate liability for CGT without having to refer back to the solicitor – perhaps many years after a file has been closed.

Release for PRs

15.22 In this particular estate, the PRs and beneficiaries are one and the same, so there is no need for the beneficiaries to release the PRs from further liability. A note of the beneficiaries' approval of the accounts might, however, be advisable as far as the solicitors are concerned. This could take the form of a simple statement on the account indicating their approval.

INCOME TAX

15.23 There has been a significant change in the way in which **beneficiaries** of an estate are assessed to income tax and this in turn has implications for personal representatives.

Personal representatives continue to pay basic or lower rate tax on income of the estate. They will pay the net income to beneficiaries with an appropriate tax credit. Up until 6 April 1995 beneficiaries were assessed to income tax on income of the estate in the tax year in which it was paid to them but at the end of the administration the total of income paid out was apportioned evenly over the whole administration period on a daily basis. This led to recalculation of the beneficiary's tax liability for each tax year of the administration. In cases where a beneficiary was close to the limit of a tax band the apportioning of income could take the beneficiaries into or out of a particular band.

Since 6 April 1995 income paid to a beneficiary is treated as income of the tax year in which it is paid and there is no apportioning of income at the end of the administration. This can result in a beneficiary paying an unnecessarily high rate of tax. For example, if personal representatives make no interim income payments and pay out all the income at the end of the administration period to a beneficiary, that beneficiary may be pushed into higher rate tax for that year, whereas had the payments been made in two tax years the beneficiary might have remained a basic rate taxpayer.

Personal representatives are now under an obligation to provide residuary beneficiaries with R185Es.

The Revenue has published a very helpful booklet explaining exactly how to treat income of the administration period called *Administration of the Deceased's Estate*. We have also set out below at para. 15.24 a helpful article by Mary Hase, partner in charge of executorship at chartered accountants, Hereward Phillips. This article first appeared in [1997] *Solicitors Journal,* 20 June and we are most grateful to Mary Hase and to the *Solicitors Journal* for allowing us to reproduce it.

'Additional tax responsibilities for solicitors

15.24 The introduction of self-assessment puts increased responsibilities on solicitors acting as or advising executors. Tax matters can no longer be left until an estate is fully administered. Put simply, good management of an estate is essential. It saves time, money and – above all – professional reputation.

As a result of self-assessment, solicitors are responsible for ensuring that an estate is administered in a tax efficient manner, with tax returns completed on time and payments made in stages for the current year according to the dates laid down by the new tax regulations.

In the past, it has been common practice for solicitors to leave sorting out the tax on an estate until the estate has been substantially completed. Such practice would now lead to a series of mounting fines for the executor and beneficiaries.

Tax planning

This is the key to success. Consider at the outset when the estate's income is likely to be received and plan the distributions accordingly.

Also consider the financial position of the beneficiaries at the beginning. For wealthy beneficiaries looking to minimise their tax liability it may be best to delay distributions and thereby postpone the impact of higher rate tax until a more convenient time. For those in the middle range the payments might be spread to avoid hitting the higher rate tax threshold. Needy beneficiaries may desire a speedy settlement but again spreading their entitlement over a number of tax years may be more likely to help them utilise allowances and fall beneath tax thresholds.

Remember too that a large income distribution in one year may affect the beneficiaries' tax payments on account in the next.

If in doubt, call in the accountants/tax advisers early to assist with the planning.

The solicitor, acting as executor, must advise the Inland Revenue of the estate's untaxed income and capital gains. The normal deadlines apply – 30 September if the Revenue are to calculate the tax, 31 January if not. However, the Revenue will not work out the income and chargeable gains for you. Beneficiaries who have an absolute interest must also be advised of the income element included in their distributions to enable them to include these figures on their personal tax forms. It is the executor's responsibility to ensure that beneficiaries can meet their deadlines, which may be 30 September if the beneficiaries do not wish to calculate their own tax.

Payments on account

Payments on account underline the importance of good management. Plan the date of cessation and work out how the resulting accounting will be done, so that the beneficiaries are provided with the necessary information in good time to complete their own tax returns and assess their own payments on account.

The basic rule is that a payment on account should be half the previous year's tax liability, excluding capital gains. This is fine when income flow is regular, but distributions from an estate may involve payments over the short term only. It can be particularly difficult for executors and beneficiaries with unreliable income sources to deal with the tax payments. Once assets are realised, and the ensuing untaxed income sources cease, the executor may seek to reduce the payment on account.

Executors should also beware of placing any cash sums received from the estate in investments which pay income gross, such as the money markets, even if this is on a temporary basis. If the liability turns out to be greater than that anticipated when the payment on account was assessed, the executors will be liable for interest and possibly penalties.

For smaller estates it is advisable to avoid these complications by selecting investments which deduct tax at source, even if it means sacrificing one or two interest points and the cash flow advantage of gross income.

For beneficiaries the problem is worse. They may be looking at total income, taxed and untaxed, and can have no idea what their payment on account should be unless the executors give them guidance on how much and when the income distributions are likely to be. Remember that for absolute interest beneficiaries, their distributions will be part income, part capital so merely telling them how much in total to expect is not sufficient.

For life interest beneficiaries, their whole distribution is income so the amounts and dates will suffice for them during the period of administration. Any balance unpaid will be taxable at the date the administration ceases so the date(s) should be planned and made known to the beneficiaries.

Trustees' responsibilities for tax returns start on the death of the person in question, though there may be nothing to report until the estate's assets are vested in them. If a discretionary trust is set up, the payment of income to the trustees or direct to the trust beneficiaries will trigger a liability at the trust rate. So the responsibility for submission of trust returns may start before the closure of the administration.

Even if no formal trust is set up under the will, often it is convenient to leave the estate's assets in the hands of the executors after completion of the administration. This becomes a bare trust and under self-assessment bare trustees are not liable to make returns or to calculate and pay basic rate tax on behalf of the beneficiaries.

Tax liabilities of the deceased

When someone dies, their tax liabilities become the responsibility of the personal representatives, who must then try to keep to the dates above. This may be difficult if the deceased's tax affairs were in arrears, or if there is a delay in obtaining letters of administration.

Problems would occur simply by a death occurring, say, in December. This is because the tax return for the previous year, with up to three tax payments, must all be paid by the following 31 January. These tax payments would be for (a) any outstanding income tax for the previous financial year, (b) capital gains tax for the previous year, and (c) the first tax payment for the current year. As yet, there appears to be no legislation giving the executor more time to assess the tax situation, or to wait until probate is granted, or, indeed for the penalties to be mitigated in these circumstances.

If delay is unavoidable, it would be advisable to write to the Revenue at the earliest opportunity (and before the relevant deadline has passed) explaining the situation, giving an indication of when matters could be dealt with and requesting no penalties.

Delays may be considerable where a will is contested and it may not be clear which beneficiary gets which assets if applications are to be made under the Inheritance (Provision for Family and Dependants) Act 1975. The rigidity of the self-assessment regime cannot cope with such uncertainties.

Early clearance of income and capital gains tax

It has, however, been announced that procedures will be introduced to facilitate the speedy completion of trusts and estates. This will include early issue of tax returns and early written confirmation that the Revenue do not propose to enquire into the return. This will assist both executors and trustees who would otherwise have to wait for a year following the next 31 January to know if the deceased's and the estate's income and capital gains tax liabilities are settled and that they are in the clear.

In summary

It is likely that further legislation will be passed or concessions granted to simplify some of these matters. Until that time, early tax planning for the entire administration of the estate is the best approach.'

RECEIPTS FOR LEGACIES

15.25 This article first appeared in [1992] *Gazette,* 14 October. It is reproduced here, edited and with a newly approved draft of the recommended receipt and discharge wording. The Land Law and Succession Committee is grateful to Mr Richard Oerton, whose revision of the original wording of the receipt and discharge appeared first in the journal *Clarity.* The newly approved version is identical to Mr Oerton's with one minor change.

'Receipts for payment of legacies

Periodically the Law Society receives complaints from beneficiaries who have been asked by solicitors administering an estate to sign receipts for their legacies before payment is made. This has been considered by the Land Law and Succession Committee (now the Wills and Equity Committee).

It should now be standard practice for all solicitors to write to legatees and beneficiaries early in the administration of an estate to inform them of their legacies and entitlements and then, when funds are available, to pay legatees and beneficiaries direct by cheque, unless other arrangements have been made.

The Committee (except as stated below) considers that it is no longer reasonable or necessary for legatees and beneficiaries to be asked to sign receipts in advance of payment and that such a practice is bound to generate additional correspondence and thus to add unnecessarily to the cost of the administration of the estate.

Precedents for simple forms of receipt for the payment of pecuniary, specific and residuary legacies are available. However, solicitors may find it more convenient to ask the legatee or beneficiary to acknowledge receipt by signing and returning a duplicate copy of the letter accompanying the cheque. In any case, Cheques Act 1957, s.3 provides that: "An unindorsed cheque which appears to have been paid by the banker on whom it is drawn is evidence of the receipt by the payee of the sum payable by the cheque".

Solicitors are also reminded of the protection for cheques which is afforded by the "account payee" crossing under the Cheques Act 1992.

With regard to residuary beneficiaries, the estate accounts will first have to be approved by the personal representatives. When that has been done, solicitors should then, in most cases, proceed with the final distribution by sending the residuary beneficiaries copies of the approved accounts, and cheques in payment, with a request that the beneficiaries acknowledge payment by signing a receipt either endorsed on the accounts or supplied separately; the receipt to include, if needed, a discharge to the personal representatives.

If difficulties have arisen during the administration, there may be occasions when solicitors, before making final distributions, wish to make sure that the residuary beneficiaries are not going to object to the amounts. In such cases the residuary beneficiaries should be sent, in advance, copies of the approved accounts and be asked to sign a form of receipt and discharge to the personal representatives on the basis that they will be sent a cheque immediately upon the solicitors receiving back the signed form.

It is recommended that the receipt and discharge should be in the following form:

THE LATE_____

The estate accounts show the final sum due to me as £_____

I approve the accounts and will accept that sum in full satisfaction of all my claims against the estate.

Please pay it by a crossed cheque in my favour and send it to me by post.

Finally, it must be remembered that a discharge will only be fully effective if the beneficiaries have been given full details of all the assets and liabilities of and all dealings with the estate.'

Problems with legacies to minors

15.26 Where a will fails to authorise executors to accept the receipt of a parent or guardian, executors have a problem in obtaining a good discharge.

The traditional options have been:

- paying the money into court;

- appointing trustees under AEA 1925, s.42;

- appropriating assets under AEA 1925, s.41.

However, in an interesting article in [1997] *Private Client Business* Issue 1, 37 Michael Waterworth of 8 Gray's Inn suggests that there is not (and has not been for some time) any problem. He says that as a result of the Children Act 1989 all parents with parental responsibility have the same rights, powers and duties as guardians appointed under section 5 of the Act. These rights are set out in section 3 and include 'the right to receive or recover in his own name *for the benefit* of the child, property of whatever description and wherever situated, which the child is entitled to receive or recover'.

The words in italic indicate that the parent or guardian will hold the property in a fiduciary capacity.

CHARITABLE BENEFICIARIES

15.27 There are a number of special factors to bear in mind if a charity is left a substantial gift. The rest of this chapter highlights the important issues. We are grateful to the Charity Commissioners for their advice, and the help of Brian Walsh of Hempsons in revising those parts of the Handbook covering charities, has been invaluable.

Charities and wills

15.28 Charities now work very hard to maximise their legacy income, and the Law Society, in its recent 'Will Week' campaigns, has highlighted the ability to leave a gift to a favourite charity to encourage will-making.

Because of the importance legacies have for charitable funding, you will find that the larger charities in particular are very knowledgeable about their rights and entitlements and are very experienced beneficiaries. You can expect them to be well organised and efficient. They will appreciate being sent early a copy of a will which leaves them a residuary gift (as will individual beneficiaries). Certain charitable and other residuary beneficiaries are entitled to obtain a remuneration certificate – see Chapter 2.

Checklist: Charitable beneficiaries

15.29   The following reminders should help avoid problems:

1.   **Changed circumstances**. A charity may feel a moral obligation to renounce part of its entitlement under a will (or even make a payment from the estate) if there are grounds for believing that, in the events which have happened, the will does not in fact carry out its maker's intentions. A charity normally needs authority from the Charity Commissioners to make an *ex gratia* payment. They have a discretion to refer individual cases to the Attorney General for a decision. Applicants can have their cases considered afresh by the Attorney General if the Commissioners refuse authority. The Charity Commission's leaflet CC7 explains the procedure (address in Chapter 30). Changes do not always work to a charity's advantage – a gift may be adeemed, for example, and clients should be warned about this possibility when making a will.

2.   **Wrong descriptions**. Problems of a different kind are caused by wrongly describing the intended charity in a will. You can check that an organisation is a registered charity, and its correct name, by contacting the Charity Commission.

3.   **Charity dissolved.** The recent case of *Re ARMS (Multiple Sclerosis Research) Ltd* [1997] 2 All E.R. 679 highlights a particular problem in relation to incorporated charities. In that case a charitable company overspent and went into liquidation. The court had to decide whether legacies to the charity taking effect after the date of the liquidation but before dissolution were payable to the liquidator – so as to be available to the company's creditors – or whether, as the Attorney General argued, the legacies were given and should be applied for the charity's purposes. The court directed that all the legacies were payable to the liquidator.

This decision shows the clear distinction between incorporated charities, which take legacies beneficially in their own right, and unincorporated charities which take for their charitable purposes. It made no difference that one of the legacies in the ARMS case was expressed to be 'for the general purposes' of the charity.

This case is significant for the probate practitioner when administering an estate and also when drafting wills including legacies to incorporated charities. The draftsman should consider adapting the standard amalgamation/dissolution clause to create a substitution or to give executors a discretion where a legatee is in liquidation.

4. **Conditional gifts.** If your client wants to give a gift on condition, find out from the charity whether the terms of the gift will be acceptable or feasible; alternatively, provide in the will for what is to happen if the charity declines the gift.

It is also important to make clear what is to happen if it is impossible to carry out the condition at the time of the testator's death (e.g. a gift which is conditional on a charity caring for the testator's pets and at the time of the testator's death there are no pets). Failure to do so will result in uncertainty and possible litigation. (See *Watson* v. *National Children's Home* [1995] *Gazette,* 18 October, 24).

5. **Delayed distribution.** If your client wants to enable the PRs and trustees to be able to distribute a gift over an extended period of time, you need to draft this carefully. The Commissioners' Annual Report for the year 1990 highlights the decision in *Re Muller's Estate* (unreported) which concerns a gift using a precedent in *Williams on Wills* (6th edition) vol. 2, p.1185. It was held that the gift implied that distribution would be made within a reasonable time, and hence this formulation may not be suitable if your client wishes to provide otherwise.

6. **R185Es.** R185Es – annual certificates of tax deduction – are especially important to charities. They need these certificates for each tax year of the administration, as evidence that tax – which they can reclaim – has been deducted. Charities can reclaim not only tax on income which has arisen during the administration period, but also tax which has accrued prior to the date of death and not been paid (e.g. building society interest which is credited half-yearly) – but not without the R185E. The repayments form a valuable addition to the funds available to charities.

Solicitors' failure to issue these forms is a complaint frequently made to the Law Society and it is the responsibility of the firm undertaking the administration, and not the bank or building society, to prepare them and send them to beneficiaries. Having to produce these forms is a chore but as the charities will continue to ask for them, producing them early will allow the file to be closed more quickly.

Complete the R185E with the tax district reference number. Without this number, charities cannot reclaim the tax shown on the certificate.

If the deceased was a non-taxpayer, and you do not have the tax district reference number, you can solve the problem by writing to your local tax office. Send a copy of the estate accounts and ask the Revenue to waive the need for tax returns for the administration period. The local tax district reference number can then be quoted on the R185E. (See also para. 15.45.)

7. **Charities Act 1993.** If a will leaves land to a charity, both the charity and the executors must comply with Charities Act 1993, ss.36 and 37. An absolute gift to a charity of a house, for example, means that the charity can require the executors to transfer or assent the property to it: from the date of assent the charity must comply with the Act's provisions in relation to sale.

A gift to a charity, for example, of a house, on condition that it will permit another beneficiary to occupy it for life, means that the executors' freedom to sell the property is curtailed. Because they hold the property on trust for the charity, the executors too are bound by sections 36 and 37 of the Act, even before assent.

8. **Interest.** Interest will be due on legacies not paid at the end of the executors' year and may be due beforehand.

9. **Form of gift.** Discuss with the charity the best way for them to receive the gift – in some cases appropriation *in specie* may allow the charity to sell an asset and thus save capital gains tax. The charity may customarily use a particular auction house or estate agency, with which they may have a special arrangement relating to fees, which may also be able to assist. Appropriation of assets can be done on paper, that is, without any necessity physically to transfer securities. The sale is then made as bare trustee on behalf of the charity. It is, however, important to have a written record of the appropriation. See point 14 and para. 15.37 below.

10. **Deeds of variation.** Consider deeds of variation to make the gift in the most effective way (see the points set out at paras. 15.41–15.42 below).

11. **Exempt and non-exempt beneficiaries.** If the residuary gift is to both exempt and non-exempt beneficiaries, the problem of how to distribute the estate in the light of *Re Benham* arises. See para. 15.30 below.

12. **Early notice.** Sending a copy of the will at an early stage alerts a charitable residuary beneficiary to its entitlement and enables it to put forward its own wishes for the PRs' consideration. Obtaining the PRs' consent to briefing the charity on progress can also be worthwhile. However, PRs remain, of course, obliged to act in the interests of the estate as a whole, not just those of one particular beneficiary.

13. **Interim distributions.** Consider whether one or more interim distributions can be made.

14. **CGT.** Capital gains tax may be more easily reclaimed by the charity if an exchange of letters has taken place between the solicitors acting in the estate and the charity beneficiary, authorising the sale.

15. **VAT.** Charities are no longer able to recover VAT on costs associated with sales made in relation to land or buildings.

The problem of Re Benham

15.30 The case of *Re Benham's Will Trust, Lockhurt v. Harker: Reed and the National Life Boat Institution* [1995] S.T.C. 210 has caused great problems for personal representatives. The notes on the case in paras 15.30–15.36 have been written specially for us by Chris Whitehouse, Barrister of 8 Gray's Inn Square and we are most grateful to him for doing do.

As a general rule a testator is free to decide where the burden of inheritance tax is to fall. Specific gifts are, in the absence of any direction to the contrary, tax free with the tax being paid out of residue. To preserve the value of exempt transfers, however, and notably of gifts to spouses and charities, Inheritance Tax Act 1984, s.41 provides that:

'Notwithstanding the terms of any disposition:

(a) none of the tax on the value transferred shall fall on any specific gift if or to the extent that the transfer is exempt with respect to the gift; and

(b) none of the tax attributable to the value of the property comprised in residue shall fall on any gift of a share of residue if or to the extent that the transfer is exempt with respect to the gift.'

In a simple case where residue is split between chargeable and exempt beneficiaries (for instance, between the testator's son and his wife) any tax attributable to the son's share must be borne out of that share; no part of that tax can come out of the portion of residue passing to the surviving spouse.

When is Re Benham relevant?

15.31 In practice, difficulties only arise if residue is split between chargeable and exempt beneficiaries. Commonly this occurs when part of the residue is left to charity with the rest passing to the relatives of the testator. A will leaving a specific legacy to charity with residue to the testator's family does not, therefore, give rise to problems. A second point to bear in mind is that *Benham* is concerned with the calculation of inheritance tax on the chargeable portion of an estate. Accordingly, if that portion falls within the testator's nil rate band, no computational difficulties can arise.

Grossing up a chargeable share of residue

15.32 Given that section 41 prevents tax on a chargeable share of residue from being borne by an exempt share, how can the wishes of a testator that the *net* residue after payment of all expenses and inheritance tax is to be divided equally between (say) his wife and daughter be satisfied? Only, it is thought, if the will provides for the chargeable share (in this example the daughter's share) to be grossed up to include the tax which is charged on it.

Illustration: Assume net residue of £100,000 to be divided equally between surviving spouse and daughter. Estate rate 40 per cent.

- *Option 1* deduct tax on £50,000 and divide balance (£80,000) equally: prohibited by section 41.

- *Option 2* divide equally so that spouse gets £50,000 and daughter gets £50,000 then bears tax so that she ends up with £30,000.

237

- *Option 3* gross up daughter's share (X) so that both end up with the same:

ie $X + \dfrac{(100X)}{60} = £100,000$

$X = £37,500$

Both receive £37,500; gross value of daughter's share is £62,500.

	Spouse (£)	Daughter(£)	Tax Man (£)
Option 1	40,000	40,000	20,000
Option 2	50,000	30,000	20,000
Option 3	37,500	37,500	25,000

The facts of Re Benham's Will Trust

15.33   In this case under Clause 3 of the will residue was left as follows:

(a)   upon trust to pay debts, funeral and testamentary expenses;

(b)   after such payment 'to pay the same to those beneficiaries as are living at my death and who are listed in List A and List B hereunder written in such proportions as will bring about the result that the aforesaid beneficiaries named in List A shall receive 3.2 times as much as the aforesaid beneficiaries named in List B and each case for their own absolute and beneficial use and disposal'.

List A contained one charity and a number of non-charitable beneficiaries; and List B contained a number of charities and non-charitable beneficiaries. By an originating summons, the executor sought, *inter alia,* the opinion of the court on the following questions:

- whether the wording in Clause 3(b) meant that each qualifying beneficiary in List A should receive 3.2 times the sum taken by each beneficiary in List B, or whether the List A beneficiaries should between them receive 3.2 times the total sum taken by the List B beneficiaries;

- whether, in view of IHTA 1984, s.41 and the terms of the will, the non-charitable beneficiaries should receive their shares subject to inheritance tax, or whether their shares should be grossed up; and

- whether the shares of legatees who predeceased the testatrix accrued by survivorship to the other legatees or became applicable for the payment of funeral and testamentary expenses and debts.

The deputy judge agreed that the choice between the two interpretations of Clause 3(b) was not so clear that it could be said that there was no real doubt or ambiguity and he admitted extrinsic evidence under Administration of Justice Act 1982, s.21(1)(b). He then concluded that Clause 3(b) directed payment of the residue to two groups of beneficiaries and, whilst the persons named in Lists A and B, respectively, took as between themselves in equal shares provided that they survived the testatrix, the part of the residue available to List A beneficiaries to share equally between them was a fund 3.2 times as large as the fund available for the List B beneficiaries.

On the second question, there were three possibilities:

- the non-charitable beneficiaries received their respective shares subject to inheritance tax, which would mean that they would receive less than the charities;

- the non-charitable beneficiaries should have their respective shares grossed up, so that they received the same net sum as the charities; or

- the inheritance tax was paid as part of the testamentary expenses under Clause 3(a), and the balance was distributed equally between the non-charitable beneficiaries and the charities.

The deputy judge agreed that the third possibility was precluded by section 41. However, he did not agree that the charities should receive more than the non-charitable beneficiaries. The plain intention of the testatrix was that each beneficiary, whether charitable or non-charitable, should receive the same as the other beneficiaries on the relevant list. That result, he concluded, was consistent with the express terms of the will and section 41. Thus, he considered that the non-charitable beneficiaries' shares should be grossed up.

Finally, Clause 3(b) made it a condition that any named beneficiary should be living when the testatrix died. Thus, the deputy judge said, the two funds should be divided between the beneficiaries in the two lists, after deleting those who had died.

Difficulties arising from Re Benham

15.34   The main difficulty posed by *Re Benham* lies not in the actual facts of the case (which were obviously somewhat unusual!), but in the assertion of the judge that 'the plain intention of the testatrix is that at the end of the day each beneficiary, whether charitable or non-charitable, should receive the same as the other beneficiaries'.

This view, if correct, would appear to result in the implication (as a matter of construction) of a grossing up clause in all cases where:

(a) the residue is left to be divided between exempt and non–exempt beneficiaries;

(b) the will provides for them to take in equal shares and there is no evidence that the testator did not intend *Benham* to apply; and

(c) the value of the estate is such that IHT is payable on the chargeable portion of residue.

This approach goes against the existing practice which had been to apply section 41 in such cases.

Attitude of the Capital Taxes Office

15.35   The attitude of the Capital Taxes Office to the *Benham* case and the consequent problems of construing and drafting wills can be gleaned from the following exchange of correspondence.

The British Heart Foundation wrote to the Capital Taxes Office in the following terms:

'*Re: Benhams Will Trusts*

The British Heart Foundation, like many other charities, is alarmed at the potential threat to its income if, as has been widely propounded in the legal press, the decision in the above case is applied in cases where the will is drawn not in the terms of the Benham will but in the very much more common terms usually applied.

The cases I refer to are of course those involving gifts of residue to exempt and non-exempt beneficiaries, where the will directs the executors to pay IHT and legacies and then divide the residue. Our concern is that if the *Re Benham* judgment is applied then non-exempt beneficiaries wrongly benefit from the exempt status of organisations such as ourselves, contrary to section 41(b) of the IHT Act 1984; that is that charities as a whole could lose a great deal of money, part of which will effectively go towards paying the IHT of non-exempt beneficiaries, contrary to our charitable objects.

We at the Foundation believe that *Re Benham* really turns on the rather unusual terms of the will and has no general application to bequests of shares of residue between exempt and non-exempt beneficiaries as expressed in the common cases outlined above. We and other charities are currently considering two cases to be put to the court, but clearly a decision may take some time. Whilst this information may hold off executors from distributing estates along the lines of *Benham,* we would be obliged however if you would confirm the following: that the CTO's view is also that the *Re Benham* decision is inapplicable for this more common type of provision and that in such cases no IHT will arise that will deplete charitable shares of residue as a result of the *Benham* decision.'

The CTO's response indicates that they will abide by a proper construction of the will (so that the fact that extra tax is payable if grossing up applies is not a factor to be taken into account):

'We consider the decision to be primarily concerned with ascertaining the intention of the testatrix and hence as not directly involving the Inland Revenue. In an attempt to be helpful, however, we would comment as follows.

Like you, our view is that the decision followed from the particular facts of the case with the court deciding that the plain intention of the testatrix was that at the end of the day and therefore after the payment of tax each beneficiary whether charitable or non–charitable on the respective lists should *receive* the same amount as the other beneficiaries in that list.

Generally speaking the court is concerned in such cases to establish the intention of the testator or testatrix from the wording of the will and admissible extrinsic evidence. If the will is drafted in common form with a direction to ascertain residue after payment of funeral and testamentary expenses and debts followed by a bequest of that residue then it is focusing on the ascertainment and division of disposable residue rather than on what each residuary beneficiary is to receive. Accordingly wills so drafted would not appear to involve *Benham* style grossing up computations.' (P. Twiddy)

Practical advice on the distribution of residue

15.36 Because of the interpretation put by the judge on residue clauses, *Benham* presents major problems in practice. The following are a number of suggestions as to how the problem may be approached: unfortunately they cannot be regarded as solutions for every case!

(a) The first matter is to decide whether the division of residue and value of the estate are such that there is a *Benham* problem at all.

(b) If the will expressly provides for the shares of chargeable beneficiaries to be grossed up then that is an end of the matter.

(c) If not, everything turns on a correct construction of the document. A relevant exercise is to calculate the inheritance tax that would be payable on the alternative bases of:

(i) applying section 41; and

(ii) grossing up.

It will normally be the case that, if grossing up occurs, the tax take is increased; chargeable beneficiaries get a greater slice of the estate and the loser will be the exempt beneficiary (i.e. either spouse or charity).

(d) When the only beneficiaries of the residue are family members (typically therefore the surviving spouse and children) it is often possible to agree an approach which will resolve the difficulties. Commonly the children will be prepared to accept that *Benham* should not apply thereby ensuring that more is received by their mother than would otherwise would be the case (and, of course, that less is received by the Capital Taxes Office!).

(e) If a 'deal' is not possible then counsel's advice may be taken and the executors may then act in accordance with his opinion. This practice is frequently adopted, but executors should always be warned that it does not prevent them from being sued by disappointed beneficiaries and in reality the absolutely safe course is to go to the court for directions. (Note, in this connection, that the court's general power to excuse executors and trustees under Trustee Act 1925, s.61 depends on the executors satisfactorily showing that a failure to obtain the court's directions before carrying out the relevant distribution was not culpable.) *Benham* itself was not appealed. However, it is understood that a further case will be heard shortly. In appropriate cases PRs may decide to wait for the result of this case before deciding what action to take.

(f) If full agreement cannot be reached between the beneficiaries as to what is to be done then the executors may decide to apply section 41 if an indemnity is given either by the charity or by the surviving spouse. Given the uncertain value of such indemnities and the difficulties of enforcement, this approach cannot be wholeheartedly recommended.

(g) In some cases, partial distributions are made with the executors retaining sufficient assets to ensure that when the law is clarified a distribution can then be made on whatever turns out to be the correct basis. The defects of this approach as a long-term solution are obvious!

What is needed in this area is judicial clarification given that the matter is basically one of will construction. Calls for amending legislation are therefore misguided. At the time of writing a further test case is under consideration but, like its predecessors, it may well be settled before coming to court.

Postscript

15.37 For practitioners who find themselves in the unenviable position of having to perform a *Benham* calculation there is an interesting article on software available to do the job in [1997] *Private Client Business,* April, 197–202. There is also a helpful article by James Sunnucks in [1998] *Solicitors Journal,* 20 November, explaining why, in his view, '*Benham* should at its highest be regarded as an exceptional case turning on the construction of that particular will'.

In *Re Ratcliffe deceased, The Times,* 19 March 1999, Mr Justice Blackburn declined to follow *Re Benham* stating that he was unable to find any principle in it. However, the case is being appealed so the area is still uncertain.

Charities and capital gains tax – importance of assent or appropriation of assets to charity entitled to residue

15.38 Charities benefit from capital gains tax exemption in respect of gains realised on the disposal of assets if the gains are applicable and applied for charitable purposes (see Taxation of Chargeable Gains Act 1992, s.256). However, the exemption will only apply if the relevant property is beneficially owned by the charity. If, during the administration of an estate, an asset, which has increased significantly in value since the date of death, is to be sold, it will be important either for the assets to be vested in the name of the charity prior to the sale, or for the executors to execute an assent declaring that they hold the asset for the charity absolutely. Failure to take these elementary steps will mean that the gain will be realised by the executors and not by the charity and the Inland Revenue may claim capital gains tax on the gain realised, even if the benefit of the sale proceeds will ultimately pass to the charity.

Many of the major charities have very helpful notes advising executors on the correct procedure. We print by way of example the note issued by The Guide Dogs For The Blind Association.

Specimen guidance note from charity

15.39   'May we please draw the attention of the executors and their advisers to the fact that as a national charity we are exempt, under the provisions of TCGA 1992, s.256(1), from payment of capital gains tax on the sale of any securities made on our behalf.

The exemption relates to any sale made on our behalf in respect of the residue or shares of the residue of the estate to which we are entitled.

The procedure to be followed to comply with Inland Revenue requirements is that the securities should be appropriated to our account by a simple but clear designation in your books, or by a memorandum or resolution signed by the personal representatives in your files. Any sales subsequently made by you are made as bare trustee on our behalf under TCGA 1992, s.60.'

Executors should be careful if they require an indemnity from the charity for the payment of administration expenses in return for the transfer of assets to the charity. The Revenue may argue that such an indemnity is to be construed as a payment for the asset and accordingly a sale by the executors, or alternatively that the gain realised by the charity is not fully applicable and applied for charitable purposes.

ADMINISTRATION EXPENSES

15.40   The notes in paras 15.41–15.42 are based on an article originally written for the *Law Society's Gazette* by Alan Jarvis, a partner in Wilde Sapte & Co. (see [1991] *Gazette*, 15 February). We are most grateful to him for allowing us to adapt and update it.

Administration expenses and inheritance tax

15.41 Most administration expenses are not deductible for inheritance tax purposes. Careful planning at the time of the preparation of the will can, however, achieve an additional benefit whereby the administration expenses will, in effect, be deductible for inheritance tax purposes. For example, a testator leaves an estate of £623,000 with a gift to charity of £200,000 and the balance of the estate passing to a nephew absolutely.

The inheritance tax position will be as follows:

	£
Value of estate	623,000
Legacy to charity	200,000
Residue to nephew	423,000
Less	
Inheritance tax on residue	(80,000)
Administration expenses	(6,000)
Net amount received by nephew	337,000

An alternative approach might be to give the nephew a specific legacy which after the payment of inheritance tax, would leave him a net sum of £337,000. The residue of the estate would then pass to the charity. The revised inheritance tax position will be:

	£
Gross legacy to nephew	413,000
Less inheritance tax on legacy	(76,000)
Net legacy sum due to nephew	337,000
Residue	210,000
Less administration expense	(6,000)
Net residue payable to charity	204,000

Similarly, a benefit can be given to charity where none previously existed at no extra cost to a beneficiary:

Intended disposition	£
Gross estate due to beneficiary	623,000
Less inheritance tax	(160,000)
Net estate	463,000
Less administration expenses	(6,000)
Net amount received by beneficiary	457,000

Alternative disposition	
Legacy to beneficiary (£457,000–£223,000 grossed up at 40 per cent + £223,000)	613,000
Less inheritance tax	(156,000)
Net amount received by beneficiary	457,000
Residue to charity	10,000
Less administration expenses	(6,000)
Net amount received by charity	4,000

Use of discretionary wills

15.42 Fine tuning to the degree mentioned in the above examples is not normally possible at the time of preparing the will since the testator's or testatrix's estate is likely to alter in nature or value before death. Consideration might be given to two alternative approaches.

First, he or she may wish to consider the establishment of a two-year discretionary trust established under the will (see Inheritance Tax Act 1984, s.144). If a discretionary trust is established by will, any distributions or appointment from the trust within two years of death will be treated for tax purposes as a disposition under the will occurring on death. The advantage, as demonstrated in either of the above examples, can be achieved with full knowledge of the value of the deceased's estate. The disadvantage of a discretionary trust is particularly that the Revenue will seek to charge inheritance tax in full on the application for the grant of representation, even if subsequent appointments from the trust may invoke spouse or charitable exemptions. This problem may be avoided by the executors exercising their discretionary powers before making the application for the grant since, unlike administrators, executors' powers commence upon death. (Do be careful not to make a distribution from the trust within the three months of the death or the advantages of section 144 will be lost. This trap is pretty well known but the recent case of *Frankland* v. *IRC* [1996] S.T.C. 735 shows that people can still get caught.)

Secondly, it is still possible to effect a post-death variation of the will of the deceased under Inheritance Tax Act 1984, s.142.

It is worth noting that a post-death variation is now effective for income tax purposes as well as for the purposes of inheritance tax and capital gains tax.

Administration expenses and income tax

15.43   As most expenses of administration are not deductible for income tax, they will be paid out of the income of the administration which has borne tax at the basic rate. This will reduce the income which is distributed to the charity and, therefore, the scope for a repayment claim as the charity cannot reclaim the tax deducted from the income used to pay income expenses. The fewer expenses which are attributable to income, the greater will be the tax repayment to the charity. However, without specific power to pay income expenses out of capital, the level of expenses which are attributable to income will not be determined according to the executors' discretion but according to the law.

It may be appropriate to include in a will a direction that the executors shall have the power to pay administration expenses out of capital or income at their discretion, thereby enabling the executors to attribute all expenses to capital and allowing the charity to effect a full recovery of all basic rate tax paid.

In the absence of this power, it is important for the executors to ensure that no more than the correct amount of expenses is set against income. The matter should, however, be given careful thought and not merely determined by reference to the usual rough and ready estimate. Certain expenses may, upon a careful analysis, be properly attributable to capital rather than income.

CHARITIES AND DIVIDENDS

15.44   Practitioners may be interested to see the following edited notes, originally prepared by the Inland Revenue. Although they relate to transitional provisions for dividends received in the tax years 1993 to 1997 they can still be relevant to practitioners until 1999.

Dividends – transitional payments for charities

15.45   **Background.** Following Finance Act 1993 the general tax treatment of dividends paid by UK companies was amended. The tax credit for dividends paid on or after 6 April 1993 is to be calculated by reference to a 20 per cent tax rate instead of the 25 per cent rate which applied until 5 April 1993.

What this means for charities. If in the tax year 1992/93 a charity received a dividend of £75 it would be entitled to a tax credit of £25 which it would claim back from the Revenue. Now a dividend of £75 paid on will carry a tax credit of only £18.75. The charity will therefore receive £6.25 less than before.

What are the transitional payments? To ease the transition to a new rate of tax credit, the Chancellor provided special transitional payments to charity. These will run for a period of four years from 6 April 1993. These payments will be calculated at the following rates:

1/15 of dividends for 1993/94
1/20 of dividends for 1994/95
1/30 of dividends for 1995/96
1/60 of dividends for 1996/97

In each instance 'dividends' for a particular year means distributions made in that year.

Why are these fractions used? These payments represent the difference between the new tax credit (based on a 20 per cent tax rate) and the tax credit which would have been available if the tax rate had been 24 per cent for 1993/94, 23 per cent for 1994/95, 22 per cent for 1995/96 and 21 per cent for 1996/97. To simplify the calculations the payments have been rounded slightly to produce the fractions set out above.

How will this work? Suppose a charity received a dividend of £75 each year. It would claim repayment of the tax credit of £18.75 and is also entitled to the following transitional payments:

1993/94 1/15 of £75 = £5
1994/94 1/20 of £75 = £3.75
1995/96 1/30 of £75 = £2.50
1996/97 1/60 of £75 = £1.25

When can these payments be claimed? Transitional payments can be claimed after 27 July 1993. There will be a special two-year time-limit for making claims. If the charity is a trust, the claim will have to be made within two years from the end of the relevant tax year. For example, the claim for transitional relief for the 1996/97 tax year will have to be made by 5 April 1999.

If the charity is a company or an association, the claim must be made within two years from the ending of its accounting period. If the company draws up its accounts for a year to 31 December, transitional payments in respect of distributions paid in the year ended 31 December 1997 will have to be claimed by 31 December 1999.

The normal six-year time-limit continues to apply in respect of claims for repayment of tax credit.

Will repayment supplement be paid? No. Repayment supplement will not be available on such payments.

How will payments be claimed? There is a special claim form for these payments (see below).

Is there anything else which needs to be done? It will help us to process your claims promptly if you could separate the dividend vouchers for each year when you send us claims for payment of tax credit or transitional payment.

The special claim form introduced for transitional relief is the R68 (TR).

The Revenue add:

1. The claim form R68(TR) can be obtained from FICO Repayments (Charities) at the address shown below. It should be used only for UK company dividends paid between 6 April 1993 and 5 April 1997.

2. The form should be completed in addition to the form R68 on which charities claim payment of tax credits on dividends. Charities will normally find it convenient to send the two forms in together; but there is no obligation to do so. The new form also allows for the possibility that charities will sometimes want to include, in one claim, dividends attributed to more than one tax year.

3. The completed claim form should be sent to:

Inland Revenue
FICO Repayments (Charities)
St John's House
Merton Road
Bootle
Merseyside L69 9BB

Tel: 0151 472 6024

Tax credits and charities

15.46 In the 1997 Budget the Chancellor announced changes to the system of tax credits. From April 1999 the rate of tax credits will be halved to 10 per cent and tax credits will no longer be payable to shareholders with no tax liability. The tax credit will continue to satisfy the tax liability of taxpayers in the lower and basic rate tax bands.

To compensate charities for the loss of tax credits the government will make payments to charities equal to a percentage of their dividend income. This will be 21 per cent in 1999/2000 falling to 4 per cent by 2003/04.

Inspection of charities' records

15.47 The Revenue have produced a helpful booklet entitled *Inspection of Charities' Records* giving the Code of Practice in this area. If you have any complaints relating to the application of this Code of Practice you should contact Liz Hill at the following address:

FICO Repayments (Charities)
St John's House
Merton Road
Bootle
Merseyside L69 9BB

Tel: 0151 472 6024

Internet

15.48 The Charity Commissioners have a useful website:
http:\\www.charitycommission.gov.uk.

Chapter 16

Checklist: Probate practice

Solicitors in private practice may adapt or adopt these checklists for the purpose set out on page iv but not for any other purpose.

PRS AND PLANNING CHECKLIST

16.1 Before you begin to deal with the assets and liabilities have you:

1. Obtained clear instructions from the PRs?

2. Explained to the PRs:

   - their duties;

   - the nature and extent of the work to be done;

   - costs, charging, expenses;

   - IPFDA, statutory advertisements, deeds of variation, plus time-limits – and noted relevant date in your diary;

   - potential hold-ups: elapse of survival period, CTO, etc.;

   - any welfare benefits relevant and how to apply? (See Chapter 9.)

   Sent to PRs:

   - information letter (see Chapter 3);

   - client care letter/leaflet (see Chapter 3);

   - copy will?

3. Obtained your clients' addresses and phone and fax numbers and their availability? Agreed reporting frequency? Logged dates in your diary?

   Agreed billing frequency? Logged dates in your diary?

4. Established an anticipated, realistic, timetable for completion of the administration?

Confirmed this to PRs?

Established target dates for completion of each stage?

Logged these into your diary? Plus six-month and 12-month anniversaries of death and other significant dates such as two-month anniversary of statutory advertisements.

5. Checked will for validity?

    Contacted witnesses if affidavits are necessary?

    Checked gifts for ademption, lapse, contingencies, etc.?

    Checked form of ownership of assets (sole name, joint tenancy, co-ownership)?

6. Obtained PRs' consent to contact residuary beneficiaries with copy will and estimated timescale?

    Obtained PRs' consent to contact legatees with estimated timescale?

7. Confirmed beneficiaries' and next of kin's addresses with PRs?

    Taken steps to trace any missing beneficiaries?

    Considered whether statutory advertisements are appropriate? The cost may not be justified where the executor is taking the entire estate.

    Inserted statutory advertisements?

8. Advised:
    - deceased's bank or building society;
    - other professional advisers;
    - insurers;
    - others? (See checklist, para. 16.7.)

    Obtained figures for balances of funds held, accrued interest, etc.?

    Included these on draft accounts?

Obtained details of deceased's tax office and current position?

9. Begun to prepare the accounts by:

    • listing all assets and estimated values;

    • deciding whether specialist advice is needed;

    • listing all liabilities?

10. Prepared list of asset holders needing to see the grant of representation?

    Arranged valuations?

11. Considered with PRs the method of payment of inheritance tax? (See para. 13.34.)

    Made the necessary arrangements? (See para. 13.35 for specimen letter to a bank to arrange a 'global' loan facility.)

12. Established the nature of money coming into the office in terms of the Accounts Rules requirements? (See Chapter 5.)

13. Considered whether variation desirable.

IMMEDIATE PRACTICAL ACTION CHECKLIST

16.2 *Items*   *For action by*
                                                                   Family   Us

1. Register death.

2. Check for directions re disposal of body in wills, personal assets log, and amongst papers.

3. Arrange funeral/cremation (as directed if appropriate).

4. Notify time, date and place to family.*

5. Deceased's house:

    • remove valuables (if to office, does our insurance cover value? Do any special conditions, e.g. regarding guns, apply?);**

Items   *For action by*
                                                          Family   Us

- arrange maintenance (e.g. drain water system) if appropriate;

- cancel deliveries, e.g. milk, papers;

- redirect mail;

- lodge keys securely, not marked with address.;

- deal with insurers, landlord and council tax as appropriate.

6. Deceased's car:

- inform insurers;

- transfer insurance, etc., if to be used by family;

- arrange for security if not to be used.

7. Livestock and pets:

- arrange for their immediate welfare;

- check if prior long-term arrangements have already been made with friends or family (the Law Society personal assets log includes a point on pets);

- if not, pedigree pets may sometimes be returned to the breeder; otherwise the Kennel Club, Cat Fancy and welfare organisations could help (addresses in Chapter 30).

* Some firms counsel clients not to announce the death in the local or national paper, nor the funeral, because many families have – almost unbelievably – come back from the funeral to find the house has been burgled.

** See the helpful article on firearms in this context by Peter Sarony in [1995] *New Law Journal*, Probate, 29 September.

TESTATE ESTATE CHECKLIST

16.3   1.   Is the will valid and properly signed and dated, with an appropriate attestation clause, and correctly witnessed? If not, list remedial action needed and advise the client.

2. Is this definitely the last will? Are there any codicils?

3. Is there likely to be any dispute about the validity of dispositions included in the will? Did the testator or testatrix marry or divorce after the date of the will? Are any of the presumptions, e.g. capacity, validity, etc., likely to be rebutted? If so, is there any evidence of the circumstances surrounding the execution? Can the witnesses be traced if affidavits have to be obtained? List remedial action, and advise the client.

4. Does the will refer to unexecuted writings, chattels by memo, etc.? Is there a letter explaining why a person has not been provided for in the context of an IPFDA claim? Is a claim likely? (See Chapter 10.) Advise the client.

5. Is there any evidence of secret or half-secret trusts? If so, have the requirements for validity been met? If the will contains precatory words, can they be complied with?

6. Is there any evidence of an agreement that wills of deceaseds should be mutual? If so, where the death is of the first testator make sure that the existence of the trust now binding on the property of the surviving testator is clearly recorded; if the death is of the surviving testator remember that the terms of any will left by the surviving testator cannot overrule the terms of the trust imposed on the death of the first testator.

7. If the will refers to contingencies, have they been satisfied?

8. Is all the property referred to in the will available for beneficiaries, or have any gifts adeemed?

9. Have all beneficiaries been traced? Do any gifts lapse?

10. Is the estate solvent?

11. Is there any evidence of PETs and other transfers?

12. Is a variation appropriate?

INTESTATE AND PARTIALLY INTESTATE ESTATE CHECKLIST

16.4 1. The death: if the deceased and spouse or partner died together in an accident, does Law of Property Act 1925, s.184 apply or Intestate Estates Act 1952? What will the effect be in this estate? Advise client.

2. Has a search for a will been made? (If it is thought a will was made, the 'Wills and Whereabouts' page in the *Gazette*, local solicitors, the deposit facility at the Principal Registry (address in Chapter 30) and enquiry of the deceased's bank, friends and relatives may all be of assistance.)

3. Will the estate be solvent? Does it exceed £125,000/£200,000? How will the existence of any undisposed-of property affect the payment of debts?

4. List the surviving relatives; in more complex cases drawing up a family tree is usually easier than describing relationship. Can they all be contacted? Will there be any problems establishing identity and relationship? Might there be an IPFDA claim? (See Chapter 10.)

5. Establish who will be entitled to the estate; note minor children's ages and the years in which they will attain majority.

6. Establish who will take the grant. Will two administrators be needed?

7. How will the statutory trusts apply, if at all?

8. Does the spouse wish to redeem the life interest and/or appropriate the matrimonial home? Log the 12 months deadline from the issue of the grant into the diary. Does the value of the matrimonial home exceed the value of the statutory legacy? What arrangements need to be made for equality money?

9. Is there any evidence of PETs and other transfers?

THE OATH AND AFTER CHECKLIST

16.5 1. List assets and liabilities.

2. Which Inland Revenue account? (See paras. 13.9-13.10).

3. Prepare oath and Inland Revenue account.

4. Send tax cheque to CTO.

Lodge papers and receipted Inland Revenue account at Probate Registry.

Order plenty of office copies – it is false economy to order too few.

Does timetable need adjusting? If so, inform PRs.

5. Prepare for payment of debts. Will assets need to be sold? If so, contact PRs and residuary beneficiaries:

- Which ones? Arrange valuations if necessary.

- Consider tax implications – deed of variation?

6. Update draft accounts.

Update other lists.

Review file generally, especially initial letters, and check expiry dates and deadlines – review schedule if necessary and advise client.

Check proceeds of sale of shares and land against probate valuations to see if assets qualify for IHT loss on sale relief (IHTA 1984, ss.178–189). If so, claim relief and file corrective account.

Check proceeds of sale of assets generally against probate valuations to see if there are gains or losses for CGT purposes.

7. Diarise due dates for IHT interest payments in relation to instalment option property, if appropriate.

8. Interim bill? (Did you agree this with the PRs in advance?)

9. Interim distribution? May be advisable to avoid a beneficiary receiving a large income receipt in one tax year pushing beneficiary into higher rate tax unnecessarily (see Chapter 15).

OBTAINING THE GRANT CHECKLIST

16.6 This checklist, with reminders, has been specially revised and reformulated by Kevin Donnelly, Chief Clerk at the Probate Registry, Somerset House, and we are most grateful to him for doing so, and for permission to use it.

YES/NO

Oath form

1. *Extracting solicitors*

- Has your name, address (including post code), DX number and reference (if required) been included at the heading of the oath?

2. *Name of deceased*

    - Does the name correspond with the will (if any)?

    - If not, or if an alias is necessary for any other reason, has the true name been identified and the reason for the alias been set out in the oath by way of a footnote?

    - Was the deceased known by any other name or was the death registered in any other name? If so, these should be included on the oath (although these names may not appear on the grant.

3. *Address of deceased*

    - Has the last residential address been included? (A short stay in hospital can be ignored for these purposes.)

4. *Names of applicants*

    - Are these the true names?

    - Do they correspond with the will (if any)?

    - Is an affidavit of identity required?

    - Has the applicant included any extra initials in his or her signature to the oath? (Any extra initials should be investigated and the oath resworn to show the true name if necessary).

5. *Survival clause in will*

    - Does the will contain a clause providing that the executor or executrix must survive by a specified period before the appointment becomes effective?

    - If yes, has the period expired?

6. *Date of death*

    - Does the date of death given in the oath agree with that on the death certificate? (If the death certificate does not give a specific date of death, the oath should state when the deceased was last seen or known to be alive and when his or her body was found.)

7. *Codicil*

   - Did the deceased leave any codicils to the will?

   - If yes, has reference been made to them in the oath?

   - If yes, have they been marked in accordance with Rule 10 of the Non-Contentious Probate Rules 1987 by the applicant and swearing Commissioner?

8. *Age of the deceased*

   - Has the age and date of birth of the deceased been included in the oath?

9. *Domicile of the deceased*

   - Has the domicile of the deceased been included in the oath? (If the deceased died domiciled out of England and Wales and different systems of law operate within the country, the *state* of domicile must be shown, e.g. the State of Victoria, the State of New Jersey).

10. *Settled land*

    - Has the clause concerning settled land been included/completed? (This clause must be included in every oath).

11. *Life/minority interest*

    - Did the deceased leave a will?

    - If yes, is the executor or executrix appointed in it applying for the grant?

    - If no, or if the deceased left no will, does a life or minority interest arise out of the estate?

    - Has the appropriate section in the oath been included/completed? (The oath must state, in terms, whether a life or minority interest arises *unless an executor or executrix is applying for the grant*).

12. *Title*

- Have all the persons with a prior entitlement to the applicant been accounted for in the oath?

- Has the applicant's title been stated in full? (Unless *all* clearings have been included and the title stated in *full* the oath is certain to be queried and is likely to require reswearing).

13. *Value of the estate: Is the estate an 'excepted estate'?* (See para. 13.9)

- If yes, have the band figures appropriate to the date of death been included in the oath?

- Have the words 'and this is not a case in which an Inland Revenue account is required to be lodged' (or similar) been included in the correct clause? (Failure to include this clause will result in the oath having to be resworn.)

- If no, and the deceased died domiciled in England and Wales, has the total of all the estate passing under the grant been included?

- Does this total agree with that shown in the Inland Revenue account?

- If not, has an explanation for the difference been included in the oath?

- If the deceased died domiciled out of England and Wales, has the relevant clause been amended to refer to estate only in England and Wales? (It is possible to have an 'excepted estate' for a deceased who died domiciled in Scotland.)

14. *Jurat*

- Has the oath and will/codicil(s) (if any) been signed by (all) the applicant(s) and swearing Commissioner(s)?

- Has the oath been dated and the place of swearing stated? (Please bear in mind that the oath and any supporting affidavits cannot be sworn before the solicitor extracting the grant or a member of his or her firm.)

Special types of application

1. *Attorney grants*

   • Has the limitation to be recited in the grant been included in the oath? (The usual limitation is 'for the use and benefit of A–B (the donor) and until further representation be granted'.)

2. *Grants for minors*

   • Are there two applicants?

   • Is it necessary to lodge a nomination of the second applicant?

   • If the application relies upon court orders, are court-certified copies available?

   • Does the oath state that a minority interest arises?

   • Does the oath have the correct limitation? (The usual limitation in such application is 'for the use and benefit of A–B (the minor(s)) until he/she/one of them shall attain the age of 18 years'.)

3. *Domicile out of England and Wales*

   • Has the domicile of the deceased been described correctly?

   • Have those facts upon which the deponent to the affidavit of law (if any) has relied when reaching his or her conclusions been included in the oath or another sworn document? (These facts are usually recited in the affidavit of law following the words 'I am informed and verily believe' or similar. If they are not sworn, the application will be delayed whilst the oath or affidavit is resworn.)

   • Have the words 'in England and Wales' been added to the clause dealing with the estate?

- Are the foreign court documents to be used in support of the application copies certified by the court?

- Has the correct form of Inland Revenue account (IHT 201) been completed and controlled by the Capital Taxes Office?

- Has any necessary order under the Non-Contentious Probates Rules 1987 been obtained or approved? (It may not be necessary to have the order drawn before swearing the oath but prior approval of the district judge or district probate registrar must be obtained.)

4. *Lost wills*

- Has the original will been seen since the deceased's date of death?

- Was the will known to have been in possession of the deceased up to date of his or her death?

- If the answer to the first question is no and the second yes, does the evidence in support of the application rebut the presumption of revocation of the will by the deceased in his or her lifetime?

- Can the authenticity of the copy will be confirmed?

- Does the affidavit in support of the application exhibit the copy will to be proved?

- Does the oath in support of the application for the grant describe accurately the copy will being proved? (It is suggested that the affidavit(s) in support of the application be prepared in draft form in the first instance to enable any further evidence required by the district judge or registrar to be incorporated.)

Wills and codicils

1. Has the testator or testatrix signed the will?

- Has the will been witnessed by two witnesses?

- Does the will contain a properly worded attestation clause?

- Has the will been dated?

  (Although these are obvious points, a large number of wills are rejected by the probate registries each year for these simple defects. The factors also apply to codicils. It may still be possible to prove a will/codicil with any of these defects if validity can be established under the Wills Act 1963.)

2. Does the will/codicil have any unattested alterations or additions?

3. Is there a valid appointment of executrix/ executor(s)? (Care should be taken to ensure that the appointment is correctly worded; if there is any doubt, evidence of the testator's or testatrix's intention will be necessary.)

4. Did the deceased leave any codicils to his or her will?

   - If yes, are they all available?

   - Is the appointment of executors affected by the codicil?

   - Does the codicil confirm the will by the correct date? (If the date is not correct, evidence that the right will is being proved may be necessary.)

5. Have the will and codicils (if any) been marked by the applicant(s) and swearing Commissioner(s) in accordance with Rule 10 of the Non-Contentious Probate Rules 1987?

Inland Revenue accounts

1. Has the correct account, appropriate to the date of death and type of application, been used?

2. Has the account been signed and dated by the applicant(s)?

    - Does the account need to be controlled by the Inland Revenue? (Although any account may be controlled, generally speaking this need be done only in the estates of persons who die domiciled out of England and Wales.)

    - Is the date of death of the deceased before 13 March 1975?

    - If the answer is yes, has the Inland Revenue account been sworn? (N.B. This is a requirement.)

    - Has the certificate regarding payment of inheritance tax been signed?

Fees

1. Has the correct fee been paid?

2. Does the payment include the fee for any copies ordered?

COLLECTING THE ASSETS, PAYING THE DEBTS CHECKLIST

16.7 1. Cancel/obtain refund/collect/return/pay/check:

    - council tax;

    - social security payments;

    - trade union or professional association subscription – and some death benefit may be payable;

    - club and other memberships such as charities, libraries, pressure groups, voluntary organisations, political parties and consumer and motoring organisations;

    - subscriptions: journals, magazines, book clubs;

- borrowed items: library books, records, videos, hospital equipment such as wheelchair;

- payments made in advance by deceased, e.g. gas or electricity account may be in credit;

- payments due to deceased which may be in arrears, e.g. pension;

- laundry or dry cleaning, or items sent for valuation or repair;

- items on hire – TV or washing machine, computer, possibly evening or formal dress;

- relevant direct debits/standing orders, etc., at bank or building society;

- milk, papers and other deliveries;

- passport;

- credit cards.

2. List all the assets and refunds and include a column for noting what happened to the asset, its value and relevant dates.

3. Is there any property abroad? How will this be dealt with? Do foreign law rules conflict with the will or the intestacy rules? Specialist advice may be needed.

4. Valuation: some items may be more valuable than one might expect.

   Certain charities, such as the PDSA, offer house clearance services (others may advertise in local papers and free sheets) but ensure that nothing possibly of value is overlooked. See specialist valuers address list (Chapter 30) for items needing an expert's opinion.

5. Send office copies of the grant to asset holders – use standard letters on a word processor to save time and get plenty of office copies – too few is a false economy. Include a request in letters to bank, building societies, etc., for all the necessary paperwork for closure of accounts to be sent.

6. Keep standard letters to creditors on a word processor to save time. Send these early so that relatives are not troubled by reminders about bills.

7. Make a list of all the deceased's liabilities, with columns for the dates and amounts of payments. Tick each off as it is dealt with.

8. Ensure that assets in your office are insured and listed, and any special regulations (e.g. re guns, antique or modern – see para. 16.2) are observed.

9. Pay bills promptly when funds becomes available – if this takes time, does the timetable need adjusting? If so, advise the client.

10. It may be helpful to keep all the paperwork related to paid debts – bills, receipts and correspondence, etc. – in a separate file once they are no longer current matters.

ACCOUNTING AND DISTRIBUTION CHECKLIST

16.8 1. Prepare any corrective account for IHT which has become necessary. For small amounts, correspondence may suffice.

2. Make interim distributions, but reserve enough money for outstanding tax, costs and other contingencies. Consider ensuring that PRs and residuary beneficiaries are satisfied with the draft accounts before making large distributions (see para. 15.4).

3. Ensure arrangements for payment of tax by beneficiaries have been made, where necessary.

4. Offer beneficiaries receiving substantial legacies your firm's investment advice service or Solicitors Financial Services (SFS). Information about SFS is available on request – (address in Chapter 30). See also Chapter 4 on undertaking investment business.

5. Do any beneficiaries need:

    * wills?

    * codicils?

    * tax advice?

    * enduring powers of attorney?

6. Have all beneficiaries received forms R185E where appropriate? This is particularly important for charities who will need to obtain refunds of income tax.

7. If problems in obtaining a discharge arise consider insurance, payment into court under Trustee Act 1925, s.63, etc.

8. Have the important dates for protecting PRs passed – two months for statutory advertisements, six months from date of grant for IPFDA claims? (See Chapter 8 on probate time-limits.)

9. Prepare accounts (or have them prepared for you).

10. Obtain receipts and discharges from beneficiaries (see para. 15.25).

CLOSING YOUR FILE CHECKLIST

16.9   1. Which documents belong to the client?

See the Guide, Principle 12.11 and 12.12, and Annex 12A, 'Guidance – ownership, storage and destruction of documents'.

2. How long must the file be kept?

See the Guide, Annex 12A para. 4 'How long should I retain old files?'.

3. Which documents should be preserved? This list is not exhaustive:

- documents belonging to the client;
- documents of title;
- significant correspondence with the Inland Revenue, returns, accounts, etc.;
- court orders;
- valuations (it may be advisable to supply probate valuations to non-residuary legatees – otherwise they will contact you in the future if CGT becomes an issue for them).

4. Consider asking the client if any old, but non-essential, documents could be of interest to a local history society or museum.

5. Could any of the letters or documents you prepared form the basis of stock letters for future use by you or within the office? If so, consider keeping these in a separate, indexed, precedent file.

EVALUATING CHECKLIST

16.10   Ten things I know now I wish I'd known then:

1.

2.

3.

4.

5.

6.

7.

8.

9.

10.

PART FOUR

Profitable Probate

Much of this Handbook is intended to help with cost-effective case and file management. This Part of the book looks more widely at practice management and the organisation of work in the office both generally and individually, so it is hoped it will be of interest whether or not you have management responsibilities.

Chapter 17

Computing and technology issues

by Charles Christian

Charles Christian was a practising barrister and is now an independent analyst and commentator on developments in law office technology. He is the publisher of the fortnightly Newsletter *Legal Technology Insider* and a special adviser on IT to Jeffrey Green Russell, Solicitors. This chapter was specially written for us by Charles Christian and we are most grateful to him for doing so.

INTRODUCTION

17.1   Thanks to the high profile coverage computer systems and information technology (IT) related matters now enjoy in the national press, there is a growing belief among not just solicitors' practices but businesses generally that computerisation is the universal panacea for all problems. However, while it might be nice to think that if you are not making enough money out of probate practice, the easiest solution is to install a new 'probate case management software' application, not only is this a far too simplistic approach – but it could also prove to be commercially disastrous.

Leaving aside the cost and inevitable disruption (including the time taken up with administration matters that would otherwise be devoted to fee earning) associated with all computerisation projects, you risk running foul of the old computer industry adage: GIGO – garbage in, garbage out. In other words, if your practice has problems, installing a computer will not fix them, it will merely computerise them.

That's the bad news. The good news is that a properly implemented law office computerisation project will yield positive benefits. And in the case of probate practitioners, at the very least this should include reducing the time and overheads associated with individual probate matters, so you can both increase the volume of work you can handle and increase the profitability of that work.

Topics covered

17.2 This chapter will therefore be looking at: (1) the type of IT systems available; (2) how they can help probate practitioners; (3) how probate practitioners should approach the purchasing of IT systems (the principles of IT procurement); (4) current trends in technology generally, including prices; (5) suppliers of probate systems; and (6) obtaining help and advice.

PROBATE SYSTEMS

17.3 Probate systems are an unusual area of law office automation in that the same term is loosely applied to a broad range of applications covering everything from will writing software through to investment trust accounting and portfolio management systems. For the sake of convenience I have broken these down into the following categories:

- **Will writing software (WW)**. Most of the packages commercially available have been designed for the DIY market or will writing businesses and so are probably unsuitable for probate solicitors in private practice.

- **Electronic forms and precedents (EFP)**. Arguably a more useful tool for practitioners are the type of systems that contain legal precedents in an electronic format (typically on a CD-Rom disk) so that clauses can be selected and automatically incorporated within a will without the need to retype any wording. There is some overlap with will writing software and to add to the confusion the term 'document assembly' system is sometimes used to describe this type of software. (Readers should also check the latest publications from mainstream legal publishers, such as Sweet & Maxwell and Butterworths as increasingly they are also producing electronic versions of their precedents, etc.)

- **Probate accounts software (PA)**. Typically these are based around the Microsoft Excel spreadsheet application and will allow practitioners to calculate estate accounts and prepare and complete IHT returns. These systems also contain some basic case management-style diary reminders and checklists. Bearing in mind that the preparation of estate accounts can be one of the most time consuming features of probate work, this is a system many practitioners could benefit from using.

- **Probate case management (PCM)**. These systems take the automation of probate work one stage further by building a workflow

272

routine that effectively controls the legal process. These can be very useful where work is being handled by a department and the partner in charge needs not only to be able to review and manage the progress of matters but also to ensure that tasks delegated to non-legally qualified staff take place within a sufficiently rigid framework, so there is no room for mistakes to be made.

For prospective purchasers, the key issue here will be whether they have the volume of work or organisational structure to justify the case management approach. For larger firms with a probate department, such systems are probably a 'must have' item, whereas smaller practices will usually only need a system to handle estate accounts. (When looking at PCM systems, readers should also consider whether the accounts element of the software is adequate.)

- **Wills and deeds registers**. Back in the days of stand-alone technology a number of suppliers sold specific software packages to handle this type of application. Today – with the emphasis in law firm IT on central databases – this type of information will usually be stored within an overall practice management system or else be one of the elements of a probate case management system.

- **Trusts and portfolio management systems**. This area of legal work sees the practitioner moving beyond the conventional bounds of probate practice and into the broader private client/investment/financial services arena which is outside the scope of this chapter. It is, however, worth bearing in mind that a number of suppliers of 'pure' probate systems also supply trust accounting and management systems.

How Probate Systems can help Practitioners

17.4 This is a potentially contentious topic, for it does not matter how good a computer system may be in theory because unless a practice is prepared to invest adequately in training – so its members really know how to operate the computers on their desks – the full benefits of the system will never be realised. Leaving aside this important qualification, there are five potential areas of benefit.

Achieving immediate objectives

17.5 There are a number of situations that can arise where computerisation is successfully undertaken to achieve immediate, relatively limited, short-term objectives.

For example, suppose an experienced probate practitioner is heading for retirement and planning to work on a part-time consultancy basis. If the firm still has a healthy probate practice then investing in a probate accounts system that can act as an *aide memoire* to another less experienced lawyer and take over some of the donkey work on the estate accounts preparation work may be a cost-effective alternative to replacement of the consultant.

Similarly, if the firm were to win a major commercial client – such as a financial institution – and with it the prospect of a major increase in the volume of its probate work, then installing IT would be a cost effective alternative to recruiting additional probate department staff.

Better information

17.6 In discussing computerisation most people tend to focus on the 'technology' aspect of 'information technology'. However, we should also remember the 'information' angle.

Although computers have earned a poor reputation in the past for generating impenetrable reports of monumental length, modern systems are excellent tools for extracting valuable business information from large volumes of data – information that would be almost impossible to obtain (or at least take a long time and prevent staff from getting on with their normal work) using manual methods.

For example, access to detailed information about clients and work types allows firms to be more precise in their marketing and cross-selling efforts – which in the past probably involved little more than sending Christmas cards to every client name on the books, regardless of whether anyone had seen them in the last decade.

For firms who anticipate that most of their probate work will be generated from the results of earlier wills campaigns (such as the annual Law Society 'Wills Week') a good information system also allows the firm to become proactive rather than reactive, so clients can be periodically contacted to see if they need to review and update their wills. After all, this year's happily married shopkeeper could be next year's lottery winner with a younger spouse, new family and an increasingly complex network of commercial interests.

Greater efficiency and productivity

17.7 One of the most obvious benefits of computerisation is that IT is very good at doing relatively dull repetitive tasks very quickly – such as adding up long columns of figures. In the probate department this means estate accounts can be prepared within hours whereas previously staff could have been tied up for days. (The lawyer drafts the accounts, the secretary types them up, the lawyer has to revise and recalculate them, the secretary has to retype them, and so on.)

Better service

17.8   Having an IT system also opens up the possibility of offering services to clients which previously firms would have been reluctant to offer because of the additional workload it would have involved. For example, producing interim accounts for the beneficiaries of an estate becomes an automated click-of-a-button operation. Leaving aside the potential for generating extra fees – or taking less time to earn the same amount of fees – the ability to offer additional services is a plus point in terms of establishing a longer-term professional relationship with a client and helping to differentiate your firm from the competition.

Increased profitability

17.9   If an IT system can help increase productivity among secretarial, clerical and fee earning staff, so the same people can get through more work in the same or less time, then this will clearly have an impact upon the firm's profitability in that it frees them to get on with additional fee earning activities. However, computerisation can also bring about an increase in profitability by its potential for reducing overheads.

For example, it is not uncommon to find that smaller firms have an administrative 'tail' with a ratio of 1 to 2. In other words, for every fee earner in the firm, there are two back office staff (including secretaries). But, if IT is introduced, so fee earners can start doing jobs that would have previously involved dictating instructions to secretaries and waiting for them to effect them – it becomes possible to reduce the size of this tail.

A 1 to 1 ratio is the minimum to aim for (typically by sharing secretaries between fee earners, assigning some secretaries to quasi fee earning activities and reducing the reliance on 'temps') but many firms have already achieved 2 to 1 or greater.

Less reliance on support staff does in turn have a number of other benefits. For example, it means it is possible to recruit more fee earners without also having to recruit a corresponding number of secretaries, which in turn means an expanding firm is likely to outgrow its existing office space less quickly than it would otherwise do.

Clearly having proportionally fewer staff means less is being spent on overheads, which in turns means increased profits. However, bearing in mind the competitive market in which solicitors operate, carrying less overheads means firms can also afford to compete on price – for example against banks and other financial institutions – by cutting their margins yet still managing to make some profit on a matter.

THE PRINCIPLES OF IT PROCUREMENT

17.10 Aside from acquiring office premises, for many solicitors' practices their investment in a new computer system – or some related form of information technology (IT) – will be one of the single largest financial commitments they ever take on.

Furthermore, unlike buying conventional office equipment, such as a new photocopier, an investment in IT is potentially going to alter the way a whole firm operates. Bookkeepers, secretaries, receptionists, fee earners, partners and clients will all find that the new technology has some impact upon them and the legal services they either supply or receive. It is, therefore, essential that the IT procurement process is as efficient and problem free as possible, for if you get it wrong, not only will a lot of time, money and effort have been wasted but the firm's commercial viability and professional reputation may have been irreparably compromised.

Strategy

17.11 Most solicitors probably know of 'computing disasters' that have occurred within other firms. However what is not always appreciated is that the bulk of these disasters stem not from choosing inappropriate hardware or software but from attempts to implement fundamentally flawed IT strategies. The key element to bear in mind here is that IT – even a stand-alone probate system – is not some self-contained entity but is instead merely an enabling technology or tool that should be regarded as an integral part of the practice's overall business development plan. If you want to get your IT strategy right, a firm must first have (or devise) an appropriate general business strategy.

276

To give a simple example, there is no point worrying about choosing a supplier of probate software, if the firm's only probate practitioner is considering retiring. In addition, any strategy should also take into account the firm's medium-term requirements and longer-term aspirations, for example opening branch offices or diversifying into new areas of practice, such as trust and portfolio management. In other words, don't buy a system that meets your immediate needs – buy one that will also meet your anticipated needs.

The first stage in devising an IT strategy therefore has nothing to do with computers but actually involves drawing up a business or practice development plan. Only once this is in place should partners begin considering how IT can be used to help implement that plan over the next few years.

Next comes the process of drawing up more detailed specifications and requirements – in effect a computerisation shopping list – that will help realise the IT strategy. For example, is the proposed system only going to be used by one fee earner as a productivity tool? In this case you will typically be looking for a stand-alone software application that will run on a personal computer. Or is probate work to be handled by a department, with different tasks delegated between fee earning and secretarial staff? In this case a networked case management product is going to be more appropriate.

Whether or not you need to draw up a formal 'Invitation to Tender' (or ITT) document is a matter of policy but you certainly must have a clear understanding of your requirements, if you are to be able to properly brief prospective suppliers and evaluate their responses on a like-for-like basis.

Budgets

17.12 It is essential at this stage to consider budgets and the availability of finance to support the proposed investment in IT (whether from cash reserves, leasing, bank loans, etc.). An important factor to bear in mind here is that calculating the overall IT spend is a lot more complicated than adding the cost of PC hardware and a single user software licence together and multiplying it by the total number of users.

Along with hardware and software, there is the cost of installing the supporting network cabling – which in older premises may mean major rewiring and redecorating exercises. There is also the cost of training –

and it cannot be stressed strongly enough that it is essential to properly train everyone who is intended to use computers. Then there are the ongoing running costs, including insurance, annual maintenance contracts, renewable software licences (where applicable), hardware and software upgrades, additional training for additional or replacement staff and computer 'consumables' such as replacement laser printer toner cartridges and pre-printed 'continuous' stationery.

As a rule of thumb today, in terms of capital costs, for a probate accounts software package, plus a PC to run it on and training, budget on between £3,000 and £5,000 per user.

Finding a supplier

17.13   Having decided what you want to buy and how much you are prepared to pay for it, you are now in a position to look for a suitable supplier. This may seem a daunting task, particularly when you consider the total number of suppliers. However, when broken down into logical stages, it becomes more manageable:

- First of all thin down the number of contenders – if you are not interested in trust accounts, the case management approach or will writing software, drop them from the list.

- Then contact the remaining suppliers for further information, such as brochures and promotional literature containing details of their track records and installations; visit their stands at exhibitions; attend any of the sales presentations they will inevitably invite you to, once they realise you are a prospect; talk to contacts within the profession; reference sites given by the supplier and anyone else who has experience of dealing with them.

- Given the size of the probate systems market, this process will help whittle down the total number of prospects to a shortlist of four or five suppliers. Send these shortlisted companies copies of your tender document (if you have one) so you can evaluate their responses on a like-for-like basis.

- Visit their premises (or user reference sites) for detailed system demonstrations and discussions about how they would propose to handle the implementation of your project, including training. (Incidentally, do ensure the staff who will actually be using the proposed new system attend these demonstrations.)

- Follow up any user references that are given and start exploring the contractual terms that are being offered, as this is frequently a protracted stage of the negotiations.

- Do take notice of your own business instincts. Your relationship with the supplier does not end the day the new computer goes 'live' – you will be dealing with them for at least the next three to five years, so be certain these are people you feel you can trust and work with on a longer term basis.

- Don't be blinded by science. A lot of suppliers are now claiming their respective products are better than those of their competition because they have been developed using 'better' software development tools. This is all 'under the bonnet' stuff. What really matters is the functionality of the software – does it do the job you want it to do, in the way you want it done?

Installation and implementation

17.14   Now you in a position to place an order. And is that it? Well actually no, for you now enter one of the most sensitive stages – and one where problems can frequently arise because law firms do not devote sufficient management resources to this aspect of the project. At the very least a partner should have responsibility for overseeing the project management side of system installation and implementation.

There is a co-ordination job to ensure that the installation of the network cabling, the delivery of the hardware, the loading of the software and the training of staff to use the new system is properly scheduled and takes place satisfactorily according to a mutually convenient and pre-agreed timetable – for example, you will probably want to avoid the holiday season and the end of your financial year – not least because you will normally be expected to pay for substantial chunks of the system on the completion of each of these stages.

CURRENT TRENDS IN LAW OFFICE TECHNOLOGY

17.15   Strictly speaking, any law office computerisation projects should primarily be concerned with the applications lawyers and staff will use – in other words software issues. However, recent changes and trends in system 'architecture' mean some reference must also be made to underlying hardware and operating platform issues.

279

Networks

17.16   At the time of writing, it is arguable that the majority of small to medium-sized law firms in England and Wales (i.e. excluding large firms with their own IT resources and very small practices who just need stand-alone systems) should not be considering buying new software applications that are based on DOS, Macintosh or UNIX operating platforms. (This argument does not apply to firms who already have such systems and merely want to extend them.)

The main reason for this is the overwhelming popularity of Microsoft's various Windows operating systems and their relative power, simplicity and cheapness when it comes to linking PCs together as part of a network, so data records can be shared between users. For smaller practices (say up to 10 users) the most common mechanism is a Windows 95 'peer-to-peer' network, whereas for larger firms Microsoft's NT 'client/server' architecture is rapidly emerging as the new industry standard.

Workstations

17.17   When it comes to buying desktop PC hardware (sometimes called 'workstations') almost inevitably the PC will come ready to run with Microsoft's Windows 95 (soon to become Windows 98) operating system software installed. Some firms may have PCs running an alternative operating system called Microsoft Windows NT 4.0 for Workstations (soon to be replaced by NT 5.0) which is essentially a different flavour of Windows.

Typically a modern PC will have an absolute minimum specification of a 166MHz Pentium processor with 32Mb of RAM, 1Gb hard disk and a CD-Rom drive. Such systems are designed to run the latest Windows '32-bit' software applications and while such products are still in the minority in the legal systems market, almost all new product development is in the 32-bit arena. It is, however, worth noting that Windows 95 and Windows NT 4.0 are both 'backwards compatible', which means that along with 32-bit programs, they can also run older '16-bit' applications designed for the earlier Windows 3.1.1 operating system and even DOS.

There is then an element of future proofing in buying the latest technology as first it will still be in use in the early years of the next century and second it means you can still run older applications, thus extending the return on your existing IT investments.

Trends in legal software design

17.18 Traditionally, legal practice computerisation projects began in the accounts department in the 'back office', where they would usually exist in splendid isolation from the wordprocessing systems being used by secretaries and any 'fee earner support systems' – such as a probate software – being used by qualified staff in the 'front office'. The more modern approach to legal IT is the 'integrated system' based around a central records and contacts management software package – a database – which can be accessed and shared by all the users on the network through all the other applications on the network. This means records need only be entered – or amended – once and are then available to all.

A second and equally significant change is the growing importance of Microsoft standards, with specialist legal applications now being developed almost exclusively to be compatible with both the latest Microsoft Windows operating systems and the Microsoft Office family (which includes the Word wordprocessing and Excel spreadsheet applications) of desktop software.

This standardisation brings with it a number of benefits, in particular:

- Because most of these modern systems have a Windows-style front end (or 'user interface'), training and support issues are simplified, as once users are familiar with how to operate one Windows software application, they are well on their way to mastering all Windows applications.

- There is a growing element of 'openness' in systems design, as all suppliers use the same relatively narrow number of system development 'tools', take advantage of the same linking technology (software components known as 'DDLs' and 'OLE') within Windows, and comply with the industry-wide ODBC standard for databases.

This in turns means that firms are no longer so dependent upon one single supplier for software, as products from different suppliers can exchange data with each other. So, for example, client information gathered by the probate department can be supplied to the firm's marketing specialist for the purposes of cross-selling some of the firm's other services. Admittedly not many firms do this but at least the potential is there!

The internet

17.19 The last few months have seen the first law firms going 'live' with projects that allow clients to send new instructions directly to a solicitors' practice via a page on a World Wide Web site. For example, Kaye Tesler & Co. in North London is using one such system to offer a fixed will writing service to the public – the idea being that a firm can 'sell' its services to a far wider catchment area than would normally be possible through conventional marketing means such as direct mail, *Yellow Pages* and advertising in 'Wills Week' supplements in local newspapers. (See also Chapter 20 on marketing.)

Although the internet is unlikely to emerge as a truly mass market phenomenon until interactive digital television becomes a mainstream technology (the first services commenced in the autumn of 1998), it is an area all lawyers would be advised to watch. But, unlike most areas of computing, it does have the advantage of being a relatively cheap technology – firms can buy a communications modem for around £150 and establish a 'home page' on the web for as little as £400 to £500 a year.

SUPPLIERS OF PROBATE SYSTEMS

17.20 The following list gives details of suppliers (in alphabetical order) and their principal products identified by the abbreviations given in para. 17.3 above.

AIM (tel: 01482 326971) – TrustCharter (PCM)
Avenue Legal Systems (tel: 01489 609000) – Wisdom (PCM + EFP)
Cognito Software (tel: 01363 775582) – Custodiens (PA)
Eleetix Software (tel: 0171 256 7777) – Excalibur (PA + WW)
Excelsior LawDesk (tel: 01273 494978) – ProbateDesk (PA)
Laserform Law (tel: 01565 755154) – Probate CaseControl (PCM + EFP)
Law Systems (tel: 01326 317529) – Probate Plus (PA)
Lawbase Legal Systems (tel: 0181 840 9994) – Lawbase (PCM + WW)
Lindon Wood (tel: 0151 236 1724) – Case Flow (PCM + WW)
Linetime (tel: 0113 250 0020) – Probate Dataflow (PCM)
MCS (tel: 0181 882 8811) – DPS (PCM + WW)
Mountain Software (tel: 01476 573718) – Probate Support System (PCM)
Oyez Legal Software (tel: 0171 232 1000) – OyezForms (EFP)
Peapod Solutions (tel: 0181 574 8288) – Workflow (PCM + EFP)

PPS (tel: 01865 201801) – PPS (PCM + WW)

Professional Technology (tel: 01634 815517) – Quaestor (PCM + WW)

Sanderson Systems (tel: 0121 359 4861) – QNIX (PCM + WW)

Solicitec (tel: 0113 226 2000) – SolCase (PCM)

Sophco Systems (tel: 0171 924 4124) – Legacase (PCM + WW)

Technology For Business (tel: 01932 781120) – Partner Suite (PCM + EFP)

Sweet & Maxwell (tel: 0171 393 7000) – ExpressWills (WW)

OBTAINING HELP AND ADVICE

17.21 Because probate practice is essentially a niche market within a niche market, the number of third-party organisations that can offer useful impartial advice are relatively few and far between. However, the following sources should be of some assistance:

- **The Law Society**. The Society has a very good and friendly IT advisory service based at Chancery Lane (tel: 0171 242 1222), which can also supply a useful fact sheet on wills, trusts and probate packages. Mention should be made of the Law Society's relatively recently set-up Probate Section, which had its second conference in July 1997.

- **Information Technology Directory**. The Law Society also publishes a regularly updated IT directory which is now, without doubt, the UK's most comprehensive listing of legal IT suppliers and their products. If you want to draw up a list of potential suppliers and want further facts and figures (over and above those given in this chapter) then this should be your starting point. The latest edition (published in November 1997) can be purchased by mail order from tel: 01235 465656.

- **Society of Trust and Estate Practitioners (STEP)**. This organisation (tel: 0171 839 3886) is going from strength to strength and while it does not specifically address the subject of technology, it will be able to put you in touch with other members who will be able to share their experiences of IT with you.

- **Society for Computers and Law (SCL)**. The SCL (tel: 0117 923 7393) has been pioneering the cause of legal technology since the mid-1970s and while most of its conferences and seminars tend to be involved with the broader areas of law and technology, it now has an enthusiastic network of local branches providing an opportunity to meet other IT-interested lawyers.

- **Exhibition and events**. Although there are a growing number of legal IT events now being organised, still the largest of these (and the one at which you will find the biggest number of probate systems suppliers) is the Solicitors and Legal Office Exhibition (SOLEX) which is held at the Barbican Exhibition Centre in London in the first week of June each year. Admission is free, call the organisers Truemist on tel: 0181 742 3388 for details.

- **Probate system suppliers**. Most IT suppliers now run free seminars to demonstrate aspects of their systems. While you will no doubt find these of interest – not least because most of the modern probate packages were designed by probate practitioners (in fact some of the supplier companies were formed by probate lawyers) – it is, however, worth bearing in mind that their ultimate objective is to try to sell you their products at the expense of their competitors, so do not expect impartial advice.

- **Independent consultants**. Theoretically IT consultants should be a good idea but in practice you are likely to find that while most of them understand about legal accounts, wordprocessing, office automation networks and broader areas of legal IT, few will be sufficiently familiar with probate practice to be able to provide you with constructive advice. Cost is another factor – IT consultants will charge on average between £300 and £1,200 a day, which is a lot of extra money to spend if you are only going to buy a stand-alone probate accounts system retailing for £2,000.

Chapter 18

Managing an efficient probate practice

We are most grateful to Simon Bray of Nelsons Practice Development for writing this chapter specially for us.

SETTING THE STRATEGY

Why plan at all?

18.1 Pressures on the management of the law firm are increasing day by day. Within recent memory, the legal profession has undergone many major reforms. Examples include the virtual abolition of the Publicity Code and the ban on 'touting', the development and introduction of sophisticated information technology packages which streamline and improve performance, and the introduction of quality management procedures.

In broad terms, the impact of these (and other) radical reforms have passed probate practitioners by. The move towards the introduction of quality management procedures has been largely driven by the Legal Aid Board's Franchise Specification which, although applicable throughout legal practice, has had its major impact on contentious departments. Until recently, there has been little investment within probate departments in integrated case management systems. Overt promotional activity has been more directed at will making than at probate work.

As a result, most probate departments, in management terms, have been able to continue to pursue a largely uninterrupted course, without having to cope with significant change. Probate practitioners have been reliable but unchanging, generating constant, profitable fees in reasonable volume.

This perception and situation should change – indeed, must change in the light of pressures affecting the profession as a whole which, for the first time, are now having a direct impact on probate practice.

Within a typical 'High Street' practice, there is often a cyclical view of the relevance and value of different departments. When the property market booms, partners congratulate themselves on having a significant penetration of the conveyancing market place – the litigation departments are seen as makeweights.

But when property prices collapse and the market slides into recession, practices are delighted with the depth and range of the litigation departments' capabilities, which provide an umbrella of income under which the firm can shelter.

In either economic climate wills, probate and trust work continues unaffected. Now, however, the profession is faced with an unpalatable economic scenario in which both traditional sources of core income are under threat.

The conveyancing market continues to be depressed and highly competitive in terms of fee structures. At the same time, litigation departments within High Street firms are also subject to severe financial constraint, with falling legal aid eligibility, reduced remuneration levels and an increasing volume of fixed fee work. Margins throughout the firm are becoming tighter.

As a result, partnerships are seeking to develop other remunerative areas of practice. The attention of the managing partner is inevitably turning towards the ever-reliable probate department as a source of significant levels of fee income and profit – and probate practitioners need to respond to this challenge by providing not only an efficient and friendly service for the client, but also an increasingly profitable income stream for the practice.

Such a situation demands a reconsideration of the way in which probate is delivered. Without in any sense compromising on the quality of work delivered or the relationship with the client, efficiency must be sought, revenue must be maximised and systems must be streamlined.

Probate practitioners need to look to their management systems to improve efficiency and enhance performance.

The planning process

18.2   The starting point is a thorough review of the issues confronting the probate department, addressing the resources available, the constraints acting upon the department and the funding available to it. In short, the first step must be the preparation of a departmental business plan.

Such a discipline may be foreign to probate lawyers. A common reaction is: 'We don't need a business plan – we have never had one before'. This, perhaps, is the very best possible reason for preparing a business plan. Without a business plan which formulates strategy, sets objectives and provides a yard stick against which to measure progress and performance, it is impossible to stretch or challenge existing perceptions.

This is true no matter how large or how small the department. Even in a 'typical' probate department consisting of perhaps one solicitor and a secretary, the preparation of a strategic departmental business plan will be of enormous benefit.

During the day-to-day activity of running client files, there is very rarely the opportunity of looking up from the desk and taking stock of the department's future needs and opportunities. Investing time in the planning process will bear significant dividends, by allowing the probate practitioner to focus on the medium and long-term issues facing the department.

The business plan should also generate a sense of common purpose and a defined path to follow. We are all members of teams (a team is, after all, a group of individuals working together to achieve a common goal) and it is unreasonable to expect the team to function at full effectiveness unless its objectives are known and understood by all of its members.

It follows that it is essential for all members of the department, no matter how large or how small its size, to understand the nature of the business plan and its contents.

This is not to say that detailed financial projections should be published to all members of the department – but it does mean that all members of the department should have a clear understanding of the department's overall aims and objectives, and of the part they play in achieving those objectives.

Preparing the plan

Defining aspirations

18.3 At the outset of the planning process, management needs to set acceptable standards of financial performance. Questions which need to be resolved include:

- What are acceptable billing figures?

- What are acceptable profit levels?

- What are the required levels of growth?

These targets will be affected by the factors which motivate the practice as a whole. Different firms are driven by different motivations and the business plan must reflect these differences. Motivation will generally be composed of a balance between:

- money;

- power;

- material gain;

- promotion;

- status;

- improving the environment;

- job satisfaction;

- helping others.

Content of the business plan

18.4 Having defined departmental aspirations, an analysis of how to meet those aspirations must be undertaken. There are two simple but effective tools which assist with this task.

STEP analysis

18.5 A STEP analysis is a review of the *external* influences and factors operating on the department. It covers the following issues:

- S – Sociological

- T – Technological

- E – Economic
- P – Political

A STEP analysis within a probate department might consider:

Sociological

Social attitude influencing demand – e.g.

- towards home ownership;
- towards marriage, divorce and the family.

Consumer awareness affecting client expectations – e.g.

- price awareness;
- heightened consumer awareness of legal rights;
- greater service standard expectations.

Demographic trends – e.g.

- population trends;
- age structures, nationally and regionally.

Technological

Office equipment:

- computers have revolutionised production and management techniques;
- methods of doing business, e.g. on-line banking facilities, telegraphic transfers, E-mail, video links and others.

Economic

General economic forces impacting on:

- property;
- increasing wealth;
- declining estate values.

Political

Structural reforms – recent political decisions that have made an impact:

- abolishing the professional prohibition on 'touting' for work;

- abolishing monopolies in probate;

- authorised probate practitioners;

- taxation issues.

Financial changes with political origins:

- reductions in fee rates.

Legislative changes:

- changes in the law we advise on, and changes in how we practise.

SWOT Analysis

18.6 A SWOT analysis is a review of the *internal* influences and factors operating on the department. It covers the following issues:

- S – Strengths

- W – Weaknesses

- O – Opportunities

- T – Threats

Consider the internal strengths and weaknesses of your department or team, and then seek to address your planning so that you:

- maximise opportunities (capitalising upon strengths); and

- minimise threats (in order to eliminate weaknesses).

A SWOT analysis is often carried out by examining the department's strengths, weaknesses, opportunities and threats in the context of:

- structure;

- administration;

- finance;

- services;

- partners;

- staff;

- clients;

- information technology;

- marketing.

A SWOT analysis carried out against these management disciplines within a probate department might consider:

Structure

- Does the department have a suitable shape? What are the partner/fee earner/support staff ratios?

- Is the department's management structure appropriate?

Administration

- Who is responsible for administration?

- Does the quality of our administration meet client and staff needs?

- Do our systems have their intended effects? What are their intended effects?

Finance

- What are our profit/billing expectations?

- Is our credit control effective?

Partners

- Do the partners have the necessary management skills to develop the department?

- What is the partnership's attitude towards delegation, teamwork and communication?

Staff

- Are our staff properly trained? Do they understand their jobs?

- Are they motivated? Are we over/under staffed?

- How do we monitor staff performance?

Clients

- Who are our clients? Where are our clients?

- What do they want of us?

- Are our clients satisfied with our performance?

Information technology

- What will the future impact of technology be?

- Can we use IT more effectively?

- Can we make better use of existing equipment?

Marketing

- Have we thought through an effective marketing strategy?

- Are we providing the right services?

- Is our marketing spend sufficient to meet our strategic goals?

Strategic plan

18.7 Having carried out the STEP and SWOT analyses in the light of the department's aspirations, the strategic goals of the department will become clear. Strategic goals will often be very simply expressed. Examples might include:

- to increase the number of wills written per month by XX per cent within the next calendar year; or

- to implement an estates accounts software package before August.

In today's volatile trading conditions, an appropriate 'strategic window' for planning purposes is perhaps two to three years. Anything longer is unrealistic, as the STEP and SWOT factors affecting the department are likely to change radically over such a length of time.

Operational plan

18.8 Once you have established your strategic goals, you must consider the implementation issues and develop an operational plan. The operational plan defines the activities the department must undertake in order to achieve its strategic goals. This is often the main body of the overall plan and it is generally short or medium term in character, covering a one to two year period.

For example, the strategic goal of increasing the volume of wills written demands consideration of a wide range of issues – research into the market place, promotional activity, allocation of additional work, and so on. The operational plan provides the structure for this activity. It should define:

- what activities need to be undertaken;

- who is responsible for their conduct;

- when they will be completed; and

- what budgets have been set for the activity.

Budgeting is vital but often poorly thought through. Unless there is a strategic reason which justifies it, there is little point in undertaking a promotional campaign if the expenditure involved will be greater than the level of profit that the promotion is anticipated to yield. The budget should therefore include profit and loss and cash flow projections for the period under consideration.

Being SMART

18.9   At all stages within the planning process, it is useful to apply SMART principles. SMART is a very useful acronym:

- S – Specific

- M – Measurable

- A – Agreed

- R – Realistic

- T – Timetabled

The plan must be **specific** – it must set specific targets or else it suffers the possibility of becoming a 'wish-list' – i.e. the aspirations of the department divorced from the reality of implementation.

The plan must be **measurable** – it must include indicators against which performance may be measured. Without introducing a means of measurement, progress against the plan's objectives cannot be evaluated. Indicators may be financial in character, but may also cover issues such as staff levels, absenteeism, client numbers, equipment in place and so on.

The plan must be **agreed** – all those affected by it should understand its broad content and the contribution that they will need to make in order to achieve the plan's fulfilment.

The plan must be **realistic** – there is no point in setting targets which are not achievable. Tripling the department's volume of instructions and income within four weeks is not realistic – however desirable.

The plan must be **timetabled** – without imposed deadlines, the plan will tend to lose impetus as short-term priorities intervene. Failure to timetable properly encourages procrastination.

Review and evaluation

18.10 All too often, a business plan is prepared and then simply locked up in a filing cabinet for 12 months. It is vital to ensure that you use the plan – it is a valuable management tool and you should refer to it constantly, as a means of monitoring how well the department is performing.

Operating conditions change constantly. You may have to amend the strategic objectives and operational tactics adopted. The plan may have been flawed from its inception and only constant monitoring will identify any problems in the concepts that it contains.

You need constant review and evaluation. The business plan should be used as the agenda for a regular management review involving the decision-making body within the department.

DEFINING THE STRUCTURE

Assessing processes

18.11 Any probate department needs a high level of technical/professional skills. However, these skills are not sufficient in themselves to produce an efficient and profitable probate department. You need to assess the processes within the department.

This will lead to the design of appropriate and effective departmental structures and systems and to the allocation of work to the member of the department most capable of dealing with it.

Can the department make better use of paralegals? Traditionally the wills/probate practitioner is all things to all men – he or she is the ambassador, the salesman, the accountant, the administrator, the progress chaser, the financial controller, the credit controller and, of course, the lawyer. Within such a wide range of responsibilities, it is inevitable that the practitioner is distracted from the core functions that he or she is employed to fulfil.

It makes more sense to break the responsibilities within the department down into their component parts, and to allocate them to appropriate team members. In undertaking this review, it is vital to take into account the level of responsibility and initiative required for each job function. For example, is it really necessary for a solicitor or senior fee earner to be involved in the process of answering routine file enquiries on progress?

Inevitably, the technical requirements of the probate function are such that it must be retained in the hands of experienced fee earners. But such fee earners need not necessarily be qualified solicitors – they certainly need not be partners! Many aspects of the department's work can be devolved or delegated for example:

- initial client research;

- home visits;

- will drafting.

What of the other functions within the department? A considerable proportion of the responsibilities undertaken within the department are routinely administrative in character. Wherever possible, it seems appropriate to give responsibility for administrative work to experienced legal secretaries who can remove the responsibility for these chores from the fee earner.

Information technology has its role to play in defining function. Computers can be used as tools to assist with the delegation of work to paralegals and junior members of the department, under the supervision of a principal, and their application should form part of the process of reviewing function and allocation of work.

Probate function

18.12 What are the core functions of the wills/probate department? An analysis of key stages might identify:

Work types

- Wills:

  - enquiry;

- funding;
- preliminary research;
- interview/instruction;
- drafting;
- client response;
- engrossment;
- signing/follow up.
- Probate:
  - initial enquiry;
  - agreeing funding (interim bills);
  - instruction;
  - collation of information re assets/liabilities;
  - grant of probate;
  - tax/Inland Revenue;
  - collection;
  - distribution;
  - closure.
- Financial services:
  - in-house IFA;
  - local broker;
  - permitted third party?

Functions
- Manager/team leader/head of department function;
- planning function;
- sales and marketing function;
- funding function;
- legal function;
- enquiry/progress function;
- administration function;

- accounts function;

- drafting function;

- secretarial and support function.

These functions are broadly the same in any wills, probate and trust department, of whatever size. The skill lies in accommodating them with available resources and in allocating them to the appropriate level. This may lead to consideration of fundamental issues such as staffing levels, reallocation or retraining of members of the department, investment in new equipment and supervision of delegated tasks.

Principal roles

The **Head of Department** holds principal responsibility for the effective and profitable operation of the department. The role encompasses:

- the development and implementation of departmental operating plans geared to meeting targets established by the firm;

- the establishment and achievement of departmental budgets and targets;

- the provision of coherent leadership and management support;

- the supervision, training and development of departmental staff;

- marketing and the development of the department's client base.

Fee earners hold principal responsibility for the delivery of prompt, effective and accurate advice and services. The role encompasses:

- provision of legal advice and assistance to the firm's clients;

- development of excellent working relationships with clients and referring agencies alike;

- familiarisation with and use of the department's information technology systems;

- familiarisation with and adherence to the department's prescribed operating systems and procedures;

- maintenance and development of relevant technical legal knowledge and skills;

- direction of support staff to maximise the performance of the department;

- resolution of client/referrer enquiries which cannot be dealt with by the support staff.

Support staff hold principal responsibility for providing secretarial and administrative support to the collective fee earning staff. The role encompasses:

- provision of word-processing services and the completion of forms as directed by the fee earners;

- attendance of clients on the telephone and the accurate taking of messages;

- establishment and maintenance of accurate filing facilities on behalf of the fee earners and Head of Department;

- data input of time records;

- maintenance of fee earners' diaries and appointments;

- provision of photocopying services to the department;

- preparation and sorting of incoming and outgoing mail;

- familiarisation with and adherence to the firm's prescribed operating systems and procedures;

- answering routine enquiries relating to progress.

The need for job descriptions

18.13   'I know what this job entails. I don't have to spell it out.'

'A fee earner's job is the same everywhere.'

'A secretary is a secretary.'

These types of statement, all too common within legal practice, disguise a reluctance to address the task of defining a job. Preparing job descriptions for all members of the department is a vital exercise which:

- clarifies the content of the job explicitly;

- ensures that everyone understands their accountabilities;

- provides a yardstick against which performance can be measured.

The job description should cover, as appropriate:

- the name of the post holder;

- the job title;

- the name of the job holder's supervisor;

- a summary of the job holder's accountabilities (e.g. relationships with clients, application of professional expertise, production of documents, efficiency);

- a summary of internal duties (e.g. managing other staff, co-operating with colleagues, allocating/delegating workloads).

Defining accountabilities and duties

18.14   Accountabilities are limited in number and do not change unless the job itself changes. In essence, they are what the job holder is paid to achieve on behalf of the department.

Duties are specific, time-targeted activities which devolve from accountabilities. They are the means through which accountabilities are met.

THE ROLE OF INFORMATION TECHNOLOGY (IT)

(See also Chapter 17)

IT in context

18.15   Information technology is now a fundamental part of almost every practice, yet its full potential and benefit has yet to be realised in most firms.

The effective, planned use of computer technology offers a means of solving many problems and enhancing profitability – without compromising standards of service, compromising fee earner/solicitor discretion, or de-personalising the whole process of client relationships.

The role of IT

18.16   The role of IT within the legal profession in general and the probate department in particular cannot be over-emphasised. In recent years, the introduction of sophisticated and user-friendly word-processing, diarising, and integrated case management packages has allowed a much wider range of individuals (in terms of experience and qualification) to undertake given tasks. This enhances departmental throughput and profitability.

A lot of probate work is administrative in character and leads to the generation of printed material – letters, enquiries, pre-filled forms, accounts data, etc. In many situations, the creation of one document is entirely contingent upon the completion of the previous stage. These factors lend themselves well to a diary-driven, computer-based probate process, operation of which may be partially delegated to junior staff.

Probate software systems are now readily available which:

- automate routine document production;

- collect and collate data relating to:

  - executors;

  - clients;

  - beneficiaries, etc;

- handle the preparation of probate accounts;

- provide precedent material;

- assist in will drafting.

Such packages are reasonably inexpensive. When considering their use, you have to be prepared to challenge preconceptions about who should be carrying out functions which, traditionally, would almost certainly have been delivered by a fee earner.

Objections to IT

18.17 **Cost**. Traditionally, the use of sophisticated IT-based applications has been seen as exclusively the preserve of larger practices. However, while the power and capacity of the hardware has increased in exponential rates of progress, the cost of such equipment has also plummeted.

As an example, in early 1998 the purchase, installation and training of a complete IT-based probate package, from scratch, involving five workstations, a shared printer with three paper bins, full networking software, and case management software might cost as little as £10,000–£15,000, which would be likely to be funded over a period of three to four years. Assess the cost in the light of the improvement you can make to productivity and profitability.

Impersonality/lack of quality. Many firms object to the computerisation of the probate process on the grounds that:

- 'we offer a premium service – our clients will deal with no one other than the partner';

- 'my clients will only deal with me – they won't be prepared to deal with an unqualified clerk';

- 'de-skilling the delivery of probate services will compromise quality and have a negative effect upon our marketing drive'.

Admittedly, these criticisms can be levelled at a poorly planned and a poorly implemented strategy. However, the criticisms cannot be justified if proper controls and systems are put in place.

Clients do not necessarily want to deal with a partner, but they do want:

- to be dealt with in a professional and efficient manner;

- proper reports;

- deadlines to be met;

- quotations to be adhered to.

These requirements are all about dealing with an efficient probate department and system. If you can achieve this without face-to-face or partner-to-client contact, what is the problem?

Practical Case Management

What difference can case management make in a probate department?

Systems

18.18 A management system provides the capacity to:

- capture information relating to the progress and conduct of the matter;

- attach timetables and schedules to this information; and

- subsequently to attach document and form production to the schedules.

Because the information relating to a given matter is stored centrally, on the computer, it is possible to:

- minimise the opportunity to miss key dates;

- avoid the duplication of data input/keyboard input;

- automate document production;

- automate the collation and calculation of financial information;

- report on the status and progress of a matter on a central basis without recourse to the file; and

- monitor the effectiveness of the service delivery.

Marketing

18.19   When information is captured on a case management system, a valid and valuable client marketing database starts to emerge. This can be used for future promotional purposes and to cross-sell services.

Time recording

18.20   By recording time in a detailed, planned manner, it will be possible to isolate those activities within a given department which are being delivered inefficiently or non-profitably.

Will drafting and precedent libraries

18.21   Modern word-processing packages running under the Windows operating system are capable of a wide range of functions including the ability to merge documents and clauses, create and maintain simple databases and carry out complex calculations within a document. Such functions allow even a moderately computer-literate probate department to automate a wide range of tasks by creating in house systems, including:

- will drafting;

- will registers and storage;

- the creation of simple marketing databases;

- the preparation of probate accounts;

- the production of standard precedents and correspondence;

- the automatic calculation and production of Inland Revenue forms.

Having installed a sophisticated word-processing package, it is vital to invest in suitable and adequate training from the chosen software supplier. Without it you will not get the most out of your systems.

Too Much to do, Too Little Time . . .

The problem

18.22   In order to implement and derive benefit from the business plan, you must set aside a sufficient volume of time for the management process. In many busy probate departments, this requires restructuring the way in which time, as a resource, is used within the department.

The efficient use of time is a constant problem. The day-to-day business of running a busy probate office can very easily be so intrusive as to prevent efficient management. The insistent ringing of the phone, the colleague who 'drops in for a chat', the beneficiary who wants to know when the will has been proved – these, together with the professional issues associated with managing the file often become so time-consuming that there is no time left for management and administrative topics.

This can result in a vicious cycle. If insufficient time is devoted to the vital functions of management and administration, it is almost inevitable that the files will start to bear errors. Phone calls will not be returned on time, deadlines may be missed and client expectations may not be met.

This feeds pressure on time as the resulting problems have to be resolved as a matter of urgent priority. Sometimes, the busy practitioner becomes so overwhelmed that he or she is unable to find sufficient time even to cost files and draw bills. Cashflow starts to slow and soon the financial performance of the probate department comes under question at partnership meetings.

It follows that a probate practitioner who is not managing his or her time efficiently is almost inevitably going to be less productive than a colleague who is able to manage time and its allocation effectively.

Just as importantly, poor time management cascades downwards, creating problems for colleagues and support staff who have to resolve the problems created by a fee earner who is not properly in control of time management.

For example, failure to keep a secretary informed as to a fee earner's whereabouts can lead to a considerable proportion of the secretary's working day being wasted in tracking down the missing member of the team. The secretary has priorities and tasks to complete which her principal has compromised.

Fortunately, there are simple, commonsense techniques which can be brought to bear to improve personal organisation and the use of time. Essentially, they are all geared to achieving one of two things:

- minimising the waste of time; and
- maximising the effective use of available time.

Minimising the time wasters

18.23 In any gathering of lawyers, a straw poll will indicate that there are four main time wasters within the law office. They are:

- the telephone;
- the client;
- administration;
- meetings.

These intrusive elements of office life are not only disruptive and time consuming in their own right, but they also divert fee earners away from core responsibilities, with a consequent 'double whammy' effect. When researching a complex estate planning issue, if the phone rings it is all too easy to lose concentration on the main task while the minor query relating to another matter is dealt with – and it takes time to regain the lost position when the phone call ends.

The principle of 'blocking time'

18.24 The use of the principle of 'blocking time' can help to reduce significantly the amount of time which goes on dealing with 'time wasters', which may occur at any time of the day, not necessarily fitting in to the daily schedule.

Blocking time is where periods of time are set aside for specific purposes, and to which definite rules are applied. Thus, a particular period of time is set aside during the course of the working day to deal with:

- responses to telephone calls and enquiries;
- client interviews;
- administration.

For example, to use time blocking techniques in the context of the telephone, arrange that:

- any incoming phone calls are fielded and screened, normally by a secretary but possibly by a switchboard operator, as they come in;
- a period of time every day is 'blocked out' for the return of all incoming calls.

As incoming calls are received, a firm but polite message should be given, explaining that the fee earner requested is not available but that he or she will return the phone call within the period of 'blocked' time. At this stage, as the fee earner is not 'made available' to the enquirer, it may be possible for the secretary to resolve the enquiry directly, without having to involve the fee earner at all.

If the enquiry must be referred to the fee earner, the telephone call must be logged and passed to the fee earner for follow up during the period of time 'blocked' for this purpose.

Using this technique, the fee earner can concentrate on core tasks without being distracted or disrupted. Consolidating all telephone calls into a single discrete period makes for a more efficient use of time, instead of dealing with telephone calls on a 'one by one' basis. From the point of view of the client, although they do not have immediate access to the fee earner on demand, they are able to plan their day around the anticipated return call, which allows them to plan the use of their own time.

Such an approach depends upon:

- ensuring that all members of the firm who are affected by this policy are fully aware of how it works; and

- ensuring that all phone calls are returned at the designated time – failure to do so will obviously severely compromise standards of client care and professionalism.

Time blocking can be applied to other issues which waste time. For example, blocks of time can be set aside on a weekly basis to carry out the routine administration without which a law office cannot function – the checking of monthly balances, regular file reviews, the preparation of internal reports and so on.

Client meetings and interviews can also be blocked, so that all such meetings are consolidated into one period of the day.

Having blocked out periods of time during the working day or week within which to deal with the time wasters, the remainder of the day is available and can be used for those professional activities and key tasks which require concentration and lack of interruption.

Setting priorities

18.25　A constant problem within probate departments are the changes in priorities that the workload and the clientbase creates. Having established a planned programme of activity for a given day, it can all too easily be disrupted by a single phone call or an urgent new instruction.

Prioritisation of the daily workload is an absolute necessity.

The simplest technique is to create a daily 'To Do' list. This can be accomplished using something as unsophisticated as a blank sheet of paper, but some probate lawyers may prefer to make use of a diary, electronic personal organiser or computer-based scheduler. Whatever the mechanism, the content of the list should be the same.

The To Do list should be a schedule of all the tasks which have to be undertaken on that day. Once listed, a simple series of priorities should be attached to each item on the list. An effective classification is:

- must do;

- should do;

- want to do.

Those tasks which are categorised under the 'must do' category are top priority jobs which must be tackled and completed without fail on the day to which they relate.

Items categorised as 'should do' are those items which ideally should be completed on the day in question, but which would not suffer if postponed.

Those items categorised as 'want to do' are everything else – typically those tasks which we enjoy doing but which are not necessarily important or urgent. Human nature being what it is, we often try to tackle those tasks under the 'want to do' category before undertaking anything else, with disastrous consequences in terms of time management.

Some people find it best to prepare the To Do list on the evening before the day to which it relates, thus providing themselves with an opportunity to mull over priorities while they rest and relax overnight. This approach also has the benefit of allowing the fee earner to 'hit the ground running' when arriving at the office in the morning, rather than having to sit down and create a To Do list before starting substantive work. Other people are more quick-thinking and creative during the morning and find they are better able to prepare and categorise their 'To Do's' at that time.

Once created, there are two fundamental rules which attach to the To Do list:

- Always undertake all of the 'must do' tasks before anything else. If this is accomplished, shifting priorities during the remainder of the day can be assimilated into the work schedule. On the other hand, if the 'must do' tasks have not been completed when the phone rings with an urgent set of new instructions, it may prove impossible to schedule the new task into the time available that day.

- Do not expect to complete all of the tasks on the To Do list each day. Inevitably, some of the tasks in the 'should do' and 'want to do' categories will remain uncompleted and will have to be carried over on a daily basis until such time as they can be completed.

Importance v. urgency

18.26 When prioritising tasks for the daily To Do list, a distinction should be drawn between the concepts of urgency and importance. A job may be urgent but not important – conversely it may be important but not urgent.

The chart below illustrates the point.

IMPORTANCE v. URGENCY

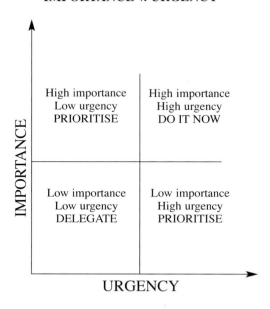

If a task is both urgent and important, it should go to the head of the 'must do' category on the daily To Do list.

If a job is of low importance and low urgency, it makes sense to consider its delegation to another, more junior member of the team, if such an individual is available. If it is not urgent and not important, why are you doing it?

Discretion and judgement must be exercised in the case of those grey areas where a task may be of high importance and low urgency or low importance and high urgency. The nature of the task will dictate where is 'sits' within the daily To Do list.

Time management and teamwork

18.27 Planning the use of time on a daily basis with colleagues will help the probate department to make the best use of available time. Everyone within the department has their own agendas and priorities to meet, many of which will interrelate with each other. For example, there is little point in dictating a large volume of work if your secretary already has a backlog of tapes to transcribe.

In order to avoid such counter-productive use of time, establish a routine daily meeting with your colleagues to establish how best to use available time. Such a meeting might review:

- incoming post;
- new instructions received;
- client appointments;
- appointments outside the office;
- workloads and 'To Do' lists.

Delegation

18.28 Many lawyers find it difficult to delegate work to colleagues or subordinates. Reasons for failure to delegate often include:

- lack of confidence in colleagues or staff;
- a consequent desire to retain responsibility for a task which is enjoyed;
- unwillingness to provide appropriate levels of authority to the delegatee.

If properly managed, delegation has a number of advantages. It makes the most of available time and skills and has the additional benefit of developing and motivating subordinates.

In delegating, it is important to recognise that responsibility can be delegated but never accountability. Accountability for the successful completion of the task in hand will always remain with the delegator. In order to delegate effectively:

- decide what tasks are appropriate for delegation (task prioritisation is useful here);
- match the tasks to the most suitable available person;
- consider – are they willing? How do you motivate them?
- consider – are they competent? Do they need coaching or training?
- set objectives. They should be SMART (Specific, Measurable, Agreed, Realistic, Timetabled);

- review progress of the task and monitor its performance;

- coach and praise;

- give authority – empower your colleagues by informing everybody affected by the delegation of the task.

Use of these time management techniques, coupled to the file management techniques discussed elsewhere in this chapter, will free up considerable volumes of time and maximise efficiency within the probate department.

Personnel Management and Team Building

Why does it matter?

18.29 The single largest overhead incurred in any probate department is likely to be the payroll and its associated costs. Given the very high ratio of payroll costs to income generated, it is vital to ensure that the best possible value is obtained from the firm's investment in staff.

As a simple example, a significant impact of poor personnel management is often high staff turnover. This not only subjects the department to the disruption encountered when a key member of staff moves on – there are also the significant costs incurred in replacing that member of staff and a learning curve to be overcome when a new member of staff begins work.

Good personnel management practices will ensure that staff are properly motivated, committed to the practice, properly trained and resourced and dedicated to meeting the needs of clients. Good personnel practice begins right at the outset of the relationship between employer and employee.

Recruitment

18.30 There is no point in filling a job vacancy with someone who is not ideal for that position. The first step is to identify the ideal candidate through the preparation of a candidate profile. This should list:

- required qualifications;

- required personal characteristics;

- required experience;

- required attitude.

This process should be accompanied by the production of a detailed job description which outlines exactly what accountabilities and duties the putative job holder will be expected to fulfil.

It is important to narrow down the range of applicants to realistic candidates as early as possible. An information pack for applicants will help candidates to assess for themselves whether or not they are likely to fit into your firm. It should describe:

- the firm's history;

- the firm's ethos;

- the firm's aspirations;

- the firm's attitude.

When recruiting, never forget to consider whether a member of your existing staff might be appropriate for the job. All too often, internal candidates are overlooked, yet they already know your firm, its clients and its systems – all of which will reduce the duration of the learning curve.

Induction

18.31   The learning curve can also be shortened through an effective and properly thought through induction process. Welcoming new members of staff on a Monday morning, showing them to their desks and dumping 20 files or tapes on them is not an adequate induction process. The induction process should cover:

- PAYE and financial matters – P45;

- training/conversion needs;

- office/department layout and colleagues;

- conditions of employment;

- health and safety;

- rules and regulations;

- history of the practice;

- welfare and benefits.

Appraisal

18.32   Appraisal should not be seen as a 'marks out of ten' exercise, nor as some sort of inquisitorial process.

Instead, it should be seen as a mutual exploration of how the performance of a given job can be improved – and this is a two-way process. The manager should not be dictating to the employee, but merely exploring alternative methodologies. By the same token, the employee may be able to propose ideas which will have an immediate, beneficial impact on the department.

Most importantly, the appraisal process should lead to some form of activity – often to develop or acquire new skills. 'Training and Development' need not equate to high levels of expenditure – it can encompass a wide range of activities, many of which can be carried out on an in-house basis including:

- traditional training;
- in-house training;
- coaching and/or mentoring;
- improved access.

The appraisal process should be conducted, as a minimum, on an annual basis. There should be a sufficient period set aside in advance of the meeting for both parties to prepare and decide the issues that they wish to discuss. After the meeting, consensus as to points agreed and action to be taken should be evidenced by both parties signing off a written report of the meeting.

Finally, the appraisal process should be followed through. It will almost inevitably identify means of improving job performance. Any action required to release that potential must be undertaken – otherwise the appraisal process becomes merely a bureaucratic process and loses its credibility amongst the department's staff.

Communications

18.33   Good communications are essential in maintaining high levels of employee commitment.

The views, concerns and proposals of staff should always be aired and taken seriously, both from the point of view of good morale and because employees are at the 'sharp end' and understand in real terms what their problems are.

There is no formula or recipe for the ideal balance of communications within a given practice. However, depending upon the size of the business concerned, consideration should be given as to whether communication systems need to be set up dealing with:

- the team;
- the department; or
- the firm.

Techniques to be adopted might include:

- the establishment of staff committees;
- social activities;
- effective and regular use of notice boards (avoid 'round-robin' memos – nobody reads them);
- use of internal E-mail (an increasingly common phenomenon within legal practice);
- the use of an intranet;
- an 'annual general meeting', reporting back to the employees on past performance and future plans;
- team/departmental meetings (but be careful when considering whether to make them fee earner only).

Many firms have dipped a toe into these turbulent waters only to withdraw very swiftly, saying 'we tried to hold meetings, but nobody contributed'. Improved communication is a cultural, long-term commitment. One staff meeting will not revolutionise the way in which people within the practice interact.

FILE MANAGEMENT

Quality management systems

18.34 There are a number of quality management standards which are appropriate for incorporation within law offices and probate departments. They are:

- ISO 9001;

- Investors in People;

- the Law Society Practice Management Standards – Lexcel.

Available options

ISO 9001

18.35 ISO 9001 is an externally audited management standard with its roots in the American defence industry. It is a self-defined standard – users establish their own management and file systems against the framework requirements of the standard itself, and are then audited against their own written systems. The standard is not specific to the legal profession but can be interpreted within a legal context. ISO 9001 tends to enjoy higher popularity within larger firms with commercial practices.

Investors in People

18.36 Investors in People (IIP) is a management standard developed within the UK and applied and audited in England and Wales through the national network of Training and Enterprise Councils. IIP is based upon the premise that a business will be successful if:

- it has a clear set of objectives which are communicated to all staff;

- all staff understand their contribution to those objectives;

- all staff are properly trained and equipped to fulfil their responsibilities;

- performance is continually evaluated and reviewed.

As with ISO 9001, IIP is not specific to the legal profession, but fits very well within it.

Practice Management Standards – Lexcel

18.37 The Law Society's Practice Management Standard (PMS) represents Law Society guidance on good management practice. Specific to the legal profession, the PMS covers:

- management structure;

- services and forward planning;

- financial management;

- managing people;

- office administration;

- case management.

The Law Society plans to introduce external accreditation and audit of the standard during the spring of 1998, under the brand name of 'Lexcel'. Accredited practices will be able to make use of the Lexcel logo and take part in Lexcel promotional initiatives. It is anticipated that the audit process will be simplified for those firms which are already accredited under other quality management standards.

There are several shared characteristics between these standards:

- all require external assessment and audit of the firm seeking accreditation;

- all measure the quality of the management systems in place within the practice, and not the quality of the legal advice and experience on offer;

- all require a measure of strategic planning to have been carried out;

- all require defined systems to be in place for the delivery of the product or service on offer;

- all require effective mechanisms for personnel management, training and development to be in place.

The quality management standards provide a framework within which efficient management practices can be developed and implemented. In particular, systems for the efficient running of client files, incorporating safeguards to minimise the possibility of error or client dissatisfaction, are a key feature of quality management systems within the legal environment.

Need for systems

18.38 The need for such systems is clear. Five per cent of SIF claims by number and 4 per cent by settlement amount are attributable to wills and probate matters. Penalty deductibles (effectively, an additional deductible of 50 per cent) apply arising from failure to:

- execute a deed of variation within two years (Inheritance Tax Act 1984, s.142(1));

- give written notice to the Inland Revenue within the six months permitted under Inheritance Act 1984, s.142(2).

The main problems encountered by the SIF within the probate arena include:

- wills:
  - delay in preparing wills – disappointed beneficiaries;
  - failure to comply with formalities for attestation;
  - failure to consider tax implications;
  - invalid gifts (e.g. severance of joint tenancy);
- administration:
  - delay – loss of value in assets;
  - failure to submit tax returns as trustees;
  - failure to review fund investments;
  - failure to act promptly in sale of shares/stocks/currency;
  - shares sold at loss within 12 months of death – failure to substitute lower value for value of shares at time of death;
- deeds of arrangement:
  - failure to consider tax consequences;
  - failure to meet time limits – deeds of variation;
  - failure to give notice of election within six months;
- beneficiaries:
  - failure to verify IHT liability prior to payment of beneficiaries;
  - failure to verify correct beneficiaries/address;
  - duty to disappointed beneficiaries;
- trusts:
  - failure to ensure trust drafted to make favourable tax treatment available.

File management systems

18.39 The checks and balances inherent in an efficient file management system can be broken down into a series of key areas:

- response to enquiry/provision of quotations;

- funding arrangements;

- allocation of confirmed instructions;

- opening a file;

- collection of marketing information;

- the legal process;

- responding to enquiries;

- post-completion and file closure.

Response to enquiries

18.40   The provision of telephone quotations is often seen as a mere irritant. Many probate practitioners, when asked to give a quotation over the phone, will do so briefly and without any attempt at 'selling' the service or the department. It is important to:

- give responsibility for responding to enquiries to the person who is best equipped to do it – not necessarily a partner but ideally someone with:

    - a good telephone manner;

    - sales experience;

    - an outgoing personality;

- prepare a checklist of all the information that must be provided to the client;

- take a positive approach – 'knocking' will be seen as a defensive attitude to competitive pricing;

- cross-sell – ensure that the client is well aware of all the issues and services attached to his initial enquiry. You may, for example, encourage clients to consider an enduring power of attorney whilst discussing wills. (See Chapter 20 on marketing);

- capture information – it is vital to keep a record of the enquiry and to find out from the client what prompted the enquiry in the first place. Knowing the source of the enquiry will enable you to monitor and plan your marketing strategy for the future.

Information on costs

18.41 This is a major source of client dissatisfaction and complaint.

The full and adequate provision of information about the likely costs of the matter, at the start and during its progress, will assist the client by providing a clear expectation. Failure to provide this information inevitably leads to shock at the size of the final bill.

Documentary follow-up

18.42 To help convert an enquiry into firm instructions, it is essential to follow up initial enquiries with a personalised letter. Ensure that the response is made on the day of receipt of the initial enquiry, unless this is patently unreasonable, and that it is accompanied by appropriate sales or promotional literature – particularly that concerning related services.

The details of the quotation, the client and the source of the enquiry should be recorded for future follow-up and in order to monitor sources of work and conversion rates.

Confirmation of instructions

18.43 The successful probate department will be efficient in confirming instructions and obtaining the necessary data from the client to progress the matter.

Upon receipt of the instructions:

- despatch terms of engagement and confirmation of quotation immediately to the client, as required under Rule 15 of the Solicitors' Practice Rules (see Chapters 2 and 3);
- agree funding arrangements and payment terms;
- allocate the work to the most appropriate fee earner. This means achieving a balance between:
  - experience;
  - workloads;
  - nature of the instructions;
  - value of the work.

Failure to control the workload being handled by an individual fee earner spells potential disaster – particularly if file management/supervision procedures are absent;

- seek written confirmation of instructions, if received by phone or from a third party;

- seek as much as possible of the information required to process the matter at the very outset.

At the same time undertake a case planning exercise to try to identify problem areas as the matter progresses. In a probate matter, such a planning exercise might check:

- difficult interpretations of law?

- beneficiaries lacking capacity?

- insolvent estate?

- all assets in possession of deceased?

- outstanding tax or other liabilities?

- deed of variation necessary/appropriate?

- IHT implications?

- statutory advertisement for creditors required?

- charities properly identified?

The case planning exercise might also seek to establish target and key dates relating to:

- assets collected;

- liabilities settled;

- time-limits (variation, etc.);

- interim billing;

- grant of probate;

- distribution – interim and final.

File set-up and opening a file

18.44 By now, the vast majority of the information required in order to carry out this function should be available. Client details are available and must be transferred on to the file and on to any electronic database or case management software, if in place.

File supervision

18.45 Supervision of the management of the matter breaks down into two areas:

- fee earner supervision; and
- file review.

Fee earner supervision

18.46 Supervision equates to effective support of the fee earner. The objective of supervision is to ensure that:

- all fee earners know who is supervising them;
- arrangements to ensure supervision of the conduct of case work are in place and understood within the department;
- arrangements are in place for a regular independent review of case files in terms of procedural and legal content; and
- arrangements are in place to supervise the conduct of work carried out by non-fee earning staff.

The supervision process tends to be divided into three areas:

- checking of incoming post;
- checking (but not necessarily signing) of all outgoing post;
- regular supervision meetings.

The level of supervision required will depend upon the experience of the fee earner concerned. Fee earners who are considered to be of sufficient experience should be granted the ability to supervise their own post, but they should still be subject to regular supervision meetings by their supervisor.

Base the frequency of supervision meetings on the fee earner's experience. Meetings should include coverage of issues such as:

- new cases taken on;
- existing workloads;

- progress on current cases;

- problem clients;

- the outcome of cases;

- training needs;

- undertakings granted or given;

- any other problems encountered.

The purpose of the meeting is for the supervisor to guide and assist the fee earner in the delivery of legal services.

File review

18.47   All files should be subject to independent periodic review. The review should cover both procedural matters and substantive legal issues and the review should be carried out by a supervisor who is independent from the day-to-day conduct of the matter.

The frequency of reviews is dependent upon the experience of the fee earner involved – five files per quarter will give an accurate, cross-sectional overview of the workload of most fee earners concerned. The file review should be evidenced by means of a file review sheet which should be signed off and agreed by both parties to the review process. The review should check at least the following issues:

- substantive legal issues properly addressed;

- papers referenced;

- file notes used consistently;

- undertakings recorded;

- conflict of interest check conducted;

- requirements or instructions of the client recorded;

- advice given recorded;

- action to be taken recorded;

- costs arrangements recorded;

- terms of business despatched;

- key dates recorded and backed up;

- client properly updated;

- changes in costs notified.

Any poor levels of compliance should be drawn to the fee earner's attention and rectified within an agreed period of time.

Professional checklists

18.48 Fee earners should complete professional checklists at key stages in the conduct of the matter.

The purpose of a checklist is to act as an *aide memoire* to ensure that all relevant professional issues have been properly addressed prior to moving forward to the next stage in the matter.

If all is as it should be, the checklist will act as evidence on the file to confirm this – if the checklist throws up an omission, no matter how major or minor, the fee earner will be prompted to go back into the file to rectify the identified problem.

Undertakings

18.49 Strict control is required over the granting of undertakings, which bind the firm and its partners. Any undertakings, other than standard wording undertakings, (e.g. those recommended by the Law Society in a conveyancing transaction) should receive a partner's prior authority.

A central register of undertakings granted should be established in addition to a clear record being placed on the file. Many firms now use a system of synopsis sheets on the front covers of files, which summarise key data relating to the file – it is sensible to include space on the synopsis sheet to show when an undertaking has been granted. Verbal undertakings should always be confirmed in writing.

Arrangement of file contents

18.50 Case files should be laid out neatly to ensure easy accessibility to all information by all fee earners and support staff and to enable supervisors regularly to review work. Working papers should be arranged so that:

- all correspondence is in sequence on a filing clip;
- all file notes/attendance notes are stored in sequence on the correspondence clip;

- a synopsis sheet is prominently attached to all files;

- deeds and other documents of title are stored in secure filing facilities, properly cross-referred to the file;

- any other papers are neatly arranged on the file, if necessary in a plastic wallet.

Updating the client

18.51 Fee earners should ensure that clients are appropriately updated throughout the matter and this includes ensuring that:

- information about action taken in a case, or its handling, is given to the client promptly;

- information relating to delays are passed on to the client immediately.

Both of the above points should be evidenced on file, either by attendance notes or by means of a copy letter to the client.

At the end of the matter

18.52 Proper procedures need to be put in place to ensure that any outstanding points are properly dealt with before the file is closed formally within the firm. This is best achieved by means of a file closure checklist. Issues addressed on the checklist should include:

- that the client has been informed of the outcome of the matter;

- that the client has been accounted to for any outstanding money;

- that interest on the client account been calculated (where applicable);

- that original documents have been returned to the client unless storage arrangements have been agreed;

- that, where appropriate, the client has been informed about arrangements for storage and retrieval of papers;

- that the client has been advised whether the matter should be reviewed in the future, and if so, when;

- that final bills have been received and settled and that account balances are zero;

- that a future review date (if applicable) has been diaried forward and that a file destruction date has been allocated.

Complaint systems

18.53   Complaint systems are not simply to provide clients with the ability to whinge. Complaint systems are a part of the process of assessing client satisfaction. They are a means of identifying problems, resolving those problems and ensuring that the resulting benefit is passed on to the client base.

Complaint systems should include a means not only of resolving the initial client complaint, but also of planning to ensure that the problem which gave rise to it never recurs.

Chapter 19

Avoiding complaints and claims

Experiences of the Office for the Supervision of Solicitors

Paragraphs 19.1–19.18 have been specially written for us by Richard Peel, and we are most grateful to him. Richard worked at the Office for Supervision of Solicitors (OSS; formerly SCB) for a number years and has recently returned to private practice with William Sturges & Co.

'Central to a civilised society are informed citizens who know and are able to access their rights.'

Ann Abraham, Chief Executive, National Association of Citizens Advice Bureaux 1995/96 Annual Report.

INTRODUCTION

19.1   Since Ann Abraham wrote these words she has become the Legal Services Ombudsman who reviews the work of OSS and therefore of complaints against solicitors. These few words illustrate graphically the demands of consumers ('complainants') in their dealings with solicitors and with OSS.

Anticipation

19.2   Probate work depends on having a system and sticking to it. This requires proper supervision from a qualified and experienced fee earner, good individual organisation and systematic work methods – and not taking on more work than the firm can handle. Probate questionnaires, standard letters and standard forms greatly assist this process.

This advice will also apply in future to the developing areas of private client work such as contentious probate, enduring powers of attorney and, as OSS is increasingly discovering, matters relating to financial services.

Beneficiaries

19.3   *'As a layman I must say that I find it surprising that solicitors administering estates do not have a greater obligation to beneficiaries.'* Michael Barnes, Legal Services Ombudsman, 1994 Annual Report

OSS experience is quite clear that a considerable number of complaints originate from beneficiaries who are not technically the solicitors' clients, i.e. are not the executors. Obviously beneficiaries are recommended to raise complaints in the first place with the executors but in many cases the solicitors are the sole executors. OSS has always entertained complaints from beneficiaries under the powers given to it by the Solicitors Act 1974. Practitioners will now be aware that beneficiaries also have rights to complain about the level of the solicitors' costs as 'entitled third parties' where the only executors are solicitors in the firm complained against. Beneficiaries' rights will not go away and will continue to be championed by the Legal Services Ombudsman, the Charity Legacy Officers Group (representing all the major charities) and consumer associations.

Client care and costs information

19.4   The Law Society and OSS have for some time made it clear that failure to supply proper client care letters and costs information to clients at the outset of the administration represents a breach of the written professional standards for which OSS has power to reduce a solicitor's costs and/or award compensation. It is obvious common sense to anticipate these problems by supplying client care letters and costs information at the outset of the administration. Assess at the first interview the time likely to be needed to complete the administration and settle at what stages the clients will be informed of progress and about costs. Tell them promptly and in writing about any adjustments which have to be made. Use the client care letter to record and follow up initial discussions.

THE DEADLY SINS

Failure to communicate

19.5   It is essential to keep clients (and beneficiaries) regularly informed of how the administration is progressing. Failure to communicate constitutes the single main instance of complaint.

Failure to explain

19.6 If there are likely to be delays in completing or progressing the administration of an estate (for example, a claim under the Inheritance (Provision for Family and Dependants) Act 1975 or queries from the Inland Revenue) early explanation will ensure that the clients are aware of the position and so do not complain about inadequate communication or delay.

Delay

19.7 After inadequate communication the main complaint is of delay. Without proper communication and explanation, clients and beneficiaries believe that all administrations can be completed within three months. Failure to achieve this is a guaranteed source of complaints to OSS.

Cost problems

19.8 In addition to complaints concerning the initial cost information/client care letter (see para. 19.4), regular complaints occur where solicitors take interim costs without informing clients or beneficiaries, sometimes without formally rendering a bill. In addition, where the original estimate of costs is exceeded it is a breach of the written professional standards not to inform the client as soon as the solicitors are aware that this is likely to happen and obtain the client's consent. Such information must be given in writing to the client.

Failure to follow instructions

19.9 This is an obvious example of breakdown in communication between solicitor and client.

Failure to give proper investment advice

19.10 This is becoming an increasingly common complaint, particularly where solicitors are holding themselves out as providing investment advice.

Loss of jewellery and deeds

19.11 If clients hand in cash, valuables or papers detailed lists should be prepared and receipts should be given. Estate valuables, cash items and personal effects should be kept in a safe or strongroom.

Failure to pay adequate interest

19.12   Failure to place estate money on deposit and obtain the best practicable rate of interest constitutes a breach of the Solicitors' Accounts Rules and is treated by OSS as inadequate professional service.

Failure to make appropriate interim distributions

19.13   Accurate and prompt distributions of estate funds should be made as soon as the extent of liabilities is clear. Legacies should be paid as soon as funds become available. Residuary beneficiaries' wishes (especially those of charity beneficiaries or others having special tax considerations) should be ascertained and discussed with the executors.

Failure to provide tax deduction certificates

19.14   These must be provided as a matter of course and promptly. It is a regular source of complaint to OSS when these are not provided or when solicitors seek to impose an extra charge for providing these.

Failure to produce adequate estate accounts promptly

19.15   These need to provide full details of assets, payments and receipts and in particular must distinguish between capital and income (see comments on tax deduction certificates and deposit interest in paras 19.14 and 19.12).

Conflict of interest/instructions from third parties

19.16   Solicitors must not accept instructions solely from third parties (who are often the source of introduction of administration work) without reference to the real client. Solicitors should also be particularly alert to possible conflicts of interest and ensure that independent professional advice is obtained by all affected parties. Complaints of conflict of interest raise some of the most time consuming (for solicitors) complaints to OSS.

Errors

19.17 If an error or mistake has been made admit this and correct the matter as soon as possible. Attempts to conceal errors are inevitably counter-productive and compound the problem (and the penalty) where a complaint is brought to OSS.

Excuses

19.18 It may be salutary for practitioners to be aware of a number of the most common excuses given to OSS when a complaint is raised:

- I have never made a mistake in . . . years of practice.
- I have mislaid the file.
- Someone else is dealing with this matter.
- We have had an office re-arrangement.
- I have been in court all day/all week/all month and have not had time to deal with this matter.
- Funny you rang. I was just planning to write to you.
- I do not reply to letters; why don't you telephone me?
- I do answer telephone calls but only on a weekly/monthly basis.
- There is/will be a letter/fax on the way to you today.

From the OSS . . .

19.19 The OSS confirms that delay and failure to keep clients (and, where appropriate, residuary beneficiaries) informed result in the majority of complaints made to it. It points out that good estate administration is greatly assisted by proper supervision by qualified and experienced fee earners, good individual organisation and systematic work methods – and not taking on more work than the firm can handle. It agrees that the majority of complaints about ordinary probate work originate in an unsystematic approach and poor client communication, rather than lack of knowledge of the law.

Interestingly, the OSS adds that contentious probate is a growing field and one with which more and more practitioners are likely to have to deal.

OSS's ten reminders

19.20 1. Inform executors (and residuary beneficiaries where appropriate) of progress and of costs incurred at the agreed stages of a probate matter. Too much information is better than too little.

2. Assess at the first interview the time likely to be needed to complete the administration, and settle at what stages the clients will be informed of progress and about costs. Tell them promptly and in writing about any adjustments which have to be made. The Law Society's publications, such as *The Personal Representative's Guide*, can be useful in giving standard information to clients (see Booklist, Chapter 29). Use a client care letter to record and follow up initial discussions – examples of information for clients are in Chapter 3. (Solicitors in private practice may adapt or adopt these specimens for the purpose set out on page iv but not for any other purpose.)

3. Develop a system and stick to it: keep lists of assets and debts, and note what happens to each asset and when it is dealt with or received, to avoid any possibility that assets or debts get overlooked.

4. It is essential not to take interim costs from estate funds until the executors have been advised and have given their approval.

5. Estate accounts should be simple enough for lay people to follow but need to give full details of assets, payments and receipts. (For example, in relation to the sale of stocks and shares, the sale prices and net proceeds per holding should be listed.) See the clients in person to explain the accounts, if necessary. (Chapter 15 includes advice from the College of Law about estate accounts.)

6. Place estate money on deposit at the best practicable rate of interest.

7. Always make attendance notes, and send letters to confirm oral instructions as a matter of course.

8. If clients hand in cash, valuables or papers, detailed lists should be prepared and receipts should be given; estate valuables, cash items and personal effects should be kept in a safe or strongroom (and remember that if the estate includes items such as guns, antique or modern, there may be additional rules – see para. 16.2).

9. Make accurate, and prompt, distributions of estate funds once the

extent of the liabilities is clear. Pay legacies as soon as funds become available and make interim distributions where possible. Residuary beneficiaries' wishes should be ascertained and the matter discussed with the executors if their views cannot be carried out.

10. If an error or mistake has been made, admit this to the clients and correct the matter as soon as possible – attempts to conceal an error are, the OSS says, inevitably counter-productive and very likely to result in a complaint.

. . . and SIF

19.21 These tips, slightly edited, relate to succession work and are extracted from the booklet *Claims Prevention I* published by SIF.

1. Time-limits

   • Check the time-limits for execution of deeds of arrangement and deeds of variation.

   • Check the time-limits for giving notice to the Inland Revenue.

2. Extent of retainer

   • Clarify at the outset with the client and confirm in writing.

   • Clarify the areas of responsibility between departments if the conduct of the file is divided.

3. Drafting

   • Ensure that the draft documentation is checked against original instructions.

   • Ensure that engrossments are checked against the final draft with someone else.

4. Delay

   • Ensure that wills are drafted and executed quickly – those for elderly and infirm clients and those in dangerous occupations or going abroad very soon may need urgent attention.

   • Beware of rushing after a delay, e.g. to distribute the estate – it might result in paying out to the wrong beneficiaries.

5.   Record of wills

- Ensure that a proper record is kept of wills held by the firm. The estate might be distributed only to discover a later will.

COMMUNICATIONS

Meeting clients' needs

Clients in distress

19.22   The debate over Rule 15 of the Solicitors' Practice Rules (see Chapters 2 and 3) highlighted the issue of client care in general. Probate clients may have special needs. Chapter 23 includes the text of a leaflet first published in Australia, entitled *Coping with a Major Personal Crisis*. Bereaved clients may be going through any or all of the emotions set out in the leaflet; while it is not a solicitor's role to act as a counsellor, in probate, as in divorce and other work, it is important for firms to be aware of and to cope sensitively with clients' feelings. Could you refer clients to local sources of help if necessary?

Plain English

19.23   At a more everyday level, clients need to understand the legal work being done for them. Otherwise, the causes of problems or delays may be wrongly attributed, resulting in unjustified complaints about individuals or firms.

'Clarity' (see para. 19.24) say that research has shown that clients may think they understand a lawyer's letter when in fact they seriously misunderstand it. Clients are not always willing to ask for explanations, nor to complain directly to the firm about perceived difficulties, unless they are aware that this is acceptable – which is why the client care provisions cover these issues fully.

Communications in plain English are usually very much appreciated by clients and can avoid misunderstandings. Some points about plain English are included in the following paragraphs.

Sources of information

19.24   Clarity (address in Chapter 30), is the lawyers' movement to simplify legal English. It produces a journal and runs seminars.

Relevant books are shown in the Booklist, Chapter 29, including the Law Society's own publication, *Clarity for Lawyers* by Mark Adler. Some computer programs are available: more information can be obtained from the Law Society's IT adviser.

Using plain English

19.25   One of the unjustified criticisms levelled at plain English is that it is 'not accurate' and so is not appropriate for legal use. This is entirely wrong. Plain English can certainly be accurate English – more accurate than 'legalese', which, because of its obscurity, may easily be misunderstood and cause confusion.

A commitment to using plain English may mean rethinking your approach, but it does not mean abandoning legal precision, technical accuracy, established legal usage, elegance of expression or useful, familiar legal terms when these will be understood by the reader; nor does it mean being undignified or patronising, nor that all your letters and documents must be written in words of one syllable.

Legal concepts are sometimes difficult, but nothing is gained by further binding them up in impenetrable language. A picture saves a thousand words, so use a chart, diagram or sketch if it would help.

A legal term can be the equivalent of a sketch, shorthand between people who know all that is implied by it. Effective plain English involves considering your readers, and if you know they will all understand a phrase such as *per stirpes* there is no reason to avoid it – as long as you bear in mind all the risks of taking a shortcut. Sometimes setting everything out in full, even just in your mind, highlights questions which would have been overlooked if the shortcut had been taken.

Writing to clients

19.26   Few clients will object to easy-to-use letters, which set out in straightforward terms what is meant and what they have to do. Most will have pressure on their time, and at best, other things on their minds; at worst, some clients will be acutely worried and distressed and not thinking clearly. Under those circumstances they need you to help as much as possible by assisting them to identify what is important, in letters and papers you send them, virtually at a glance. Good organisation and layout help immensely. Have the confidence to be unassuming and clear rather than impressive but incomprehensible!

Clarity's suggestions are not carved in stone, and have probably been transgressed (inadvertently) many times in this volume, but are intended to give an idea of where to start and to act as a reminder.

Document planning

19.27   The following points will help with document planning – the first step in clear communication:

- As you are putting pen to paper, or picking up your dictaphone, picture your reader(s) and ask yourself:

  - what is this document for?

  - who is going to read it? Are their interests in its content all the same? If not, whose take priority? What do I need to do about the others?

  - what will its reader(s) want to get out of it?

  - what do I *really* want to say?

- Consider how the answers to those questions will affect the way your message needs to be formulated and set out.

- Identify the kinds of things you will be doing in the document – summarising the relevant facts, asking somebody to do something, reviewing the options open to your client, explaining the law, recording an agreement, reassuring, warning, advising; decide how those should be arranged to make your points clear to your reader(s).

- Work out the headings which will summarise the points you have to make; decide the order in which you are going to put those points.

- Plan how layout, headings, paragraph numbering and so on can help make the document easy to read and how these can make the most important points stand out:

  - Use bullet points (like this).

  - Number paragraphs or sections to make cross-referring easier.

  - Use sub-headings.

  - Put important points at the beginning (of letters or paragraphs) and if need be mention them again at the end. Don't lose them in the middle where they may be overlooked.

  - If you have to use expressions which are likely to be unfamiliar or even slightly threatening ('an order of the court'), explain.

- Use lists for series of items.

- Underline the most significant part.

- Add a summary at the end, referring to the relevant paragraphs for detail.

- Read the finished document critically to check that you actually said what you intended – and if you didn't, start again (or at least make a note for next time).

- To paraphrase a famous saying, avoid being unintentionally pompous, ambiguous, vague or rude!

Your client will appreciate this kind of forward planning and, when you check your file to see that everything has been done, so will you.

Picturing your readers

19.28   Picturing your readers will highlight the differences and similarities between you and them – and how your document needs to reflect these. Readers may well come from a completely different professional, educational or cultural background from writers: what seems commonplace to one side may be entirely new to the other. Documents may have multiple uses, and some readers may not be aware of all of them. Accordingly your readers may well not share your assumptions about what is clear and what is not, nor about what is implicit and what is not.

Common shortcuts, such as 'where the context so admits', 'the singular includes the plural' and 'the masculine includes the feminine' can be traps. People may disagree about whether the context admits or not; one trustee's powers are not always the same as those of two; and many people do not automatically assume that the word 'he' is sometimes intended to mean 'he and/or she'. At least one Canadian jurisdiction is using 'gender neutral' language in all official publications, including statutes, because of this social change. (The old usage, and un-thought out questions like, 'What is your Christian name?' may also upset clients unnecessarily.)

Some shortcuts and habitual formulations shift what is properly the writer's burden – clarifying meaning – to the reader. Problems can then arise. It is better to be plain about exactly what you mean at the outset and ensure your document expresses it without ambiguity. After all, there's no point in saying, 'Well, it's obvious what I meant' when a glance at the law reports shows that virtually nothing is beyond dispute.

Not using plain English

19.29   Although some firms are actively changing to plain English for all work, others remains dubious. Lawyers who are comfortable using it in letters and informal documents may balk at using it in wills because of fears that plain English documents will not 'work' if tested in court. This is not the place to cover all the arguments; these are issues firms and individuals have to consider carefully if they share these concerns. If the verdict is against plain English, this means being extra-conscientious about explanations, in letters and meetings; and good layout and sensible document organisation can do a lot to clarify meaning.

Do not underestimate the amount of explanation that may be needed. Clients who have never been involved in estate administration may need an outline of the whole process, including what a grant is, why one is needed and what their duties are as PRs. The Society has a range of publications which may be of help (see Booklist, Chapter 29). Specimen letters and leaflets are included throughout this book (which solicitors in private practice may adapt or adopt for the purpose set out on page iv but not for any other purpose). Use of these materials and careful explanations should help prevent another person being in the position of the client who telephoned the Law Society to ask, 'What is probate?'

Chapter 20

Marketing wills and probate

This chapter was specially written for us by Kim Tasso BA (Hons) DipM MCIM MBA. She is an independent consultant specialising in marketing for the professions. She works with large and small firms in the law, accountancy, surveying, insolvency, psychology and other high value services. She was previously director of marketing at Nabarro Nathanson and a marketing manager at what is now Deloitte & Touche Management Consultants. She started her marketing career in the technology sector.

INTRODUCTION

20.1 This chapter aims to achieve the following:

- to dispel the myths about marketing and to explain the core concepts of marketing to prepare you, the probate practitioner, for effective marketing;

- to provide an analysis and planning framework to help probate practitioners understand their present position, articulate what they want their marketing to achieve and to develop a plan of attack;

- to provide some practical guidance on selecting which of the many marketing tools are appropriate to the marketing tasks practitioners face;

- to help the probate practitioner develop and implement effective marketing action plans.

UNDERSTANDING THE BASIC PRINCIPLES OF MARKETING

What is marketing?

20.2 *'Marketing is the management process responsible for anticipating and meeting client needs profitably'* is the official definition of marketing and one that few professionals would argue with – after all, isn't every

337

lawyer there to meet the needs of their clients whilst making a modest profit? But the definition is of little value on its own.

Marketing operates at three levels. First, there is a marketing function. Someone within your practice needs to take overall responsibility for marketing to ensure that the appropriate resources are available, that all the different marketing activities throughout the firm happen in a co-ordinated and effective way and to manage the various marketing information systems that you need to draw upon. Second, marketing is a series of tools and techniques (for example, advertising, direct mail, publications, selling, etc.) designed to do different marketing tasks and these are described further below. Third, marketing is a philosophy that focuses – at every point in the firm – on the needs of the client.

Marketing typically comprises a number of elements that are blended together into what is called 'the marketing mix'. The elements are:

- product (the legal advice and the way in which that advice is processed and delivered);
- place (the market where the services are promoted and delivered);
- price (ensuring clients perceive value for money);
- promotion (all those activities designed to alert clients and potential clients to the services and benefits available);
- people (the lawyers and their support staff who are the marketers, sellers, producers and deliverers of the services).

These different elements are explored further in the remainder of this chapter but it is important that all elements are considered together – a promotional campaign alone is unlikely to succeed.

There is often some confusion within the legal profession about the terms 'marketing', 'selling' and 'business development'. They are distinct activities aimed at different parts of an ongoing and integrated cycle.

SO WHAT IS SELLING?

The marketing cycle

Marketing

Client development

Selling

20.3   Marketing is concerned with identifying needs in the market, identifying or developing the services that meet those needs and communicating the appropriate messages to the market. It is where the firm 'broadcasts' a message to many members of a market (for example, a market might be all the wealthy people within a 10-mile radius or it might be all accountancy practices with between one and eight partners). If marketing is successful enquiries will be generated.

When you move from communicating with a market to communicating with a particular organisation or individual you have moved into the selling phase. Here the focus is on the specific needs of that one organisation or individual rather than the generalised needs of the whole market. Some argue that selling is more oriented to 'pushing' the product or service you want to sell although in the legal market the most successful selling is driven by the needs of the buyer.

Converting a prospect through successful selling results in a client. However, one set of instructions does not a client make. The continued marketing and selling to that client (within a framework of relationship management) – to ensure further instructions are received for additional or new services – is a vital activity in every law firm as usually around 80 per cent of a firm's annual income is from existing clients. This should dispel the myth that marketing is only about new business – a major component of law firm marketing is about developing the existing client and referrer base through relationship marketing.

Consumer verses business-to-business marketing

20.4   Before we embark on a practical framework to get you marketing your probate and wills practice we need to appreciate that marketing techniques vary depending on the nature of your target client. We will also consider the importance of segmenting the market into smaller, more manageable segments with common characteristics or needs.

When we are promoting wills, we are typically targeting private individuals or families. There are 58 million people in the UK and they can be grouped by socio-economic group, by age, by location, by household, by lifestyle and in various other ways. Even though you have focused on a particular group, it would be difficult and not very cost-effective to try to mail all members of that group or to spend hours in one-to-one meetings with them. So, more indirect methods of marketing might be adopted – such as advertising or media relations. The members of each group or segment will have common interests or needs that you can address within a marketing campaign. The smaller and more focused your segment the easier it will be to reach the members with a suitable marketing tool and the easier it will be to tailor your message to address their specific needs.

However, you might adopt a different approach and decide to target businesses in your area, offering a will writing service to their employees. There are significantly fewer businesses than individuals in the country and there is a great wealth of information about them in various public directories and publications. Business people are less likely to be reached effectively through advertising so you might adopt a more direct approach to marketing to this group – by direct mail, through seminars or perhaps by having a lawyer make visits to employers' premises. Their needs will be different too – whereas individuals might need a will for peace of mind, to provide for their children, to minimise their tax liabilities on death, etc., a business will have different needs. If it offers a will writing service to its employees it might be because it is genuinely concerned with staff welfare, it might be more concerned with minimising time away from the place of employment to sort such matters out, or it might wish to minimise difficulties in the event of death in service for the company's pension scheme. So, the way of reaching the business audience needs to be different and the message you communicate needs to be different.

An alternative might be that you decide to reach referrer organisations to generate wills business. You might look at retirement homes, hospices, doctors, accountants or advice centres. Here you are targeting organisations so the business-to-business techniques are more likely to be effective.

In marketing terms, we are talking about the difference between consumer (private client) and business-to-business (commercial client or referrer) marketing. Often, lawyers do not make the distinction and use the wrong technique. As a rule of thumb (there are always exceptions!), if you are marketing to consumers you use indirect methods and for businesses you use more direct approaches. The following table shows the various techniques that would perform these tasks:

Indirect methods	Direct methods
Advertising	Networking
Signs/posters	Selling
Media relations	Tenders
Sponsorship	Presentations
Literature (left on display)	Literature (mailed)
Web sites	Seminars/briefings
Word of mouth	Hospitality
	Telemarketing

A marketing framework for probate practitioners

20.5   Having reviewed the main marketing ideas, what follows now is a framework to guide you through the various steps you should take to prepare yourself and your firm for effective marketing and to prepare a marketing plan to focus your marketing, selling and client development activities. It may seem that a lot of analysis, thinking and planning has to take place before you get to any real 'action'. However, most solicitors' marketing fails because insufficient attention is paid to precisely these issues.

ANALYSING YOUR PRESENT SITUATION

Analysing your current work, clients and sources

20.6   Let us start by looking at the sorts of sources of work and clients you might have:

Those inside your firm:

Private clients
- Matrimonial
- Personal
- Residential conveyancing
- Financial services

Commercial clients
- Corporate/commercial – directors, senior employees, shareholders
- Employment – senior employees

Other staff
- Friends and family

Those outside your firm:

Private individuals
- Low income
- People with ageing parents
- High net worth/rich clients
- Company directors

Referring individuals
- Existing/past clients
- Those who know of you

Referring organisations
- Accountants
- Surveyors/agents
- Advice centres/bureaux
- Banks
- Carers
- Hospitals/homes
- Funeral directors
- Other law firms

This illustrates the great variety of clients and prospects (both private and commercial), sources of referral or work and needs with which will and probate practitioners must get to grips. Prepare a similar diagram for your own firm – ensuring that you check the various information sources in your firm to get an accurate feel for the amount of work coming from each source. If your firm does not have the information then an early priority is to ensure that systems are established to collect this information in the future. Marketing without sound information is rather like building on sand – it is without foundation and liable to crumble away.

Understanding your major sources of work will help you develop a strategy to focus your marketing efforts in those areas where they are most likely to bear fruit. You cannot possibly market to all sources and markets effectively so you will need to make choices. Your choices should be based on information as accurate and as up to date as possible. You need to know the amount of fee income, the type of work, the profitability and the importance to the firm (e.g. to other departments) of each type of work.

This analysis should provide you with three or four areas on which you need to concentrate. Once you have identified the types of clients or referrers you want to target, you should start collecting information about them. This should include their names and addresses, their needs and concerns, any links within your firm, background information about them and ideas on how you might approach them or build the relationship if they are existing clients.

If you have the time available, you will find talking to a number of existing clients and referrers an invaluable aid to future marketing. It will help you to identify why people come to your firm, what they like (and don't like) about the service, what additional help or advice they would like and what it is about your firm that is different from others. Time and effort spent investigating the perceptions and satisfaction of existing clients is always paid back.

Reviewing your skills, staff and services

20.7 The next thing is to review the skills and abilities of the staff who are promoting, doing and servicing the wills and probate work. Do they have any specialist expertise – for example, in complicated tax issues, in contested wills, in situations of cohabiting couples, with overseas assets? If your firm has some expertise that is unlikely to be found in other, comparable firms then you are on your way to finding a key point of difference which will make targeting and marketing much easier.

Are there any gaps in your expertise? It is important to be clear if there are any areas where your advice is likely to be less than optimal – either training or skills development is required or you need to steer your marketing away from these areas on to other stronger offerings.

Are your staff able and motivated to sell? Perhaps you need to consider some interpersonal skills training to develop their enthusiasm and confidence for generating new business. Even if you decide to take on the major share of marketing work yourself you will still need to be sure that the others who have contact with clients (whether they are support staff on switchboard or reception or junior paralegals), understand what you are trying to achieve, deliver the services in the way you have promised and achieve a high level of client satisfaction.

Looking at the market

20.8   Now you understand where your work comes from, and the resources you have to develop and deliver work in the future, you must look outside your firm to the local market.

You should start by assessing local demands and needs. The demand in your area may be different to that in other parts of the country depending on, for example, the demographic and socio-economic spread of the local population, the prevailing attitudes towards planning and professional advice of the local people, the extent of nursing and private care homes and facilities and the nature of the competition in the area. You can obtain this information either by researching at local reference libraries or by seeking help from your local Training and Enterprise Council who often have concise overviews of areas and the main economic and social trends. Networking at local events will also enable you to learn about the dynamics within your marketplace and will provide vital marketing intelligence.

It is important to remember that effective marketing requires you to identify and anticipate needs. Without a need it will be impossible to sell anything. Be objective when researching and considering local needs. You may have to rethink the nature and packaging of the services you are providing – e.g. living wills being more important than traditional wills, DIY probate packages for lower income families rather than high value services for wealthier clients or employee support packages for local employers with large workforces.

A key issue to consider will obviously be the strengths, weaknesses, strategies and activities of your competitors. These may not all be solicitors. You will also need to consider banks, accountants (especially those with tax and trust departments), financial advisers and independent will writers. In any market you will face a variety of competitors. The key will be to identify the main ones and develop your strategies accordingly. Information about your competitors is not sufficient. You must use this information to modify your approach and activities in order to find a different marketing position offering different benefits.

Pulling your research together

20.9   You may find that an analysis of your internal strengths and weaknesses and how these translate into external opportunities and threats helps identify the key issues on which you need to act.

As you consider each opportunity and threat think what you need to do – as a specific action – to resolve or grasp the situation. The more time you spend on synthesising the key findings of your internal and external research, the easier it will be to develop a marketing strategy and action plan that works for you.

DECIDING WHAT YOU WANT TO ACHIEVE

Setting objectives

20.10   The first action will be to determine what your firm's overall objectives are – both in terms of financial targets (what fee income and profit contribution is expected from the wills and probate team?) and in terms of the perception and impression the firm wishes to create in the market and the nature of the key clients it wishes to target. It is at this stage that many wills and probate practitioners find a difficulty – especially if the firm is focusing on developing commercial clients and work rather than private client work. It may also be difficult if there are other practice groups targeting similar client and referrer groups to those targeted by the probate and wills team. You will need to work together carefully in this case to produce an integrated plan (see the comments in the case studies section below).

Once you have identified the firm-wide objectives and the short-term (usually one year forward and based on utilisation, fee income and profit) objectives set for the wills and probate team, you can start to draft some more specific long- and short-term objectives for your team. Setting objectives that are measurable and realistic (see the discussion of SMART in Chapter 18) is hard but without them it will be difficult to focus your marketing efforts appropriately and impossible to measure the success of your marketing.

Selecting your targets

20.11   With clear objectives set, it will help considerably if you can be as specific as possible about the amount and type of work you hope to obtain from existing clients and contacts (in the short term) and from new clients and contacts in the longer term.

Producing lists of referrer organisations, the names of existing clients and other detailed information at this stage will save much time later. Again, such lists will focus the mind and help you assess whether your marketing is working effectively.

AGREEING A STRATEGY

Position in the market

20.12   From previous studies into lawyer marketing, a common mistake is to try to be all things to all people. For example, lawyers often try to provide a high quality, high value-added service at the lowest possible price. Not only is this a recipe for working 24 hours a day with no return but also for financial disaster!

You need to decide what position you want to achieve in the market. If all the other wills and probate service providers are pushing the low cost, pre-packaged wills 'product' then look at whether there are opportunities for firms offering a higher priced, more tailored 'service'. If others are targeting the low income families, consider targeting the wealthy. If others are focusing on reaching the 'man on the street', why not consider reaching the executive in the boardroom or local employers?

A key element of your positioning will be trying to identify what it is that you offer that others don't – it may be expertise in a particular area, it may be your accessibility, it may be your client care philosophy, it may be your level of computerisation or the degree of integration with other legal and financial services. Unless you are pursuing a 'cost leadership' strategy, you will need to identify a suitable differentiation strategy.

If you are unable to differentiate your firm across the whole local market, then you may need to identify and select a particular niche in the market. For example, a suitable 'segment' might be accounting firms over a certain size with no tax planning capabilities or agricultural estates.

It is important that your strategy takes a slightly longer-term view as well. You already have financial targets for the next year so use the positioning stage to identify where you want your wills and probate practice to be in, say, three or four years' time. It will take this long for the market to learn and understand a new positioning statement.

Packaging the product and the people

20.13 An integral part of deciding your strategy and positioning will be agreeing what it is you are selling in the market. Some firms have differentiated the services of their wills and probate team by packaging together a range of services such as wills, living wills, enduring powers of attorney and advice on financing long-term care either in an 'elderly citizens' package or as a 'families with ageing relatives' package. Some firms 'package in' tax, financial, trust and conveyancing services in different combinations to suit the particular needs of slightly different audiences.

The actual legal 'product' is similar in all such packages – what differs is the particular needs of the particular target audience being addressed and the emphasis. The packaging can shift the emphasis away from things people are reluctant to consider (the lack of a will when they die) to more positive issues such as financing the education of grandchildren.

Another approach might be to package the way you offer or deliver the advice – for example, there are some highly innovative web sites which offer a fixed price procedure for straightforward grants of probate in low value estates or will drafting.

In addition to packaging what you are actually offering you need to consider the way in which you deliver the advice and this involves taking a long and hard look at everyone (lawyers, paralegals, secretaries and switchboard staff) involved in client communications for wills and probate services. Clients are unlikely to be able to tell whether they are getting good or bad advice from their solicitors, so they will infer your 'quality' through the impressions that are generated by the way in which you answer the phone, the speed with which their queries are answered, the accuracy and layout of the letters and documents they receive, the friendliness of the legal and support staff they meet and the tidiness and comfort of the reception areas and office they visit.

Often getting people to be a valued and integral part of your service promise will require training, communication and involvement in the marketing, planning and implementation process so if you haven't involved them so far, do so now, through an informal discussion where you explain what you are trying to achieve and ask them to discuss the barriers they perceive and the help they require in delivering the promise.

Pricing

20.14   Clients will choose on price alone if they perceive no other differences in what is being offered by different suppliers. Therefore, if there is no perceived difference in the will writing or probate service offered by your firm or any other provider then price will dominate the decision. Remember the need to make a decision between trying to offer 'cost leadership' service in the market (i.e. the cheapest) and providing something different or better.

A key element of marketing is to move clients away from thinking about the price to thinking about the benefits of the service and other factors – such as speed, accessibility, ease of use, friendliness, personal service, etc.

The price must equate to the value of the service as perceived by clients. They are not interested in the cost of providing that service. Therefore, you must think of price in both strategic terms (what are my broad hourly or fixed fee rates) and in tactical terms (how much for this particular piece of work). Some firms are becoming more creative in pricing, moving away from hourly rates to fixed price deals, value billing, retainer arrangements or shared risk arrangements and bonus arrangements. This gives clients the benefits of certainty.

Promotions and internal marketing

20.15   At last we get to the phase with which most lawyers will be more familiar – the marketing and selling of the services they provide. The objectives and earlier analysis should reveal where your efforts are to be focused and should have indicated the types of marketing tool that are going to be most effective in achieving them.

The following section identifies some of the key issues to consider when planning to use some of the most common marketing tools. You might seek further information and advice from marketing books – there are plenty written for the specific needs of solicitors.

Advertising

20.16 Advertising is where you pay a media owner (e.g. a directory, a newspaper, a magazine, a radio station, a poster site operator, a TV channel) to reproduce your message exactly as you require. There are two elements to the cost – the cost of designing and producing the advert and the cost of the space.

Advertising is a tool to get a simple message to a large audience that is perhaps difficult to reach by other means. It is generally more suited to winning legal aid or private client work. Common places where probate practitioners advertise for private client work include telephone directories, local newspapers and poster sites near advice centres. There are a growing number of magazines targeted at the older generation which may prove useful to will and probate practitioners – especially if they have produced a package of advice and services tailored to the needs of the older client.

There are over 1,400 trade and technical journals which are targeted at specific business, professional or trade audiences. For example, there are magazines aimed at funeral directors, nursing home staff, those who care for the elderly and accountants.

One-off adverts are rarely effective so if advertising is your chosen tool then make sure your adverts will appear on more than one occasion over a suitable period of time. You must be clear of the following before you attempt any advertising:

- Who is my target audience and what media might reach them efficiently?

- What message am I trying to convey?

    - Is it simple and clear?

    - Does it focus on a specific need and mention benefits?

348

- Is it sufficiently different from other solicitors' advertisements?
- What action does it prompt the reader/viewer to take?

With all marketing activities, you should be sure you can respond to any enquiries that are generated (have your switchboard and reception staff been briefed?) and that you can measure the response from any specific activity to assess its effectiveness.

Most solicitors focus on display adverts. Other types of advertising to explore include inserts into printed media, messages on appointment cards or internal posters, leaflets in counter top dispensers, door-to-door leaflet drops, cable television (considerably cheaper than national or terrestrial television and much more focused on particular areas or audiences) and within the promotional materials of non-competing organisations providing services to the same audience.

Direct mail

20.17   Direct mail is a cost-effective method of reaching commercial clients and referring organisations – as opposed to advertising which is probably best for reaching private clients. The starting point is some form of database which contains, as well as the name of the individual, their position, the organisation name, the address and telephone number. Other useful information would be specific areas of interest (e.g. tax advice), other relationships or services used within the firm, a log of past contacts and any other information that helps with analysis and segmentation.

Short, simple letters following the AIDA rule (Attention, Interest, Desire and Action) are often effective – especially when the follow-up action is low commitment (e.g. sending in for an information pack, requesting a copy of a helpful checklist) rather than high commitment (e.g. a meeting). A covering letter will increase the chances of any brochures or newsletters being read. You should also look at ways to facilitate an easy response such as reply-paid envelopes, freephone telephone numbers or proforma fax sheets.

Be creative in thinking what you might send to people that will be of value – items should be focused on specific messages or issues. Copies of articles or of speeches you have delivered, feedback or testimonials from clients facing similar situations, invitations to informal briefings or receptions, notification of books or speeches your lawyers will be preparing could all be used.

Although there has been a tendency for law firms to produce high quality, glossy promotional materials, direct mail will work just as well (sometimes even better) if the materials are produced smartly and inexpensively in-house. Such items can often feel more immediate and more personal than their glossy counterparts. They can also be tailored to specific needs, topical issues or special audiences with ease.

Direct mail can be used to communicate on a regular basis with existing clients and referrers as well – helping to build relationships, provide added-value service and keep your firm's name 'front of mind'.

Public relations (including media relations)

20.18 This is a broad term which covers a whole range of activities involving the firm in two-way communications with the various publics it serves. Relevant publics for probate practitioners might include existing wills/probate clients, other clients of the firm, potential clients, local referrers, the local media, existing staff, potential staff, the legal profession and government officials.

- **Media relations** is one of the most useful tools for probate practitioners, i.e. communications with the printed and broadcast media. Press releases about topical events, offering the expert views of your leading tax, probate or private client experts, short articles providing practical advice, articles containing checklists to help readers assess their situation and 'legal problem pages' are all inexpensive (but time intensive) ways of getting your message across. However, unlike advertising, the editor will always have the final say on whether your items are used and the manner in which the material is used so you have much less control. Unless you have some experience of dealing with the media it is often useful to employ the services of someone who does – freelance press officers can be used on an occasional basis and their rates are often very reasonable. If you choose wisely you will find a public relations officer with good knowledge of and contacts within the media you have targeted.

- **Publications** is another aspect of marketing that falls broadly into public relations too. You might have a firm brochure, a private client brochure or leaflets describing the services offered by your wills/probate team. Again, the key words here are focus and benefits. Too many solicitors' publications focus on 'we' the firm rather than 'you' the client and contain features rather than benefits. Truly client-facing publications will be written from the clients' point of view (e.g. problems, needs, questions, concerns, issues, etc.) rather than the firm's point of view (location, departments, services, etc.). Newsletters will serve a number of purposes. Whether they are general and aimed at all clients or focused on the needs of particular groups (such as private clients, elderly clients, professional carers, etc.), they will:

- alert readers to changes in the law;

- educate them on possible needs they might have;

- provide simple advice so they can help themselves;

- explain difficult legal issues in simple terms;

- remind them that the firm is proactive and able to assist;

- cross-sell services of the firm; and

- secure the loyalty and memory of existing or dormant clients.

- **Events** for existing or potential clients or referrers would also fall under the public relations umbrella. Some firms take exhibition or stand space at local county or town shows – an opportunity to meet, face-to-face, local people who might be clients or potential clients. Stands at trade exhibitions (e.g. for professional carers or home operators) can also be useful if targeted properly.

- **Speakers**. You might also provide 'expert' speakers to address the audiences of local business, trade or social groups. Organisations such as the Institute of Directors, the Chambers of Commerce and Business Links are often heavily targeted by other solicitors so seek out more unusual organisations. Similarly, you might send representatives of the firm out to network at these events – the aim being both to develop contacts that might generate or refer business in the future and also to gather vital information or market intelligence about local needs and competitors and to ensure that the firm's name appears regularly at local events.

Seminars are covered separately below (see para. 20.20).

Internal marketing

20.19 This area of public relations – communicating with those within your firm – is vitally important to will and probate practitioners because often other members of the firm will be an important source of referrals for you and because sometimes you may be targeting similar audiences to others in your firm.

In smaller firms it is easier to talk informally to the partners, assistants, trainees and secretaries within other departments without having to arrange special meetings or prepare lists of the services provided, the clients served and ways in which you can help each other develop business.

Internal marketing is important because you have limited resources within the wills and probate team. However, the marketing and communication load can be significantly spread if all members of your firm understand what you are offering, to whom, the relative benefits and how to 'pass across' clients or referrers with the sorts of questions or problems that the probate and wills team can deal with.

Organising events and networking

20.20 These again are aspects of public relations. You might consider planning your marketing on the basis of events that your firm will organise and those that others will organise but your firm will attend.

Organising events can take a huge amount of time and preparation. You will need to call upon your support staff to assist with preparing invitation lists, monitoring the response and the myriad of logistical arrangements (e.g. room preparations, catering, cloakrooms, handouts, audio visual materials, etc.).

At the most informal level, you might invite a selection of clients, potential clients or referrers to your office for lunch or a glass of wine. This provides them with an opportunity to network with other people.

However, many people are invited to 'plain' cocktail parties and receptions so it will help considerably if you can think of something that will make your event different – for example, by having an external guest of honour or by theming the event in some way. Better still, provide a business rationale for the event – so, for example, invite a group of staff involved in residential and nursing homes to an informal round table discussion where issues of common concern (with a legal flavour but not entirely legally focused) can be discussed.

The events taking most effort are where you are presenting or showcasing your legal expertise – a briefing for small firms of accountants on inheritance tax planning, a seminar for high net worth people on future changes in estate planning. It is often better with high net worth clients to package any wills, tax and probate topics with other private client topics such as property transactions, trust creation and maintenance, overseas funds, etc. Inviting external speakers to your events will both increase the attractiveness to your invitees and reduce the burden on your staff of preparing materials.

Networking can be used to achieve a number of purposes and can be done at your own and other people's events. For example, you can raise the profile of the firm in the local business community or amongst a particular audience (e.g. local social services people or local GPs). You can effect introductions and start to establish personal relationships with referrers or potential clients. Networking may also be used to help develop your understanding of the needs, interests and motivations of your target audience.

Talking to people (and listening carefully to what they say) – especially potential clients – is one of the best ways to gather market intelligence. Regular attendance at the same organisation's meetings or events will increase your chances of being recognised and establishing ongoing contacts. Offering to present topical subjects or to explain complicated legal issues with a wide appeal in a simple way – and getting yourself on their speakers' platforms – will help raise your profile. People at the events will then feel a little easier about approaching you.

Presentations

20.21   Typically, probate practitioners are not marketing to the end user (private clients) of their services but to other intermediaries such as doctors, social services people, professional carers, banks, accountants, surveyors, bereavement counsellors, etc.

After establishing contact (or, indeed, to create an opportunity to establish contact) a short presentation about a topical issue alongside some information about the credentials and experience of your firm, your team and your services will ensure the relevant information is conveyed efficiently and accurately.

Yet not everyone is comfortable making presentations and some lawyers have little experience. It is helpful to prepare audio visual materials (whether these be pre-written sheets to talk against, overhead projector slides or PC-based presentations) to guide the speaker and provide additional interest for the audience. Advance planning and rehearsals are vitally important if the quality of your talk is not to undermine your professional skills. Summaries of talks should always be distributed –

with your name, the firm's name and contact details marked discretely but clearly on each separate sheet.

Process and physical evidence

20.22   These are two aspects of the service you provide that will have an impact on your marketing effectiveness.

Physical evidence covers a number of things including the appearance of your offices and meeting rooms, the appearance of your legal and support staff, the style and layout of your marketing materials and correspondence and even the type of cups you use to serve tea and coffee. As mentioned above, clients are rarely able to determine the quality of the legal advice they receive and will therefore make assumptions about the quality of advice on the basis of those more tangible things they can observe.

Process brings us back to the product element of the marketing mix. Here you need to be concerned with aspects of case or matter management, project control, efficiency and the use of computer systems to assist in the production and management of legal work. We know that price is often driven by costs in law firms (how many hours to do this or do that) rather than by the value perceived by the client. Reducing the time and level of skilled staff involved in processing the work will reduce the cost and increase the profitability margin.

But process is not simply a 'behind the scenes' production issue. Your process should be designed to maximise client perception and value – through regular communication, keeping them up to date with progress, showing exactly what legal work has been completed, and providing copies of key documents. Too often, clients are unhappy with bills because either they were not informed of progress or they were unaware of just how much work the solicitor has undertaken for them.

IMPLEMENTING YOUR PLAN

Developing an action plan

20.23   You have established your objectives and overall marketing strategy and the sections above should have provided you with a number of ideas about how to implement that strategy. You now need to prepare a short, clear, task-oriented action plan – assigning the names of the responsible individuals and the target dates by which the tasks will be completed.

The action plan will achieve a number of things:

- ensure you select those activities which will help you achieve your objectives;

- ensure you assign priorities to those actions;

- ensure you are realistic about what can be achieved with the human and financial resources you have available;

- communicate to everyone in the probate team (and in the wider firm) exactly what is planned and their role and responsibilities;

- help you monitor progress.

An example extract of a suitable action plan for a probate department is shown below:

Sol. 1   Jan   Analyse past information about sources of work

Sol. 1   Jan.   Analyse past information about nature/types of client

Sol. 2   Jan.   Talk to 10 intermediaries to ask them for their views on the services provided by the firm

Sol. 3   Jan.   Attend two meetings with other private client practice groups in the firm to identify ways in which joint marketing can be conducted

Sol. 1   Feb.   Research a list of 30 local financial advisers

Sol. 2   Feb.   Research a list of the 20 nearest small accounting firms

Sol. 3   Feb.   Attend a meeting of the corporate and commercial group to identify 10 high net worth directors who may be interested in estate planning

Sol. 4   Feb.   Identify the main local business and consumer media and read some back copies to identify opportunities for placing articles

Sol. 1   Mar.   Prepare a checklist of the sorts of legal questions most likely to be asked by old/nursing home residents and their families

Sol. 2   Mar.   Prepare a short article for the local hospital about the issues surrounding relatives and enduring powers of attorney

Sol. 3   Mar.   Visit the three main referrers of past work

Sol. 3   Mar.   Identify two local organisations that should be targeted for networking

Agreeing a budget

20.24   In the view of the author of this chapter, the main cost in marketing probate services will be the time of the solicitors involved in the marketing. Firms often budget out-of-pocket marketing expenditure very carefully but fail even to think about how much time will be used and whether sufficient return on that time investment will be achieved.

Therefore, you need to prepare your budget in two parts. The first is the out-of-pocket expenditure and should cover items such as advertising (especially directory entries), postage for mailings, catering for events, membership and attendance of local events, the cost of entertaining people at lunches and dinners, the production of marketing materials such as leaflets and presentation aids (although many of these can be produced in-house at no cost using advanced word-processing or desk top publishing facilities) and sponsorships.

As a rule of thumb, professional firms should spend between 1 per cent and 2 per cent of their gross annual fee income on marketing and business development. Consider the overall fee income of the probate team and think about what proportion you should spend on marketing. Remember that if you have done little or no marketing in the past, you will probably need a little more cash to get you started in the first year than in subsequent years.

The second and more important part of your budget is agreeing how much time each fee earner and support person will spend on marketing each week or each month. The action list – having broken the various marketing activities down into their component tasks – might help with the estimating.

Alternatively, you can allocate a specific amount of time each week or month for each fee earner to spend marketing and selling. You may need to adjust your time recording system to capture and report on non-chargeable time spent on marketing. One of the main reasons why solicitors (particularly non-partners) do not do marketing is because they feel they only receive recognition and reward for chargeable time.

Monitoring the results

20.25 After an initial burst of enthusiasm, many law firm marketing initiatives flounder and fade away. This is often because there are no mechanisms for:

- monitoring what is happening (and taking action to ensure that it does); and

- feeding back the results and success stories to keep motivation high.

You need to monitor two parts of your marketing – the process and the results. In the early days there may be few results (it is likely to take a few months before any results materialise) so you must monitor the process. You can use the action plan to tick off what actions have been completed. You can review the amount of non-chargeable time being spent by various solicitors. You can count how many events are attended, how many mailings are issued, how many press releases or articles are produced and so on.

Monitoring the results may require some changes to your internal systems. You need to be able to monitor additional work from existing clients or referrers and to pinpoint enquiries and work as a direct result of each marketing activity. Logging calls, enquiries, meetings, instructions, income or the amount of press coverage are all valid ways to measure the success of marketing.

However, at the end of the day the only true measure will be whether the marketing activity delivers the objectives which you set at the beginning of your planning process. That is why it is so important that you spend time ensuring that the objectives are clear and measurable at the outset.

The marketing planning process is summarised below:

Step 1   Analysing your present situation

- current work, clients and sources;

- skills, staff and services;

- the market;

- pulling your analysis together.

Step 2   Deciding what you want to achieve

- setting objectives;

- selecting targets.

Step 3   Agreeing a strategy

- position in market;

- packaging the product and the people;

- pricing;

- promotions and internal marketing;

- process and physical evidence.

Step 4   Implementing your plan

- developing an action plan;

- agreeing a budget;

- monitoring the results.

SOME CASE STUDIES

20.26   The following case studies originally appeared in an article by the author of this chapter in [1997] *Gazette,* 11 June, 21.

Cole & Cole

20.27   Cole & Cole is a 31-partner Thames Valley firm with offices in Oxford and Reading. Heather Redman is the senior solicitor in charge of the four-strong probate team within the private client department. She says 'The safe full of wills is no longer a guarantee of probate work. The increasing mobility of people means that if they have moved away they will simply request the will to be transferred. This means that initiatives such as Make a Will Week and WillAid, in which we have participated in the past, need to be very carefully assessed.'

However, she is keen to point out that having analysed the source of probate work over the years it mostly comes from the firm's existing clients. An interesting discovery was that work from intermediaries was mostly from accountants – despite concerns about accountants trying to lure this work away from the legal profession.

An early marketing exercise for Heather was in segmenting her market – looking at the different types of clients and referrers and building marketing programmes that suited the needs of each segment specifically. Separating out the high net worth individuals (e.g. directors at commercial clients, agricultural clients, etc.) with high value estates and more complicated will, tax and trust requirements from the lower value clients was an important breakthrough. A close liaison between those doing lifetime tax planning and others concentrating on probate matters was necessary.

Another important distinction was between marketing to existing clients and to those without prior contact with the firm. Developing programmes to reach existing clients of the firm – through articles in the firm's tax and commercial newsletters, preparing a number of Plain English packages to help clients when considering enduring powers of attorney, etc., using the databases in the residential conveyancing and family departments, raising awareness internally of the services available and 'cross-selling' – is the cornerstone of her marketing success. Heather also recalls an exercise aimed at one of the intermediary segments: 'We invited the senior staff from local residential and nursing homes to attend an informal seminar designed to brief them on the range of questions – wills, enduring powers of attorney, living wills, etc. – that their residents were likely to ask.' As well as establishing important referrer relationships the seminars helped Heather's team to learn more about their clients' needs and perceptions – market research is a vitally important aspect of any marketing programme.

Mundays

20.28 The experiences of Mehboob Dharamsi, private client partner at the 14-partner practice Mundays in Esher supports Heather's views. He says 'We used an innovative advertising campaign immediately after the election to raise awareness of possible IHT changes and we have presented talks to nursing homes and elderly clubs. We have developed inserts for newsletters of similar organisations and have produced a range of comprehensive guides helping people understand their duties and responsibilities as personal representatives and trustees'.

'But', he says, 'by far the most successful marketing we do is as the private client team overall which is aimed at establishing and developing relationships with a range of intermediaries – accountants, banks, agents and financial advisers – for whom we do a substantial amount of probate-related work such as sales, etc. We have a regular programme of informal and social events where we get together. We are also running workshops for intermediaries looking at case studies. But the main source of work remains others within the private client department – whether it is conveyancing, family or tax work.'

Mehboob's firm took segmentation one stage further than Cole & Cole: 'We decided to concentrate on the higher value and more complex wills and probate work which enables us to provide a higher level of personal service – visiting clients at locations and times that suit them and taking time to explore and explain different options and opportunities. These are the clients that value a quality service, a high degree of specialisation and the back-up that a firm of this size can provide.'

Kaye, Tesler & Co.

20.29   Michael Kaye, of two-partner High Street practice Kaye Tasler & Co., uses an innovative web site to target a very different segment. 'We are targeting those in the 35–50 year age group with parents who have smaller estates – there is rarely any inheritance tax. They don't want advice – they know how to gather and distribute the estate – they want a finished product in applying for the relevant grant. [He offers a grant of probate for £185 plus VAT.] The interactive web site makes them read through some explanatory material and prompts them for the information we require. This information then goes direct into our computer system so the relevant forms and documentation are produced. We state the relevant warnings and disclaimers for those with more complicated needs.'

He goes on to talk about how the market will change in the future: 'People my age ask each other for recommendations. Those at university and the younger generation think nothing of getting on-line and seeking the information they need that way. It is a fundamental attitude and buying shift. Our site has generated enquiries and probate work. More surprisingly, it has generated a lot of enquiries from the United States (which of course we cannot service). However, the USA is a little ahead of the UK in terms of internet use so we will be ready when the UK catches up. Technology means we can provide an efficient, interactive service that meets the specific needs of our target clients. The internet environment means that the small firms like mine are on an even playing field with the largest firms in the country.'

PART FIVE

Further Information

This Part contains information on a range of topics related to probate work which it is hoped will be of interest and assistance to practitioners.

Chapter 21

Warnings

PINK CARD – WARNINGS ABOUT UNDERTAKINGS

21.1 This is the slightly edited text of the Pink Card produced by the Law Society's Professional Ethics Division and the Solicitors Indemnity Fund (SIF) in May 1993 to remind practitioners of the pitfalls involved in giving undertakings and to encourage good practice. If undertakings go wrong, it can cost the profession money through claims to SIF, as well as causing difficulties to the individuals involved. Most undertakings in probate work will probably relate to sales of estate property, but avoid being trapped by loose wording or otherwise into giving an undertaking, for example, to a bank, to repay PR clients' loans for the payment of IHT.

WARNING ON UNDERTAKINGS

Cost to the profession

The giving of sloppy or negligent undertakings is a considerable drain on the Solicitors Indemnity Fund and the Compensation Fund. SIF estimate that such undertakings cost in excess of £5 million per annum. However, many undertakings may result in a liability within the deductible (i.e. excess) – exposing solicitors to considerable personal liability. Your work is made easier because people know they can rely on a solicitor's undertaking. However, it can be a two-edged sword. The wide and routine use of undertakings can result in a lack of care. The profession can no longer afford to underwrite the bill!

Remember – there is no obligation on a solicitor to give an undertaking, even to assist the progress of a client's matter.

Financial guarantees

Think twice before standing guarantor for a client – you could be personally liable for a substantial sum. There can be cases where SIF provides no cover if an undertaking is given which amounts to a bare guarantee of the financial obligations of a client or third party. Moreover, you would have no cover from SIF if you give an undertaking to a lender to repay money which you have borrowed and which you then re-lend to a client who subsequently defaults.

Be **SMART** when giving undertakings – make sure they are:

- **S Specific**

Undertakings should refer to a particular task or action which has been clearly identified and defined. Do not give general or open-ended undertakings, such as an undertaking to discharge 'all outstanding mortgages on a property' or the 'usual undertaking'. Make sure that any undertaking to pay monies out of a fund is qualified by the proviso that the fund comes into your hands, and that it is sufficient.

- **M Measurable**

Undertakings should include agreed measures or steps which are understood by both parties and can easily be monitored or checked, so that there can be no dispute as to whether an undertaking has been fully discharged. If an undertaking involves the payment of a sum of money, make sure the amount is clear or that it is easy to calculate. Ambiguous undertakings will be construed in favour of the recipient.

- **A Agreed**

Undertakings should be expressly agreed by both the person giving and the person receiving them and should be confirmed in writing. They may be given orally or in writing and *need not necessarily include the word 'undertake'* – beware of inadvertent undertakings.

- **R Realistic**

Undertakings should be achievable. Before giving an undertaking consider carefully whether you will be able to implement it. If any events must happen before you will be able to implement your undertaking, it is good practice to spell out those events on the face of the undertaking. An undertaking is still binding even if it is to do something outside your control. As you give the undertaking – you can stay in control.

- **T   Timed**

Undertakings should indicate when, or on the happening of which event, they will be implemented. In the absence of an express term, there is an implied term that an undertaking will be performed within a reasonable time, having regard to its nature.

General points

Costs

- Don't ask other solicitors to provide an undertaking in terms you wouldn't give yourself. This applies particularly to undertakings as to costs: it is unfair to expect another solicitor to give an open-ended undertaking to pay your costs. Be prepared to give an upper limit or agree a basis of charging.

- An undertaking to pay another party's costs is generally discharged if the matter does not proceed to completion. If you intend some other arrangement, make this clear.

Conveyancing, property and succession

- The Law Society's formula for exchange of contracts and its Code for Completion by Post contain certain undertakings. Are you sure that you and your staff really know what undertakings they are giving in a normal conveyancing transaction?

- Make sure that each of your replies to requisitions on title concerning mortgages specifies exactly which mortgages or charges you intend to discharge. Vague replies will probably result in you being liable to discharge all charges – whether you know of them or not.

- Do not give unconditional undertakings without sufficient enquiry into the amount owed on prior charges - don't rely on what your client tells you.

- If your ability to comply with an undertaking depends upon action to be taken by another solicitor, make sure that he or she will be able to comply, e.g. by obtaining an undertaking to a similar effect.

- Beware of bank 'standard form' undertakings – they sometimes go beyond what is in your control – it may be necessary to amend them.

Good management

- Principals are responsible for undertakings given by staff. Clear guidance should be given to staff, specifying those permitted to give undertakings and prescribing the manner in which they can be given. Find out how safe you are by doing an 'undertaking audit' – ask staff to check files for undischarged undertakings. Note how many have been given in a sloppy or negligent manner and calculate the size of the potential claims if things go wrong. Then introduce a system to put things right. This might be to:

  - draw up standard undertakings for use, where possible, by all fee earners, with any deviation from the norm to be authorised by a partner;
  - have all undertakings checked by another fee earner prior to being given;
  - confirm all telephone undertakings (given or received) in writing;
  - make sure that undertakings are not overlooked by:
  - copying undertakings and attaching them to the file;
  - indicating on the file cover, using coloured labels, that an undertaking has been given and its date.

The Guide to the Professional Conduct of Solicitors 1996 has a chapter about undertakings (Chapter 18) which contains useful guidance – please read it!

BE SMART!

GREEN CARD – WARNINGS ABOUT PROPERTY FRAUD

21.2   The text of the Green Card is now included in *The Guide to the Professional Conduct of Solicitors 1996* as Annex 25.9. It is designed to help practitioners spot and avoid involvement in fraud. Although the warning is primarily directed to conveyancing transactions, it is important for probate practitioners to be familiar with the content since many estates involve the sale of properties.

Warning signs of property fraud include:

- **Fraudulent buyer or fictitious solicitors** – especially if the buyer is introduced to your practice by a third party (for example a broker or estate agent) who is not well known to you. Beware of clients whom you never meet and solicitors not known to you.

- **Unusual instructions** – for example a solicitor being instructed by the seller to remit the net proceeds of sale to anyone other than the seller.

- **Misrepresentation of the purchase price** – ensure that the true cash price actually to be paid is stated as the consideration in the contract and transfer and is identical to the price shown in the mortgage instructions and in the report on title to the lender.

- **A deposit or any part of the purchase price paid direct** – a deposit, or the difference between the mortgage advance and the price, paid direct, or said to be paid direct, to the seller.

- **Incomplete contract documentation** – contract documents not fully completed by the seller's representative, i.e. dates missing or the identity of the parties not fully described or financial details not fully stated.

- **Changes in the purchase price** – adjustments to the purchase price, particularly in high percentage mortgage cases, or allowances off the purchase price, for example, for works to be carried out.

- **Unusual transactions** – transactions which do not follow the normal course or the usual pattern of events:
  - client with current mortgage on two or more properties;
  - client using alias;
  - client buying several properties from the same person or two or more persons using the same solicitor;
  - client reselling property at a substantial profit, for which no explanation has been provided.

If you have any suspicions that a transaction is fraudulent, take the steps set out on the Green Card (e.g. question your client, check that the true price is included on all documentation).

Any failure to observe the signs and to take the appropriate steps may be used in court as evidence against you if you and your client are prosecuted, or if you are sued for negligence.

Further guidance can be obtained from the Law Society's Practice Advice Service.

Blue card – Warning on Money Laundering

21.3 The text of the Blue Card Warning on Money Laundering is now included in *The Guide to the Professional Conduct of Solicitors 1996* as Annex 16D. In rare cases, funds in an estate or funds from the deceased's investments may be the product of money laundering. As with property fraud, the issue is more likely to arise in conveyancing work, but again it is important that probate practitioners are familiar with the content. More information about money laundering can be obtained from the address given at the end of this chapter. (See also Chapter 6.)

Signs to watch out for include:

- unusual settlement requests, e.g. cash or third party cheque;

- unusual instructions, e.g. a client with no discernible reason for using the firm's services;

- large sums of cash;

- a secretive client;

- suspect territory, i.e. an introduction from a third party based in a country where drug trafficking is prevalent.

Other training and reference materials can be obtained from:

The Joint Money Laundering Steering Group
Information Transfer Ltd
Burleigh House
15 New Market Road
Cambridge CB5 8EG
Tel: 01223 312227
Fax: 01223 327017

An article on money laundering by Rowen Bosworth-Davies appeared in [1994] *Solicitors Journal,* 24 June, and a series of articles by Leonard Jason-Lloyd appeared in [1995] *New Law Journal* 17 February, 219 and 24 February, 278.

Chapter 22

High street banks' charges for estate administration

22.1 This chapter gives a summary of what are understood to be the major high street banks' 1999 charges for estate administration. Practitioners are advised to confirm details and obtain fuller information from the bank concerned where necessary. Leaflets advertising banks' executorship services are available and these usually give details of definitions, conditions and any right reserved to make additional charge over and above the standard fees.

BARCLAYS BANK

Setting up and responsibility fee (based on the gross value of the estate):

£500 plus:

on the first £250,000	2.5%
on the excess over £250,000	1.5%

Activity fee:

£265 for every relevant beneficiary

£50 for every asset

MIDLAND BANK

Administration fee (based on the gross value of the estate):

For a simple case:

on the first £250,000	4%
on the excess over £250,000	1%

369

For an intermediary case:

on the first £250,000	5%
on the excess over £250,000	1%

For a complex case:

on the first £250,000	6%
on the excess over £250,000	1%

LLOYDS BANK

Acceptance and responsibility fee (based on the gross value of the estate, excluding joint property):

on the first £500,000	3%
on the remainder	1.5%

There is a **minimum charge** of £1,000.

There is a service fee which is unit based and depends on the number of assets. The unit basis of charging for each asset is £19.00 for each unit. In general each asset is charged at five units and each liability at three units. Quoted investments are charged at 1.5 units.

NATWEST

Administration fee (charged on the gross value of the estate and normally payable on issue of a grant of representation):

on the first £300,000	3.5%
on the excess over £300,000	2.5%

Chapter 23

Disasters and major accidents

Sources of Help and Information

Appeals

23.1 There are chapters on appeals and fundraising in *Charities: Law and Practice* by Elizabeth Cairns published by Sweet & Maxwell.

The Red Cross has developed its own Disaster Appeal Scheme. This is designed to provide a set of procedures and mechanisms local authorities (and appropriate major institutions) can adopt to establish an appeal fund quickly and correctly. Contact the British Red Cross, 9 Grosvenor Crescent, London SW1X 7EJ, 0171 235 5454.

The Law Society's Multi-Party Action Co-ordination Service

23.2 This was established in 1987 after the Zeebrugge ferry disaster. The Service links solicitors' firms instructed in multi-party actions to enable them to share information and work together.

The Service also helps by providing facilities for solicitors to meet and discuss common issues at a central location.

The Service is available to members of the public who may be directly or indirectly involved in an action and who want to establish their legal rights. In such cases details of firms which have been instructed and which have contact with the Service, together with details of other recognised specialists, are given.

The Service is run by the Law Society's Practice Advice Service (address in Chapter 30).

'Coping with a Major Personal Crisis': Australian Leaflet

23.3 The following pages reproduce, unedited, materials originally published as a leaflet in Australia, compiled by the Prince Henry's Hospital Community Outreach Service, Victoria, Australia, by Dr Paul Valent, Dr Ellen Berah and Dr Julie Jones. Several bodies in the UK have reproduced this information, including Dorset Social Services and CRUSE. The CRUSE version is the one we have reproduced.

Coping with a Major Personal Crisis

Someone close to you may have died. You may have been injured yourself or you may have witnessed the death and injury of others. Your experience was a very personal one but this leaflet will help you to know how others have reacted to similar situations. It will also show how you can help normal healing to occur and to avoid some pitfalls.

Normal feelings and emotions always experienced

FEAR	– of damage to yourself and those you love.
	– of being left alone, of having to leave loved ones.
	– of breaking down or 'losing control'.
	– of a similar event happening again.
HELPLESSNESS	– crises show up human powerlessness, as well as strength.
SADNESS	– for deaths, injuries and losses of every kind.
LONGING	– for all that has gone.
GUILT	– for being better off than others, i.e. being alive, not injured, having things.
	– regrets for things not done.
SHAME	– for having been exposed as helpless, 'emotional' and needing others.
	– for not having reacted as one would have wished.

372

ANGER   – at what has happened, at whoever caused it or allowed it to happen.
– at the injustice and senselessness of it all.
– at the shame and the indignities.
– at the lack of understanding of others, and their inefficiencies.
– WHY ME?

MEMORIES   – of feelings, of loss or of love for the other people in your life who have been injured or died.

LET DOWN   – disappointment for all the plans that cannot be fulfilled.

HOPE   – for the future, for better times.

Everyone has these feelings after a disaster and they are normal. Nature heals through allowing their expression. They usually last only a short period at any one time and can be controlled in an emergency. Experience has shown that they may be particularly strong if many people died, if their deaths were sudden or violent or if no body was recovered.

Feelings do not lead to loss of control of the mind, but blocking them may lead to nervous and physical problems. Do remember crying can give relief.

Physical and mental sensations

You may feel bodily sensations with or without the feelings described. Sometimes they are due to the crisis, even if they develop many months after the event.

Some common sensations are tiredness, sleeplessness, bad dreams, fuzziness of the mind including loss of memory and concentration, dizziness, palpitations, shakes, difficulty in breathing, choking in the throat and chest, nausea, diarrhoea, muscular tension which may lead to pain, e.g. headaches, neck and backaches, dragging in the womb, menstrual disorders, change in sexual interest.

Family and social relationships

New friendships and group bonds may come into being. On the other hand, strains in relationships may appear. The good feelings in giving and receiving may be replaced by conflict. You may feel that too little or the wrong things are offered, or that you cannot give as much as is expected. Accidents are more frequent after severe stresses. Alcohol and drug intake may increase due to the extra tensions.

The following may make the event easier to bear:

NUMBNESS   Your mind may allow the misfortune to be felt only slowly. At first you may feel numb. The event may seem unreal, like a dream, something that has not really happened. People often see this wrongly either as 'being strong' or 'uncaring'.

ACTIVITY   Be active. Helping others may give some relief. However, over-activity is detrimental if it diverts attention from the help you need for yourself.

REALITY   Confronting the reality, e.g. attending funerals, inspecting losses, recalling memories, returning to the scene, will help you to come to terms with the event.

GOING OVER THE EVENT   As you allow the disaster more into your mind, there is a need to think about it, to talk about it, and at night to dream about it over and over again. Children play and draw about the event.

SUPPORT   It can be a relief to receive other people's physical and emotional support. Do not reject it. Sharing with others who have had similar experiences can help.

PRIVACY   In order to deal with feelings, you may find it necessary at times to be alone, or just with family and close friends.

Healing

Activity and numbness (blocking of feelings) may be overused and may delay your healing. Remember that the pain of the wound leads to healing. You may even come out wiser and stronger.

Some Do's and Don'ts

DON'T bottle up feelings.

DON'T avoid talking about what happened.

DO take every opportunity to review the experience.

DO allow yourself to be part of a group of people who care.

DON'T expect the memories to go away – the feelings will stay with you for a long time to come.

DON'T forget that children experience similar feelings.

DO take time out to sleep, rest, think and be with your close family and friends.

DO express your needs clearly and honestly to family, friends and officials.

DO try to keep your life as normal as possible after the acute grief.

DO let children talk about their emotions and express themselves in games and drawings.

DO send your children back to school and let them keep up with their activities.

DO drive more carefully.

DO be more careful around the home.

Warning: Accidents are more common after severe stresses.

When to seek professional help

1.   If you feel you cannot handle intense feelings or bodily sensations.

     If you feel that your emotions are not falling into place over a period of time and you feel chronic tension, confusion, emptiness or exhaustion.

375

If you continue to have physical symptoms.

2. If after a month you continue to feel numb and empty and do not have the appropriate feelings described.

   If you have to keep active in order not to feel.

3. If you continue to have nightmares and poor sleep.

4. If you have no person or group with whom to share your emotions and you feel the need to do so.

5. If your relationships seem to be suffering badly, or sexual problems develop.

6. If you have accidents.

7. If you continue to smoke, drink or take drugs to excess since the event.

8. If your work performance suffers.

9. If you note those around you are particularly vulnerable or are not healing satisfactorily.

10. If as a helper you are suffering 'exhaustion'.

Do remember that you are basically the same person as you were before the event.

Do remember that there is a light at the end of the tunnel.

Do remember that if you suffer too much or too long help is available.

Where to find help

- Your family doctor.
- The Social Services Department of your local council.

- Cruse Bereavement Care
  126 Sheen Road
  Richmond
  Surrey TW9 1UR
  Tel: 0181 940 4818

  Bereavement Line: 0181 332 7227

- Local representatives of:

  • British Red Cross

  • Relate

  • Samaritans

Your Citizens Advice Bureau will have the address of these and other voluntary organisations that can help you.

Chapter 24

CREST

INTRODUCTION

24.1 Since July 1996 the CREST system has provided electronic settlement in shares and other corporate securities in the UK and Ireland. The system maintains electronic records of holdings and the credit available to make payments. It receives and validates electronic instructions for making securities transfers or payments. It checks that the buyer and seller have given the same instructions for the settlement of the transaction and on the settlement date CREST checks that the seller has sufficient stock and the buyer sufficient credit available to cover the transaction. Thereupon simultaneous instructions to transfer legal ownership of the security and to make payment are issued through the system to effect the transaction.

The institution of CREST has coincided with increased speed of settlement. At present trades are settled on the London Stock Exchange on T+5, that is settlement must be transacted within five days of the trade. The period between trade and settlement is likely to be reduced further to three days as in most other countries in the near future.

The CREST system itself does not create difficulties for solicitors: the shorter settlement periods do. In particular it may be difficult to meet the deadline if a client's assets are held as physical share certificates. It is possible to reach arrangements with brokers for longer settlement but that is likely to incur higher charges.

As a result solicitors are being encouraged by brokers to dematerialise securities and to transfer them to their nominee companies to facilitate transactions. Solicitors will need to consider the advantages and disadvantages for their client and themselves of following that advice.

General guidance on various aspects of CREST appears regularly in the *Gazette*. The following article appeared in the *Gazette* in June 1998 and deals with the particular question of the security of assets deposited in a broker's nominated company.

USE OF STOCKBROKERS' NOMINEE COMPANIES

24.2 As one of its initiatives, the Law Society's Financial and Investment Services Working Party has given detailed consideration to the use of stockbrokers' nominee companies by solicitors. This article sets out some of the results of that work and provides guidance to solicitors which the Working Party hopes practitioners will find useful.

Pressure on solicitors to transfer securities held by them on behalf of clients and trusts to banks' or brokers' nominee companies is intensifying. Settlement periods have been reduced to five days, and are likely to be further reduced. This may create difficulties for solicitors needing to obtain authority, share certificates and payment in order to complete a transaction. Brokers maintain that to facilitate trading in future it is better for securities to be held by them in a paperless form and have drawn attention to the possible termination of the fast track service provided until now by registrars for the dematerialisation of securities into CREST holdings. Some also claim, wrongly, that the new Solicitors' Investment Business (Custody) Amendment Rules 1998, which came into force on 31 March 1998, will be difficult to comply with by those solicitors who offer custodial services themselves [see [1998] *Gazette*, 28 January, 36 – 'Custody of investments – new rules', 11 February, 30 – 'Custody rules – a practical guide' and 25 March, 31 – 'Custody of documents – common questions'].

It should be remembered that use of the CREST system is voluntary and dematerialisation may not be worth considering for the majority of small investors and trusts with few transactions. Solicitors should make their own informed decision as to the advice to be given to clients about the use of CREST and brokers' nominee companies. In a broker's nominee company the shareholder remains the beneficial owner of the shares but will probably lose voting rights, shareholders' concessions and communications from the company. If a client should wish to retain share certificates, it may be possible for solicitors to reach an agreement with their brokers for settlements beyond the normal five days and to deal up to Transaction +25 to allow sufficient time for delivery and to avoid penalties for late delivery. However, CRESTCo, which operates the system, may impose additional charges for settlements beyond T+5. Those charges could be significant and will either have to be borne by the broker or passed on to the client. In effect they will be an additional cost for paper settlement and solicitors should make clients aware of any penalty arising.

Some firms of solicitors have established their own nominee companies providing ease of transactions without losing the valuable contact with their client. For, once the custody function has been passed to a stockbroker's nominee, the future role of the solicitor in the client's personal affairs may be substantially diminished. An article has appeared in the *Gazette* on the topic of solicitors setting up and running their own nominee companies [1998] *Gazette*, 13 May, 26 – 'The full service'. For those solicitors who do decide to recommend to clients and trusts that they should transfer assets to a broker's nominee company, there are a number of factors which they may need to consider.

The primary concern must be to ensure that clients, whether individuals or trusts, are fully aware of the implications of the use of a nominee company to hold their securities and give consent to the transfer of their assets. Where the firm appoints a third party custodian, for example, a stockbroker or the stockbroker's nominee, the firm must exercise due skill, care and diligence in their selection and appointment and must comply with the relevant new Custody Rules. There may be occasions when a client chooses to appoint a broker without consulting the solicitor. In that case, the firm must agree with the broker in writing any consequential arrangements, for example, for settlement.

Solicitors need to be able to satisfy themselves that a broker's nominee is secure, that liability will lie with the broker in the event of default or fraud and will not revert to the solicitor. To that end it would be appropriate for solicitors to check the adequacy of a broker's indemnity insurance arrangements. Unlike solicitors there is no absolute requirement for brokers to carry indemnity insurance and the level of cover of individual brokers varies. Some of the larger brokers carry up to £20 million for each claim in addition to the Investors' Compensation Scheme and in recent years brokers have become more willing to provide information about their indemnity cover. Client literature will often provide details of the amount of cover carried and compensation arrangements. Remember that brokers are regulated by the Securities and Futures Authority at present and will be regulated by the Financial Services Authority in the future. Their regulatory regimes should provide considerable comfort for solicitors and their clients.

The Law Society has reviewed the standard Securities and Futures Industry indemnity policy which is provided by C.E. Heath. A legal opinion has been obtained on the policy which indicates that remaining concerns over some of the finer grounds for excluding claims are not so significant as to undermine fundamentally the protection of solicitors and their clients. It should, therefore, be relatively straightforward for a solicitor on first contact with a broker to enquire as to whether they have appropriate insurance cover, their insurers, the amount of cover and any limitations or exclusions as to liability. The Law Society understands that the C.E. Heath policy is used by two-thirds of brokers and has been liaising with APCIMS (the Association of Private Client Investment Managers and Stockbrokers) with a view to persuading its members to be more forthcoming when faced by such requests from solicitors. One result of that contact is the inclusion at clause 17 in the model agreement annexed to this article of an undertaking by the broker to provide details of its indemnity insurance policy on request. The Law Society considers this to be a significant advance as only a few years ago some brokers were refusing to divulge their indemnity cover.

Solicitors are urged to review the terms of the broker's agreement and any supporting literature. This should help to establish the respective duties of the broker and the client and the responsibility of a broker for any default of its nominee company. Annexed are the terms of a broker's nominee and safe custody service agreement which the Law Society has discussed with a leading firm of private client brokers and with APCIMS with a view to providing a model form of agreement. In the light of Law Society comments, the form of the agreement has been revised substantially and is now in a form which the Law Society considers to be both comprehensible in language and as offering reasonable protection for clients and their solicitors.

The Law Society wishes to draw solicitors' attention to some of the provisions in the agreement. The agreement provides for the payment of income from the client's assets to be paid to the client only quarterly unless other dates have been agreed with the broker. The solicitor may wish to discuss the best options for the client and to agree, if appropriate, monthly or fortnightly instead of quarterly payments. It is a question of balancing the possible cost against the benefit to the client. Solicitors may also wish to establish the position with regard to the payment of interest on dividend income received between payments to clients. Brokers are required to pay interest on monies held unless there is an agreement between the broker and the client not to pay interest. This may be covered by a provision in the broker's agreement as is suggested in the model. Similarly the solicitor/client may wish to come to a specific agreement as to the timing of the production of the consolidated tax certificate by the brokers.

It would be helpful for solicitors to familiarise themselves with the provisions of the model agreement. General points of which solicitors should be aware are that the agreement:

- specifies that the broker's nominee company is operated solely for the holding of clients' securities;

- guarantees that clients' assets are held separately from those of the brokers;

- indicates whether the client's securities are pooled with those of other clients in an undesignated nominee or are differentiated from other clients in an designated nominee: in the case of undesignated nominees solicitors should explain to clients that their investments will be registered in the same name as those of other clients, that they may be used with those of other clients to settle transactions, and that one client's investments may not be identifiable immediately which could cause delays in recovering assets in the event of insolvency;

- ensures that regular statements of a client's holdings will be provided but requires that these should be checked by the client. Brokers should identify any changes from previous statements as a matter of routine;

- specifies the basis upon which instructions to the broker for dealings in the securities can be made;

- indicates that, although the client remains the beneficial owner of the securities, some shareholder benefits may be unavailable to the investor;

- draws attention to the fact that clients have recourse to the Investors' Compensation Scheme.

The form of the agreement annexed to this article is intended only as a model. It is likely that individual brokers will wish to incorporate their own particular provisions in their agreement. It would, therefore, be worthwhile for solicitors to identify those variations and to give further consideration to them. The Law Society would certainly advise solicitors that they should not be party to an agreement which will provide the client with a standard of protection and indemnity cover inferior to that given in the model agreement.

The Law Society is grateful to APCIMS for its assistance in the drafting of the model form of agreement and for presenting it to its constituent members with a recommendation for its adoption or the incorporation of similar provisions in existing agreements across the industry. The Law Society now has good contacts with APCIMS enabling future developments affecting investments to be discussed for the benefit of our mutual clients and to keep the use of nominee companies under review.

Model nominee and safe custody agreement

24.3 *Safe custody service*

1. All securities accepted by us [insert name of firm] for this service are registered in the name of an eligible nominee company as defined by SFA rules or that of our overseas agents or their nominees ([SFA] approved banks, depositories or eligible custodians) hereinafter referred to as the firm's eligible custodian.

Different methods of holding investments

2 (i) UK registered securities may be held in dematerialised form in the CREST system and the firm's eligible custodian is bound to comply with the rules of that system.

   (ii) UK government securities may be held in the Central Gilts Office and the firm's eligible custodian is bound to comply with the requirements of that system.

   (iii) Non-UK securities may be held in an approved clearing house. The settlement, legal and regulatory requirements which apply to those securities and the clearing house may be different from those which apply in the UK.

   (iv) All certificates, bearer instruments and other documents of title will be held by us or our overseas agents or by a bank in the United Kingdom, in segregated accounts maintained solely for clients' securities.

Lien

3. All securities held in this safe custody service will remain free of any lien, claim, right of retention, or any right of sale, against any liability on our account. We shall, however, have the right to withhold delivery from this service or realise any security in the event that you fail to pay any amount due to us in settlement of any transaction including commission or any other fees or charges due to us. [It should be noted that this clause would not apply in Scotland and therefore an alternative clause may be required if one of the parties to the agreement is based in Scotland.]

[Designated investments] [Undesignated investments]

4. Our Nominee and Safe Custody System is [undesignated] [designated] and the record of your securities is held by us electronically. [Undesignated investments are pooled and, accordingly your securities may not be identifiable by separate certificates, other physical documents of title or equivalent electronic record of securities held by eligible custodians.] [Investments registered in the name of the firm's eligible custodian with a designation individual to you will be identifiable as separate from the investment of other clients.]

Acceptance of responsibility

5. We accept responsibility for all securities registered in the name of the firm's eligible custodian an eligible nominee company as defined by SFA rules, but not in the event of a default for those held by eligible custodians, save where any loss arises from fraud, wilful default or negligence on our part. Accordingly in the event of an unreconcilable shortfall this would be shared by you on a pro rata basis.

Dividends and payments

6. We shall be responsible for claiming and receiving dividends, interest payments and, subject to clause 9 below, other rights accruing to you. [It may be necessary to provide for a situation where a company does not allow a partial election for a corporate action in respect of undesignated nominees.]

Reinvestment

7. Unless you have elected to reinvest your income it will be disbursed electronically at regular quarterly intervals, or on such dates as are mutually agreed, to the bank account nominated by you at the end of this Agreement. **[No interest will, however, be paid on income accruing during the periods between such payments.]** [Interest will be paid on income accruing during the periods between such payments.] Each income payment will be accompanied by a statement of account. Consolidated tax certificates will normally be issued annually as soon as practical following the Tax Year End.

Any income due to you on securities held abroad or from an overseas entity, is not payable by us [into customer/dividend collection or other specified account] until received and converted into your reference currency.

Issue of statements

8. Regular statements showing the securities held for your account will be forwarded to you in accordance with the rules of the SFA. You are requested to check this statement and [to notify us of any errors that it may contain] [discuss any discrepancies between the statement and your own records with the firm].

Scope of facilities

9. We [do not] [do] normally provide facilities in any of the following matters. Accordingly users of this service may lose some of these benefits:

[(i) scrip in lieu of dividends;]

[(ii) shareholders report and accounts and other material issued by the entities for which we are providing nominee facilities;]

[(iii) voting rights;+]

[(iv) shareholders concessions;*]

[Notes to 9 above

+ we may exceptionally and at our discretion contact you in relation to voting rights
* shareholders concessions are not normally extended to nominee companies. Shareholdings must remain in your own name if you wish to continue receiving such concessions]

10(a) Please note, **discretionary clients excepted**, that as regards investments, which we are holding on your behalf, we [shall not] [shall] be responsible for:

[(i) taking up any rights;]

[(ii) exercising any conversion or subscription rights;]

[(iii) dealing with takeovers or other offers or capital re-organisations;]

[unless you respond to our advice on these matters within the time stated.]

[(b) We reserve the right to use our discretion in this respect when it appears advantageous to you. Such decisions will be taken in our absolute discretion based on the circumstances prevailing at the time they are made and we cannot be held responsible for subsequent events. They will normally be made [three to five business days] prior to the action date and will vary according to the location of the relevant agent with whom documentation is to be lodged.

Transfers

11. This Agreement provides authority for us to transfer securities from your account to meet sales effected for your account, acceptance of offers or other matters covered by this Agreement. We will normally accept telephonic or facsimile instructions to transfer securities held by us into your own name, but require written instructions for any other arrangements. In the case of trusts, we can only accept the instructions from all of the trustees and cannot take instructions from beneficiaries, settlors, etc.

Taxation

12. You confirm that your residence for tax purposes is as set out in the address overleaf and recorded on our books. If this is incorrect, please notify us, providing all necessary information. If you are non-resident and wish to receive income free of UK tax on qualifying investments you should ask your normal contact at [insert name of firm] to supply the appropriate Inland Revenue form for completion and return to us. We cannot be held responsible for any UK tax deducted unless these formalities are completed. No tax relief can be given until the appropriate Inland Revenue forms have been completed.

Client instructions

13. [Your obligations and liabilities set out in this agreement shall, in the case of two or more persons as client, be joint and several obligations of each person. We shall be entitled to act in accordance with the instructions of any one such persons without incurring any

liability to any other such person and any one of such persons shall be able to give an effectual receipt for any security or money.]

[For trustees – We shall be entitled to act only in accordance with the instructions of all the trustees.]

Application of rules

14. Nothing in this Agreement shall prevent us from carrying out our duties in compliance with all applicable rules of the SFA and of the London Stock Exchange [or Tradepoint] [or other Recognised Investment Exchange] and all other relevant laws, rules, regulations codes and practices from time to time applicable to our obligations hereunder and to which this Agreement is hereby declared subject. Nor shall we be in breach of any of the provisions of this Agreement where such provisions are or appear to be inconsistent with our compliance with such laws, rules, regulations, codes and practices.

Disclosure of information

15. [Insert name of firm] is authorised to disclose information relating to the client and/or the client's investments to the SFA, [or the Panel of Takeovers and Mergers] and as otherwise required by law.

Severance

16. Should any part of this Agreement be held by any court of competent jurisdiction to be unenforceable or illegal or contravene any rule, regulation or by-law of any exchange or Self Regulating Organisation, the same shall be deemed to have been excluded from this Agreement from the beginning, and this Agreement shall be interpreted and enforced as though the provision had never been included.

Insurance

17. [Insert name of firm] and the firm's eligible custodian are covered against fraud and negligence by a professional indemnity insurance policy. Details of the policy are available upon request.

Indemnity

18. You will indemnify us and our agents from and against any and all claims, proceedings, damages, loss and liability made or taken against or suffered or incurred by us in our capacity as nominees or custodian hereunder (including, without limitation, any liability to taxation anywhere in the world) except in so far as the same arises as a result of our negligence or wilful default.

Charges

19. Our charges for this service will be in accordance with the published rates which are in effect at the time the charges are incurred. [A copy of our charges is attached to this Agreement.]

Termination

20(a) Our appointment hereunder will terminate in the following circumstances:

 (i) the termination of the agreement between us constituted by the Client Agreement Letter,

 (ii) upon the expiry of at least one month's written notice from us to you;

 (iii) upon the expiry of at least one month's written notice from you to us.

 (iv) immediately in writing in exceptional circumstances (for example, in the event of your bankruptcy);

 (v) immediately in the event of the loss of authorisation by the Firm's eligible custodian; or

 (vi) immediately in the event of [insert the name of the eligible custodian] being placed in liquidation or receivership.

 Any notice given pursuant to this paragraph shall be sent by post addressed to the address given [below] [overleaf] or [such other address as has been notified in writing for that purpose.]

 (b) Following termination, within a reasonable period, we shall deliver to you all records, registered documents of title, deeds and assets in respect of the securities belonging to you which are in our possession or control.

Indulgences

21. Our failure to seek redress for violations or to insist upon strict performance of any condition or provision of this Agreement or our failure to exercise any right or remedy to which we are entitled hereunder, shall not constitute a waiver thereof.

Jurisdiction

22. The terms of this Agreement shall be governed by and construed in accordance with English law and subject to the non-exclusive jurisdiction of the English Courts.

[Investors' Compensation Scheme

[23. As a private client of a firm regulated by the SFA you would receive the protection offered by the Securities Investment Board's Compensation Scheme in the event of [insert name of firm] failing. This cover extends to clients using our Nominee Service who have signed the necessary Client Agreement Letter.]

Name of account:..
(with [insert name of firm])

Existing account number(s): ....

Address:...

....

....

Postcode:..............................

I/We agree to the terms and conditions of this Agreement which augments and therefore becomes part of the terms of business or Client Agreement Letter that I/we have received or entered into with you, or which is received or entered into with you, or which is received or entered into contemporaneously with or after this Agreement.

For corporate bodies: I/We are fully authorised to sign on behalf of the account.

Signature   ....   Date:...............................

    ....   Date:...............................

[Note: for trusts – all trustees must sign this form]

Please retain a copy of this Agreement and return one copy to us in order for this arrangement to become effective.

[insert name of firm]

[Member of [London Stock Exchange/Tradepoint/other Recognised Investment Exchange]]

Regulated by The Securities and Futures Authority

Income is remitted directly to your nominated bank account detailed below (please complete)

Name of Bank/Building Society:..

Branch/Address:..

Bank/Building Society Account Name:..

Account Number:................................. Sort Code:...............................

POSTSCRIPT

24.4 Solicitors for Independent Financial Advice (SIFA), the network for solicitor independent financial advisers, has compiled a handbook on trustee investment and sponsored a trust fund initiative designed to wean solicitor trustees away from stockbrokers to what it regards as more appropriate investment vehicles such as unit trusts and investment bonds.

SIFA managing director Ian Muirhead warned in [1998] *Gazette*, 21 October, that the typical stockbroker does not have the research resources to match city fund managers. Trustees are likely to face increasing litigation from disappointed beneficiaries alleging underperformance.

Chapter 25

Advance directives and 'living wills'

INTRODUCTION

25.1 Advance directives or statements and living wills are intended to allow individuals to specify the extent and nature of the medical treatment they would or would not find acceptable should they lose capacity in the future. The term 'living will' can be confusing since such documents have no connection with ordinary wills but this term is probably too well established to change.

Gordon Ashton, in *The Elderly Client Handbook* (published by the Law Society – see Booklist, Chapter 29) considers these documents in detail. The following cases, he says, appear to support advance directives: *Airedale NHS Trust* v. *Bland* [1993] 2 W.L.R. 316, H.L. and *Re C.* [1994] 1 All E.R. 819. The courts have clarified that competent patients can authorise or refuse consent to treatments, both contemporaneously and in advance, but cannot make legally enforceable demands about specific treatments they wish to receive.

The British Medical Association (BMA) published a statement in 1992 on advance statements, revised most recently in May 1995. It stated that the BMA 'strongly supports the principle of an advance directive' and points out that 'patients have a legal right to decline specific treatment, including life prolonging treatment'. It stresses 'the significant ethical and legal difference between the concept of an advance statement and the issue of euthanasia . . . [which] is illegal' and emphasises that its conclusion on advance directives should not be seen as supporting euthanasia. This distinction was supported by the House of Lords Select Committee on Medical Ethics (HMSO, 1994, HL Paper 21–I), which commended the development of advance directives, but recommended no change in the law to permit euthanasia. The BMA has published 'Advance Statements about Medical Treatment', a Code of Practice for health professionals, together with explanatory notes as recommended by the Select Committee.

The Law Commission published a report (Law Com. No. 231: 'Mental Incapacity') in 1995, which also supports the use of advance directives, and calls for legislation in order to clarify the current common law position that an advance refusal of treatment made with capacity survives any supervening incapacity. On 13 October 1997 the Lord Chancellor, Lord Irvine of Lairg announced that he was considering a Bill to give statutory force to living wills. This was followed up by a consultation paper *Who decides? Making decisions on behalf of mentally incapacitated adults* issued by the Lord Chancellor's Department in December 1998 seeking views on the introduction of legislation based on the draft Bill in the Law Commission report. The Government has not yet announced its response to this consultation exercise.

Information on the assessment of capacity to consent to or refuse medical treatment is contained in the joint Law Society/BMA guidance *Assessment of Mental Capacity* (1995, available from the Law Society).

There is an interesting article on this subject by Anne Wilkinson of the University of Bristol in [1997] *New Law Journal,* 12 December.

The Legal Aid Board Costs Appeals Committee recently issued guidance on a point of principle (LAA 17) setting out the circumstances in which legal advice and assistance may be available in connection with living wills (see [1998] *Gazette,* 4 February, 32).

There are numerous precedents for living wills and advance directives in existence. *The Elderly Client Handbook* by Gordon R. Ashton contains one example, drafted by Denzil Lush, and others are obtainable from the Voluntary Euthanasia Society and the Terrence Higgins Trust. EAGLE (Exchange on Ageing, Law and Ethics) has published further articles on the topic. (All addresses are in Chapter 30.) Much of this information has been usefully summarised and updated in the chapter on 'Living Wills' in *Elderly Clients: A Precedents Manual* by Denzil Lush (Jordans 1996). We have reproduced the precedent from *The Elderly Client Handbook* below and are most grateful to Gordon Ashton and Denzil Lush for allowing us to do so.

Within the Law Society these matters are the responsibility of the Mental Health and Disability Committee, in the Policy Directorate (address in Chapter 30).

Living Will Precedent

25.2 THIS LIVING WILL

is made on

by me

of

born on

I WISH these instruction to be acted upon if two registered medical practitioners are of the opinion that I am no longer capable of making and communicating a treatment decision, AND that I am:

- unconscious, and it is unlikely that I shall ever regain consciousness; or

- suffering from an incurable or irreversible condition that will result in my death within a relatively short time; or

- so severely disabled, physically or mentally, that I shall be totally dependent on others for the rest of my life.

I REFUSE any medical or surgical treatment if:

- its burdens and risks outweigh its potential benefits; or

- it involves any research or experimentation which is likely to be of little or no therapeutic value to me; or

- it will needlessly prolong my life or postpone the actual moment of my death.

I CONSENT to being fed orally, and to any treatment that may:

- safeguard my dignity; or

- make me more comfortable; or

- relieve pain and suffering,

even though such treatment might unintentionally precipitate my death.

SIGNED by me

in the presence of:

Name

Address

Occupation

Chapter 26

Problems of capacity and disability

CAPACITY

26.1   Questions of capacity frequently arise in connection with the validity of a will. In cases where there is room for doubt the solicitor drafting a will should have considered the question of capacity at the time. If capacity is in question the solicitor should consult the client's medical practitioner as to the client's capacity in general and should try to have the doctor present at the time the will is signed so as to be able to give an opinion on the client's capacity at that point. In *Buckenham* v. *Dickinson* [1997] C.L.Y. 661 the court pronounced against a will where the solicitors had not followed the 'golden rule' applied in *Kenward* v. *Adams* [1975] C.L.Y. 3591 and followed in *Re Simpson* (1977) 121 S.J. 224 that a medical practitioner should be present where there are doubts as to a testator's capacity.

Denzil Lush in an article in [1996] *Gazette,* 24 January, 24 points out that capacity is not an absolute concept. It is relative to the particular transaction. Thus, the lawyer has a duty to explain to any doctor involved the test relevant to the particular activity. We have set out below a form of letter which may be adapted and used when writing to a client's general medical practitioner for a report as to mental capacity. The letter was originally prepared for the *Law Society's Elderly Client Handbook* by Gordon R. Ashton and we are most grateful to Gordon Ashton for allowing us to reproduce it. The letter assumes that the solicitor has already attended the client and received preliminary instructions but that there is a doubt as to mental capacity which may need to be resolved.

'Dear Dr_____

Our client and your patient: *Mrs A. B.*

of *[address]*

We act for your patient and are presently advising *her* in regard to the preparation of a new Will. [We have previously made several Wills for *her* the last one being some ___ years ago.] She has [only a small estate] [a fairly substantial estate] – *amplify if there are any complications.*

We seek from you a report as to the mental capacity of your patient to sign this Will. The legal test of capacity in these circumstances is whether *she* understands first, that *she* is giving *her* property to persons of *her* choice on *her* death, second, the extent of that property and third, the nature and extent of *her* obligations to relatives and others. Your report should relate specifically to these questions and you may if you wish qualify the report by stating that you do not express any further opinion with regard to the mental capacity of your patient. Legal tests of capacity vary according to the nature of the transaction, and there is no universal test of capacity. However, you may form your view on the balance of probabilities and do not need to be satisfied beyond reasonable doubt.

If the capacity of this patient tends to fluctuate please mention this in your report and we may then need to ask you to be one of the witnesses so as to confirm your view of capacity at the time of signature. You will no doubt need to attend on *her* before preparing your report and we confirm that we shall be pleased to pay your reasonable fee for such attendance and the preparation of the report. She is presently at [*her* home] and expecting you to contact *her* there.

Yours sincerely'

The Law Society and the British Medical Association have joined together to publish *Assessment of Mental Capacity: Guidance for Doctors and Lawyers* (1998, available from The Law Society) which is extremely useful reading and provides answers to many awkward questions. It sets out the specific legal tests of capacity to make particular decisions or carry out legal transactions, and explains how these relate to the medical practicalities of assessing capacity.

MIND has issued two booklets on wills and trusts to help people with mental health problems gain greater financial control of their lives. *Find Peace of Mind* is a step-by-step guide to wills. *Making Provision* is aimed at parents and carers of people with mental health problems and explains how the carers can make financial provision for such people. Both are obtainable free from Valerie Harland, MIND, 15 Broadway, London E15.

DISABILITY

26.2   One of the most difficult disabilities for wills and probate solicitors to deal with is visual impairment. The RNIB offers a visual awareness course which gives guidance on best practice for helping clients with impaired vision. A benefit of attending the course is that the RNIB's Wills and Legacies Advisory Service is then able to recommend the firm to the visually impaired.

As a result of the Disability Discrimination Act 1995, solicitors must ensure that they do not discriminate against disabled people by, for example, refusing to provide a service or providing one at a lower standard. Over the next few years, other obligations will be brought into force, which will require all service providers, including solicitors, to change the way in which their services are provided to ensure they are accessible to disabled people. In December 1996, The Law Society issued guidance to solicitors: *How to comply with the Disability Discrimination Act 1995.*

Chapter 27

Wills

BEST PRACTICE – WILLS

27.1 This guidance was approved by the Law Society's Standards and Guidance Committee and Property and Commercial Services Committee in 1991.

1. It is for clients to ensure that their wills are kept up to date and solicitors may help clients to do this by retaining in a manual or computer database (note the requirements of the Data Protection Act 1984 and forthcoming European legislation in relation to manual records and databases) the names of clients for whom they have drawn up wills in the past. Solicitors may write to these clients from time to time reminding them of the need to review a will regularly and of their firms' services.

2. The preparation of a will for a client is in the ordinary case an entire contract so that when the work is completed and the final bill is submitted, the relationship of solicitor and client may be assumed to have ended as far as will preparation is concerned. Of course, the relationship of solicitor and client may continue with that client on other matters. Where solicitors have a continuing relationship with clients, they may wish to consider agreeing with those clients whether or not the client wishes the firm to maintain a watching brief on legal changes or tax changes which might affect their will; the Society considers that it would be appropriate for a charge to be made for such a service in addition to charges for preparation of a will.

3. Without specific instructions from the client, a retainer for will preparation would not entail the solicitor in maintaining any such 'watching brief', but it is possible for a solicitor by his or her conduct to change a retainer so that a client comes to have a reasonable expectation that such a watching brief will be maintained. Solicitors would be well advised to ensure that these matters are clear between themselves and their clients.

4. Many firms store clients' wills as a free service and a courtesy to their clients. The storage of a will does not of itself create a retainer. Solicitor and client may agree otherwise.

5. In relation to wills stored by firms, should a solicitor or clerk named as executor or executrix in such a will retire, move to another practice, or die, or otherwise become unable or unwilling to act, the firm should consider writing to the testator or testatrix at the client's last known address detailing the changed circumstances. Informing clients of such internal changes to a firm is not considered to be any indication that a watching brief on matters of law has been agreed upon, but is, rather, part of the necessary changes which follow retirement or resignation, etc., of a solicitor from a firm, such as changes to the notepaper.

6. Some firms may retain large numbers of wills for clients from whom they have not heard for many years. Solicitors wishing to clarify the position in relation to these wills may wish to consider writing to a testator or testatrix at the last known address. However, even if no reply is received, such wills should never be destroyed as they remain the clients' property or the property of the clients' PRs.

[Note the interesting article by James Sunnucks in [1995] *New Law Journal* Probate Supplement, 29 September, where he points to an Australian case (*Hawkins* v. *Clayton* [1988] C.L.R. 539) which holds that a solicitor retaining a will has duty to take reasonable steps to find the executor. Also note the case of *Cancer Research Campaign* v. *Ernest Brown & Co.* [1997], S.T.C. 1425, which emphasises the importance of clarity in the terms of a solicitor's retainer.]

APPOINTMENT OF SOLICITOR–EXECUTORS

27.2 Probate registries report frequent problems with the wording of clauses appointing solicitor–executors. The clause included in *Williams on Wills*, 6th edition, p.1049 has the approval of the Principal Registry of the Family Division. The footnote usefully outlines the issues.

CLAUSES EXCLUDING LIABILITY FOR NEGLIGENCE IN RESPECT OF PROFESSIONAL EXECUTORS/ TRUSTEES

27.3   Many people feel that it is inappropriate to include in wills and settlements clauses which seek to limit a solicitor's or other professional trustee's liability, when acting as an executor or trustee, to loss or damage through fraud or dishonesty and to exclude liability for negligence. Solicitors should in any event be fully insured against their own negligence.

However, in *Armitage* v. *Nurse* [1997] 3 W.L.R. 1046, CA and *Bogg* v. *Raper*, *The Times*, 22 April 1998, CA, the Court of Appeal stated that such clauses were not contrary to public policy nor to the nature of a trust. Millett L.J. stated that although many people felt such clauses had gone too far, it would require legislation to change their validity.

Bogg v. *Raper* confirmed that a solicitor who prepares a will or settlement which appoints him or her or a partner as an executor or trustee and which then restricts or excludes liability for negligence, does not receive a benefit. The clause merely limits liability.

Whatever you may think about the correctness of such clauses in general there are clearly special cases where it would be reasonable for the trust document to exclude or restrict liability for negligence (for example assets held overseas in countries with unreliable legal systems, long-running and serious family or other disputes, continuing litigation).

STEP: STANDARD CONDITIONS FOR WILLS

27.4   On behalf of the Society of Trust and Estate Practitioners (STEP – address in Chapter 30) barrister James Kessler has prepared a set of standard administrative clauses for wills and settlements (see Booklist, Chapter 29). STEP's aim in publishing the standard provisions was to enable wills and settlements to be shortened, and to provide 'the necessary standard powers . . . in language which is lucid, contemporary and easily understood' by non-lawyers. A Practice Direction from the Principal Registry of the Probate Division dated 10 April 1995 allows wills incorporating the STEP provisions by reference to be proved in the normal way without providing the text of the provisions themselves.

GREEN FORM ADVICE AND WILLS

Responsibility

27.5 Despite the cutbacks in legal aid some people are still entitled to advice and assistance to make a will. Form GF4 gives details.

It is your responsibility as a solicitor, not the client's, to consider legal aid and whether the client is entitled.

Extract from Legal Advice and Assistance (Scope) Regulation 1989, Reg. 4(2)

27.6 4(2) Advice and assistance in the making of a will are not excluded by paragraph (1) from Part III of the Act where they are given to a client who is:

(a) aged 70 or over; or

(b) blind (or partially sighted), deaf (or hard of hearing), or dumb, or suffers from mental disorder of any description, or who is substantially and permanently handicapped by illness, injury or congenital deformity; or

(c) a parent or guardian within the meaning of section 87 of the Child Care Act 1980 of a person to whom any description in (b) applies, where the client wishes to provide in the will for that person; or

(d) the mother or father of a minor who is living with the client, where the client is not living with the minor's other parent, and the client wishes to appoint a guardian for that minor under section 4 of the Guardianship of Minors Act 1971. [Now see Children Act 1989.]

WILLS AND PROPERTY ABROAD

27.7 Some of your clients may own property abroad because of a family connection; others because more and more people are buying overseas holiday retreats or businesses. Potentially disastrous consequences can ensue if those clients are not fully advised about local laws regulating the inheritance of land and other property. In certain civil law jurisdictions, for example, children are automatically entitled to a fixed share of the estate regardless of any will to the contrary. Sometimes an English will dealing with foreign property will put the testator or testatrix's wishes into effect, but a will in accordance with the requirements of the other jurisdiction may also be needed.

A solicitor in the UK with the necessary knowledge and experience or a local lawyer in the jurisdiction should be instructed. The Law Society can help with the names of appropriately qualified lawyers (contact the International Division – address in Chapter 30).

The publications listed below may also be of interest – those dealing with conveyancing usually contain a section on wills and probate.

Property in France

Buying Residential Property in France (French Chamber of Commerce, Knightsbridge House, 197 Knightsbridge, London SW7 1RS).

Buying Property in France by W.H. Thomas (Law Society *Gazette* Practice Handbooks).

Property in Portugal

Buying Property in Portugal (Portuguese Chamber of Commerce and Industry, 4th Floor, New Bond Street House, 1–5 New Bond Street, London W1Y 9PE).

Property in Spain

Your Home in Spain (Institute of Foreign Property Owners).

WILLS PROCEDURE CHECKLIST

27.8 This checklist was compiled after discussions with the various probate registries around the country. It draws attention to common mistakes which can lead to delay in obtaining the grant and other points, certain of which are mentioned in this Handbook, which can easily be overlooked. Probate registries report difficulties in relation to the drafting of clauses appointing solicitor–executors (see para. 27.2).

The Law Society publishes a comprehensive Will Preparation Checklist, to be used while taking instructions, as an *aide–memoire* of the topics to cover and record of those instructions. The Will Preparation Checklist is available through the Law Society (address in Chapter 30).

1. Did you obtain full, clear instructions from the client?

2. Did you check the client's eligibility for Green Form: age; capacity; intention?

3. Did you check that any charity mentioned is really charitable, and the charity number and address and that the estate is likely to be solvent and all the legacies can be paid?

4. Have you explained to the client (in no particular order):

    - The pros and cons of appointing members of the family/solicitors/others as executors?

    - The implications of the clauses extending or varying the executors' general law powers and duties?

    - The impact of the general law on the will (e.g. effect of marriage)?

    - The implications of any charging clause?

    - The need for parents to appoint guardians of minor children?

    - The position of single parents under the Children Act 1989?

    - The law relating to specific, general or demonstrative legacies, where appropriate, e.g. the need to review specific legacies if the property the subject of the gift alters or is sold or destroyed?

    - The terms and effect of any residuary gifts made?

    - Whether there will be any secret or half-secret trusts?

    - Whether the will is to be mutual, i.e. not to be revoked unilaterally?

- The effect of mutual wills? (Are they appropriate for the client?)

- Whether the will incorporates any document – was that intended?

- The general law concerning the payment of tax, testamentary expenses or other liabilities (especially those items which will not be paid out of residue)?

- The tax planning consideration which affect the terms of the will, e.g. lifetime gifts within seven years of death?

- The likelihood of a claim under the Inheritance (Provision for Family and Dependants) Act 1975 and, if any, what should be done?

- About the position of a cohabitee (with and without an interest in the home)?

- The consequences for the beneficiaries if the residue is much larger (say because of an unexpected windfall) or smaller (say because a property has had to be sold to pay for care) than anticipated?

- The advisability of making an enduring powering of attorney and discussed with the client a procedure for making the will available to the attorney (to avoid problems such as accidental ademption)?

- The need to sever a joint tenancy if the client wants to make a gift of property held as beneficial joint tenant. See Postscript below.

5. Have you agreed the arrangements for valid execution of the will, and advised the client accordingly? (See Postscript below.) What is to happen about any previous wills or codicils?

6. Have you asked the client if there are any other practical or legal steps they want to consider in relation to their financial and other arrangements – writing a life insurance policy in trust, drawing up an enduring power of attorney making an advance directive or living will?

7. Was the will executed within a reasonable time? If not, have you:

- Explained to the client the implications of not executing the will i.e. intestacy or non-revocation of existing will?

- Sought instructions about new provisions, if the client is unhappy about the terms or effect of the draft will?

- Ensured that existing provisions have not been overtaken by events in the intervening period?

8. After the will has been executed, have you:

- Checked it was executed and witnessed properly by people who are neither beneficiaries nor married to beneficiaries?

- Kept a copy for your files?

- If you are holding the original, have you given a copy to the client?

- Advised on the importance of placing the will where it will be found, and telling executors and family where it is?

- Advised on the desirability of the client placing a Personal Assets Log (available from the Law Society Shop) with their papers?

- Explained to the client that it is necessary to review a will every two to five years and sooner if there is a major change of financial or personal circumstances?

- Agreed the extent of your retainer? Is the client aware that you will/will not be reminding them of the need to review their will in five years' time or in any other situation, and will/will not be notifying them about tax changes affecting provisions made?

- If partners of the firm have been appointed as executors have you a separate record of this so that the client can be approached if a partner leaves, retires or dies?

POSTSCRIPT

27.9 The case of *Carr-Glynn* v. *Frearson* [1998] 4 All E.R. 225 suggests that solicitors may be negligent if they do not prepare a notice of severance for a client where there is any doubt as to whether property is held as beneficial joint tenants or tenants in common. The case of *Esterhuizen* v. *Allied Dunbar*, *The Times*, 10 June 1998, has raised worrying questions as to the extent of a solicitor's duty with regard to execution of a will.

Longmore J. said that the process of signature and attestation of a will is not straightforward and that a testator is entitled to expect reasonable assistance without having to ask expressly for it: 'It is in my judgment not enough just to leave written instructions with the testator. In ordinary circumstances just to leave written instructions and to do no more will not only be contrary to good practice but also in my view negligent'.

He suggested the following procedure:

1. Invite the client to come into the solicitor's office to sign the will.

2. If the client does not wish to, the solicitor should ask the client if he or she would like the solicitor to attend at home to get the will signed and witnessed.

3. If the client says 'no', that is the end of the matter.

Chapter 28

The future – the work of the Probate Section

28.1   The Probate Section was launched in July 1997 by the Law Society and now has close to 2,400 members. Since many probate solicitors also deal with other work, the Section embraces a number of related areas of legal practice. It is a service aimed at all practitioners working in the areas of:

- wills and trusts;

- tax planning;

- financial planning;

- Court of Protection;

- care planning;

- estate administration.

The Section intends to give practical help to solicitors, with member benefits including a regular newsletter, low-cost local seminars, information on marketing and information technology, and an internet site. The Section is a new departure for the Law Society and will give individual solicitors the opportunity to have a direct say in deciding the nature of services provided to them. Members run the Section and set its agenda. Membership is open to all those holding a current practising certificate, who pay an annual fee.

Historically, those members of the profession practising in probate and allied areas have been quite isolated. This, coupled with the fact that probate-related practice is still profitable, is why the area was chosen to test trial the idea of sections. Generally lawyers in this field do not meet their fellow professionals to exchange ideas and information about law and practice. This lack of contact between solicitors can in part be ascribed to the nature of the work which, unlike litigation or conveyancing, presents very limited opportunities for contact with fellow professionals from different firms and in different parts of the country. Relative isolation may have also resulted in part from the perception of other solicitors as competitors. The Law Society is keen to alert solicitors to the wider picture, having undertaken research which found that most solicitors have not fully considered the threat of competition coming from outside the profession, whether from accountants, banks or unqualified legal advisers – a threat that may in fact prove to be the greatest challenge to the profession undertaking probate-related work in the next century.

One of the most important functions of the Section is to ensure that all members are made aware of new developments in law and practice, through the provision of accessible information, thus helping to equip practitioners to meet future challenges.

If you want to join the Probate Section or make enquiries about the services it offers to members please write to Sharon Miles at the Law Society, 113 Chancery Lane, London WC2A 1PL or DX 56 London/Chancery Lane.

Chapter 29

Booklist

1. Probate and Estate Administration

Butterworths Wills, Probate and Administration Service. Richard Bark-Jones (Gen. Ed.) *et al.* Looseleaf. Butterworths.

Distribution on Intestacy. Mark Halliwell.
1st ed. 1996. Sweet & Maxwell.

Executorship and Administration. Roland D'Costa.
2nd ed. 1995. Cavendish Publishing.

Inheritance Act Claims: Law and Practice. Sidney Ross.
2nd ed. 1993 with supplement 1997. Sweet & Maxwell.

Know-How for Trust and Estate Practitioners. Philippa Blake-Roberts *et al.*
1st ed. 1995. Sweet & Maxwell.

Law and Practice of Intestate Succession. Chris Sherrin and Roger Bonehill.
2nd ed. 1994. Sweet & Maxwell.

Probate and the Administration of Estates. Philip Rossdale.
2nd ed. 1996. Sweet & Maxwell.

Probate Disputes and Remedies. Dawn Goodman and Brendan Hall.
1st ed. 1997. Sweet & Maxwell.

Probate Practice and Procedure. A K Biggs and A P Rogers.
6th ed. 1998. Tolley.

Probate Practice Manual. Thomas Eggar Verrall Bowles.
Looseleaf. Sweet & Maxwell.

Ranking, Spicer and Pegler's Executorship Law, Trusts and Accounts. Tony Sherring and Michael Sladen.
24th ed. 1996. Butterworths.

Spencer Maurice's Family Provision on Death. Alexandra Mason and Marian Conroy.
7th ed. 1994. Sweet & Maxwell.

Tyler's Family Provision. R D Oughton.
3rd ed. 1997. Butterworths.

Tristram and Coote's Probate Practice. R F Yeldham *et al.* (Eds.).
28th ed. 1995. Butterworths.

Williams on Wills. C Sherrin *et al.* (Eds.).
7th ed. 1996 with 1997 supplement. Butterworths.

Williams, Mortimer and Sunnucks on Executors, Administrators and Probate. J H G Sunnocks *et al.*
17th ed. 1993 with 1996 supplement. Sweet & Maxwell.

Wills, Administration and Taxation: a Practical Guide. John Barlow *et al.*
7th ed. 1997. Sweet & Maxwell.

2. Inheritance Tax

Dymond's Capital Taxes. Roy Greenfield.
Looseleaf. Sweet & Maxwell.

Foster's Inheritance Tax. R A Wallington (Gen. Ed.) *et al.*
Looseleaf. Butterworths.

Mellows: Taxation for Executors and Trustees. Updated by Julie Anderson.
1997. Butterworths.

Post-Death Rearrangments: Practice and Precedents. Matthew Hutton.
5th ed. 1995. Sweet & Maxwell.

Practical Trusts: Law, Tax and Precedents. Peter White.
1st ed. 1994. Sweet & Maxwell.

Ray's Practical Inheritance Tax Planning. Ralph P Ray.
5th ed. 1999. Butterworths.

Tolley's Estate Planning 1999-2000.
Tolley.

Tolley's Inheritance Tax 1999-2000.
Tolley.

Tolley's UK Taxation of Trusts. Matthew Hutton and Ian Ferrier.
9th ed. 1999. Tolley.

3. Wills and Will Precedents

Brighouse's Precedents of Wills. David Endicott.
12th ed. 1997. Sweet & Maxwell.

Parker's Modern Wills Precedents. Eric Taylor (Ed.).
3rd ed. 1996. Butterworths.

Practical Will Precedents. Murray Hallam *et al.*
Looseleaf. Sweet & Maxwell.

Sweet & Maxwell's Express Wills. Digital Drafting Software.
Sweet & Maxwell.

The Will Draftsman's Handbook. Robin E Riddett.
7th ed. 1995. Sweet & Maxwell.

Theobald on the Law of Wills. J G Ross Martin and the late Professor J B Clark.
15th ed. 1993. Sweet & Maxwell.

4. Trusts and Trust Precedents

Drafting Trusts and Will Trusts. James Kessler.
3rd ed. 1997. Sweet & Maxwell.

Parker and Mellows: The Modern Law of Trusts. A J Oakley.
7th ed. 1998. Sweet & Maxwell.

Pettit: Equity and the Law of Trusts. Philip H Pettit.
8th ed. 1993. Butterworths.

Practical Trust Administration. Michael Sladen.
3rd ed. 1993. Chartered Institute of Banking.

Practical Trust Precedents. Richard Underwood *et al.*
Looseleaf. Sweet & Maxwell.

Riddall: The Law of Trusts. John G Riddall.
5th ed. 1996. Butterworths.

Underhilll and Hayton: Law Relating to Trustees. David J Hayton.
15th ed. 1995. Butterworths.

5.   Other Relevant Reading

A. General

Berry, Bailey and Schaw-Miller: Personal Insolvency - Law and Practice. Christopher
Berry *et al.*
3rd ed. 1999. Butterworths.

Change of Name. Helen Mead (Ed.).
15th ed. 1995. Sweet & Maxwell.

Child Support: A Practitioner's Guide. Wendy Mantle.
2nd ed. 1996. Sweet & Maxwell.

Cohabitants. Stephen Parker and John Dewar.
4th ed. 1995. Sweet & Maxwell.

The Elderly Client Handbook: The Law Society's Guide to Acting for Older People.
Gordon R Ashton.
1st ed. 1994. Law Society.

Elderly Clients. A Precedent Manual. Denzil Lush.
1st ed. 1996. Jordans.

Enduring Powers of Attorney. Stephen M Cretney and Denzil Lush.
4th ed. 1996. Jordans.

Law Society's Guide to Oaths and Affirmations. Robin Spon-Smith.
2nd ed. 1996. Law Society.

B. Practice Management, Costs, Client Care, etc.

Checklists for Solicitors. Alan J Juylan. (Gen. Ed.).
7th ed. 1998. Sweet & Maxwell.

Client Care. James Alexander.
1st ed. 1993. Blackstone.

Client Interviewing for Lawyers: An Analysis and Guide. Avrom Sherr.
2nd ed. 1998. Sweet & Maxwell.

Cordery on Solicitors. Anthony J Holland (Gen. Ed.).
Looseleaf. Butterworths.

Encyclopedia of Data Protection. Simon Charlton (Ed.) *et al.*
Looseleaf. Sweet & Maxwell.

Handbook of Practice Management: a Guide to Best Practice in Law Firm Management. Will Newbold.
1992. CLT Professional Publishing.

Keeping Clients: A Client Care Guide for Solicitors. Patrick Stevens.
1st ed. 1997. Law Society.

Legal Aid Handbook 1997/1998. Prepared by the Legal Aid Board.
Sweet & Maxwell.

Legal Practice Management and Quality Standards. Craig Klafter and Gordon Walker.
1st ed. 1995. Blackstone.

Managing the Law Firm. Alan Pannett.
2nd ed. 1995. Blackstone.

Practice Management Standards Kit.

All books in the kit are available separately: *The Office Procedures Manual, A Guide to Implementing the Practice Management Standards, The Assessment Guide, An Introduction to Quality Systems.*
1st ed. 1997. Law Society.

Professional Management of a Solicitor's Practice. Martin Read (Gen. Ed.).
Looseleaf. Sweet & Maxwell.

Solicitors' Guide to Good Management. Trevor Boutall and Bill Blackburn.
1996. Law Society.

Solicitors' Partnerships: The Law in Practice. Charles Bonney.
Looseleaf. Sweet & Maxwell.

C.   Media and Marketing

Marketing for Lawyers. Matthew Moore.
2nd ed. 1994. Law Society. (Gazette Practice Handbooks.)

Marketing Professional Services: A Handbook. Patrick Forsyth.
1992. Pitman.

Media Relations for Lawyers: practical guidance on using the media for solicitors, barristers, legal executives and their staff. Sue Stapely.
1st ed. 1994. Law Society.

D.   Legal Writing and Research

Clarity for Lawyers: the use of plain English in legal writing. Mark Adler.
1st ed. 1990. Law Society.

Dictionary of bias-free usage: a guide to non-discriminatory language. Rosalie Maggio.
1991. Oryx Press.

Effective Communication. Anthony King.
1992. Blackstone.

Effective Interviewing. Helena Twist.
1992. Blackstone.

Legal Research Guide. Guy Holborn.
1993. Butterworths.

Legal Research. David Stott.
1993. Cavendish.

Legal Research: Law Finding and Problem Solving. V Tunkel.
1992. Blackstone.

Legal Writing. Margot Costanzo.
1993. Cavendish.

Legal Writing and Drafting. P Rylance.
1994. Blackstone.

6.   Journals

British Tax Review. Sweet & Maxwell.

Capital Tax Planning. Sweet & Maxwell.

Personal Tax Planning Review. Key Haven.

Private Client Business. Sweet & Maxwell.

Tax Journal. Butterworths.

Taxation. Tolley.

Taxation Practitioner. Tolley.

Tolley's Practical Tax. Tolley.

Trust Law International. Tolley.

Trusts and Estates. Legal Studies and Services.

7.   Law Society Materials

Making a Will Won't Kill You. (Client information booklet.)

Personal Assets Log. (Checklist for clients.)

Personal Representative's Guide.

Questionnaire for Personal Representative Clients.

Your Will: Client Questionnaire.

Chapter 30

Addresses

Probate Registries

PRINCIPLE REGISTRY

Somerset House
Strand
London WC2R 1LP

Tel: 0171 936 6000/6983
Fax: 0171 936 6946
DX: 396 Lond/Chancery Ln WC2

DISTRICT REGISTRIES

Birmingham
The Priory Courts
33 Bull Street
Birmingham B4 6DU

Tel: 0121 681 3414
Fax: 0121 681 3404
DX: 701990 Birmingham-7

Brighton
William Street
Brighton
East Sussex BN2 2LG

Tel: 01273 684071
Fax: 01273 688281
DX: 98073 Brighton-3

Bristol
The Crescent Centre
Temple Back
Bristol BS1 6EP

Tel: 0117 927 3915/926 4619
Fax: 0117 925 9377

Ipswich
Level 3
Haven House
17 Lower Brook Street
Ipswich
Suffolk IP4 1DN

Tel: 01473 253 724

Fax: 01473 280 889
DX: 3279 Ipswich

Leeds
3rd Floor
Coronet House
Queen Street
Leeds LS1 2BA

Tel: 0113 243 1505
Fax: 0113 243 1505
DX: 26451 Leeds Park Sq

Liverpool
The Queen Elizabeth II
Law Courts
Derby Square
Liverpool L2 1XA

Tel: 0151 236 8264
Fax: 0151 236 5575
DX: 14246 Liverpool-1

Manchester
9th Floor, Astley House
23 Quay Street
Manchester M3 4AT

Tel: 0161 834 4319
Fax: 0161 834 5651
DX: 14387 Manchester-1

Newcastle upon Tyne
2nd Floor
Plummer House
Croft Street
Newcastle upon Tyne NE1 6NP

Tel: 0191 261 8383
Fax: 0191 233 0868
DX: 61081 Newcastle 14

Oxford
10a New Road
Oxford OX1 1LY

Tel: 01865 241 163
Fax: 01865 204 402
DX: 4337 Oxford

Winchester
4th Floor
Cromwell House
Andover Road
Winchester
Hants SO23 7EW

Tel: 01962 853 046
Fax: 01962 877 371
DX: 96900 Winchester-2

Probate Registry of Wales
PO Box 474
2 Park Street
Cardiff CF1 1TB

Tel: 01222 376 479
Fax: 01222 376 466
DX: 122782 Cardiff-13

Sub-Registries
Bangor
Council Offices
Ffordd Gwynedd
Bangor LL57 1OT

Tel: 01248 362 410
DX: 23186 Bangor-2

Bodmin
Market Street
Bodmin
Cornwall PL31 2JW

Tel: 01208 72279
DX: 81858 Bodmin

Carlisle
Courts of Justice
Earl Street
Carlisle CA1 1DJ

Tel: 01228 21751
Fax: 01228 590 588
DX: 63034 Carlisle

Carmarthen
14 King Street
Carmarthen SA31 1BL

Tel: 01267 236 238
DX: 51420 Carmarthen

Chester
5th Floor
Hamilton House
Hamilton Place
Chester CH1 2DA

Tel: 01244 345 082
DX: 22162 Chester (Northgate)

Exeter
Finance House
Barnfield Road
Exeter
Devon EX1 1QR

Tel: 01392 274 515
DX: 8380 Exeter

Gloucester
2nd Floor
Combined Courts Building
Kimbrose Way
Gloucester GL1 2DG

Tel: 01452 522 585
DX: 7537 Gloucester-1

Lancaster
Mitre House
Church Street
Lancaster LA1 1HE

Tel: 01524 36625
DX: 63509 Lancaster

Leicester
5th Floor
Leicester House
Lee Circle
Leicester LE1 3RE

Tel: 0116 253 8558
Fax: 0116 262 7796
DX: 17407 Leicester

Lincoln
Mill House
Brayford Side North
Lincoln LN1 1YW

Tel: 01522 523 648
DX: 11048 Lincoln-1

414

Maidstone
Law Courts
Barker Road
Maidstone
Kent ME16 8EQ

Tel: 01622 202 000
DX: 130065 Maidstone-7

Middlesbrough
Teeside Combined
Court Centre
Russell Street
Middlesbrough
Cleveland TS1 2AE

Tel: 01642 340 001
DX: 60536 Middlesbrough

Norwich
Combined Court Building
The Law Courts
Bishopsgate
Norwich NR3 1UR

Tel: 01603 761 776
Fax: 01603 760 863
DX: 5202 Norwich

Nottingham
Buttdyke House
33 Park Row
Nottingham NG1 6GR

Tel: 0115 941 4288
Fax: 0115 924 3374
DX: 10055 Nottingham

Peterborough
1st Floor, Crown Building
Rivergate
Peterborough PE1 1EJ

Tel: 01733 562802
DX: 12327 Peterborough-1

Sheffield
PO Box 832
The Law Courts
50 West Bar
Sheffield S3 8YR

Tel: 0114 281 2596
DX: 26054 Sheffield-2

Stoke on Trent
Combined Court Centre
Bethesda Street
Hanley
Stoke on Trent ST1 3BP

Tel: 01782 854 065
Fax: 01782 854 067
DX: 20736 Hanley 1

York
Duncombe Place
York YO1 7EA

Tel: 01904 624 210
Fax: 01904 624 210
DX: 61543 York

Other Useful Addresses

THE LAW SOCIETY

The Law Society's Hall
113 Chancery Lane
London WC2A 1PL

DX: 56 Lond/Chancery Lane
Tel: 0171 242 1222
Fax: 0171 831 0344
www.lawsociety.org.uk

Ipsley Court
Berrington Close
Redditch
Worcestershire B98 0TD

DX 19114 Redditch
Tel: 0171 242 1222
Fax: 01527 510213

Office for the Supervision of Solicitors
Victoria Court
8 Dormer Place
Leamington Spa
Warwickshire CV32 5AE

DX: 292320 Leamington Spa-4
Tel: 01926 820082
Fax: 01926 431435

You can also use the following national rate telephone numbers for the enquiry services listed below.

Central Switchboard: 0870 606 2500
Library Enquiries: 0870 606 2511
Practice Advice: 0870 606 2522
Professional Ethics: 0870 606 2577

SPECIALIST VALUERS

Central Association of Agricultural Valuers
Market Chambers
35 Market Place
Coleford
Gloucestershire GL16 8AA

Tel: 01594 832979
Fax: 01594 810701
E mail: CCAVAgVal@aol.com

Fleurets
Chartered Surveyors – Hotel and Licensed Property Valuers
18 Bloomsbury Square
London WC1A 2NS

Tel: 0171 636 8992
Fax: 0171 636 7490
E mail: ldn@fleuretsltd.demon.co.uk

For auctioneers, surveyors and valuers whose sole or main business is concerned with the sale and valuation of hotels, public houses and licensed property generally.

Incorporated Society of Valuers and Auctioneers
3 Cadogan Gate
London SW1X 0AS

Tel: 0171 235 2282
Fax: 0171 235 4390
E mail: hq@isva.co.uk

Represents the interests of valuers, auctioneers, estate agents and surveyors.

Institute of Revenues, Rating and Valuation
41 Doughty Street
London WC1N 2LF

Tel: 0171 831 3505
Fax: 0171 831 2048
E mail: enquiries@irrv.org.uk

Rating and local revenues administration; valuation for rating and general purposes; valuation appeals.

LAPADA, The Association of Art and Antique Dealers
Suite 214
535 Kings Road
Chelsea
London SW10 0SZ

Tel: 0171 823 3511
Fax: 0171 823 3522
E mail: lapada@lapada.co.uk

For established antiques and fine art dealers and related ancilliary trades - fine art packers/shippers, restorers, valuers.

National Association of Goldsmiths
78a Luke Street
London EC2A 4PY

Tel: 0171 613 4445
Fax: 0171 613 4450
E mail: nag@easynet.co.uk

Society of Fine Art Auctioneers
St Edmund's Court
Oakhampton Street
Exeter EX4 1DU

Tel: 01392 204 470
Fax: 01392 422 804

Fine art auctioneers, antiques and chattels auctioneers.

Stanley Gibbons Ltd
399 Strand
London WC2R 0LX

Tel: 0171 836 8444
Fax: 0171 836 7342
E mail:
stamps@stangibbslondon.demon.co.uk

Valuation of postage stamps and postal history. Philatelic auctioneers.

Wildy & Sons Ltd
Lincoln's Inn Archway
Carey Street
London WC2A 2JD

Tel: 0171 242 5778
Fax: 0171 430 0897
E mail: info@wildy.com

Valuation of legal books for probate matters.

REGULATORY ORGANISATIONS

Adjudicator's Office
(Inland Revenue, Customs & Excise and
Contributions Agency)
3rd Floor
Haymarket House
28 Haymarket
London SW1V 4SP

Tel: 0171 930 2292

Fax: 0171 930 2298
E mail: adjudicator@gtnet.dov.uk

Banking Ombudsman
70 Gray's Inn Road
London WC1X 8NB

Tel: 0171 404 9944
Fax: 0171 405 5052
E mail: bankingombudsman@obo.org.uk

Building Societies Ombudsman
Millbank Tower
Millbank
London SW1P 4XS

Tel: 0171 931 0044
Fax: 0171 931 8485
E mail:
bldgsocombudsman@easynet.co.uk

Financial Services Authority
25 The North Colonnade
Canary Wharf
London E14 5HF

Tel: 0171 676 1000
Fax: 0171 676 1099

COUNSELLING AND SUPPORT

Age Concern England
Astral House
1268 London Road
London SW16 4ER

Tel: 0181 679 8000
Fax: 0181 679 6069
www.ace.org.uk

Age Concern Wales
4th Floor
1 Cathedral Road
Cardiff CF1 9SD

Tel: 01222 371566
Fax: 01222 399562
E mail: enquiries@accymru.demon.co.uk

British Association for Counselling
1 Regent Place
Rugby
Warwickshire CV21 2PJ

Tel: 01788 578328

Child Poverty Action Group
94 White Lion Street
London N1 9PF

Tel: 0171 837 7979
Fax: 0171 837 6414
E mail: staff@cpag.demon.co.uk

CRUSE
CRUSE House
126 Sheen Road
Richmond
Surrey TW9 1UR

Tel: 0181 940 4818
Fax: 0181 940 7638

Bereavement care.

Gingerbread
16–17 Clerkenwell Close
Clerkenwell
London EC1R 0AN

Tel: 0171 336 8183
Fax: 0171 336 8185
E mail: advice@gingerbread.org.uk

Information, advice and social support for one-parent families

National Association of Widows
54–57 Allison Street
Digbeth
Birmingham B5 5TH

Tel: 0121 643 8348

ANIMAL WELFARE

Blue Cross
Shilton Road
Burford
Oxon OX18 4PF

Tel: 01993 822651
Fax: 01993 823083
E mail: info@bluecross.org.uk

Cats Protection League
17 Kings Road
Horsham
West Sussex RH13 5PN

Tel: 01403 221927
Fax: 01403 218414

Governing Council of the Cat Fancy
4–6 Penel Orlieu
Bridgwater
Somerset TA6 3PG

Tel: 01278 427575
Fax: 01278 446627
E mail: GCCF_CATS@compuserve.com

Kennel Club
1–5 Clarges Street
Piccadilly
London W1Y 8AB

Tel: 0171 629 5828
Fax: 0171 518 1014
E mail: info@the_kennel_club.org.uk
www.the_kennel_club.org.uk

National Canine Defence League
17 Wakley Street
London EC1V 7RQ

Tel: 0171 837 0006
Fax: 0171 689 0482
www.ncdl.org.uk

People's Dispensary for Sick Animals
Whitechapel Way
Priorslee
Telford
Shropshire TF2 9PQ

Tel: 01952 290999
Fax: 01952 291035

RSPCA
Causeway
Horsham
West Sussex RH12 1HG

Tel: 01403 264181
Fax: 01403 241048
E mail: webmail@rspca.org.uk
www.rspca.org.uk

MISCELLANEOUS

Advertising Standards Authority
2 Torrington Place
London WC1E 7HW

Tel: 0171 580 5555
Fax: 0171 631 3051
www.asa.org.uk

British Medical Association
BMA House
Tavistock Square
London WC1H 9JP

Tel: 0171 387 4499
Fax: 0171 383 6400
www.bma.org.uk

British Red Cross
9 Grosvenor Crescent
London SW1X 7EJ

Tel: 0171 235 5454
Fax: 0171 245 6315
www.redcross.org.uk

Charity Commission
St Albans House
57–60 Haymarket
London SW1Y 4QX

Tel: 0171 210 4477
Fax: 0171 210 4545
www.charity-commission.gov.uk

Clarity
c/o Mark Adler
Adler & Adler
74 South Street
Dorking
Surrey RH4 2HD

Tel: 01306 741055
Fax: 01306 741066
E mail: adler@adler.demon.co.uk
www.adler.demon.co.uk

Court of Protection
Public Trust Office
Stewart House
24 Kingsway
London WC2B 6JX

DX: 37965 Lond/Kingsway

Tel: 0171 664 7000
Fax: 0171 664 7705

DSS
Newcastle Benefits Directorate
DSS Central Office
Benton Park Road
Newcastle upon Tyne NE98 1YX

Tel: 0191 213 5000

DTI
1 Victoria Street
Westminster
London SW1H 0ET

Tel: 0171 215 5000
www.dti.gov.uk

EAGLE (Exchange on Ageing, Law, and Ethics)
c/o Age Concern England
Astral House
1268 London Road
London SW16 4ER

Tel: 0181 765 7377
Fax: 0181 765 7218
E mail: moorec@ace.org.uk

Ergonomics Society
Devonshire House
Devonshire Square
Loughborough
Leicestershire LE11 3DW

Tel: 01509 234904
Fax: 01509 234904
E mail: ergsoc@ergonomics.org.uk
www.ergonomics.org.uk

General Council of the Bar
3 Bedford Row
London WC1R 4DB

DX: 240 London
Tel: 0171 242 0082
Fax: 0171 831 9217
E mail: GeneralOffice@Barcouncil.org.uk
www.barcouncil.org.uk

HUSAT Research Institute
The Elms
Elms Grove
Loughborough
Leicestershire LE11 1RG

Tel: 01509 611088
Fax: 01509 234651
www.lboro.ac.uk\research\husat\
index.html

Inland Revenue
Capital Taxes Office
Ferrers House
PO Box 38
Castle Meadow Road
Nottingham NG2 1BB

DX: 701201 Nottingham 4
Tel: 0115 974 0000
Fax: 0115 974 2432

Insolvency Service
Bankruptcy Search Room
Commercial Union House
22 Martineau Square
Birmingham B2 4UZ

Tel: 0121 344 3799

Institute of Advanced Legal Studies
University of London
Charles Clore House
17 Russell Square
London WC1B 5DR

Tel: 0171 637 1731
Fax: 0171 436 8824 (Library)
0171 580 9613 (Other departments)
E mail: ials@sas.ac.uk
www.sas.ac.uk\ials

Legal Aid Board Head Office
85 Gray's Inn Road
London WC1X 8AA

DX: 450 London
Tel: 0171 813 1000
Fax: 0171 813 8631

Lord Chancellor's Department
Selborne House
54–60 Victoria Street
London SW1E 6QW

Tel: 0171 210 8500
Fax: 0171 210 8549
E mail: lcd@gtnet.gov.uk
www.open.gov.uk\lcd

Official Solicitor's Department
81 Chancery Lane
London WC2A 1DD

DX: 0012 Lond/Chancery Ln
Tel: 0171 911 7127
Fax: 0171 911 7105

PDSA House Clearance Service
491–493 Liverpool Road
London N7 8NS

Tel: 0171 609 0411

Principal Registry of the Family Division
Somerset House
Strand
London WC2R 1LP

DX: 396 Lond/Chancery Ln
Tel: 0171 936 6000
Fax: 0171 936 6995

Royal Courts of Justice
Strand
London WC2A 2LL

DX: 44450 Strand WC2
Tel: 0171 936 6000
Fax: 0171 936 6946

Society of Computers and Law
Administrative Secretary
10 Hurle Crescent
Clifton
Bristol BS8 2TA

DX: 37017 Clifton
Tel: 0117 923 7393
Fax: 0117 923 9305
E mail: ruth.baker@scl.org
www.scl.org

Society of Trust and Estate Practitioners
PO Box 13272
Eagle House
110 Jermyn Street
London SW1Y 62H

Tel: 0171 839 3886
Fax: 0171 408 1081

Solicitors Benevolent Association
1 Jaggard Way
Wandsworth Common
London SW12 8SG

DX: 41608 Balham
Tel: 0181 675 6440
Fax: 0181 675 6441
E mail: sec@solben.force9.co.uk

Solicitors Indemnity Fund Ltd
100 St John Street
London EC1M 4EH

DX: 46601 Barbican EC1
Tel: 0171 566 6000
Fax: 0171 566 6006

TEC National Council
10th Floor
Westminster Tower
3 Albert Embankment
London SE1 7SX

Tel: 0171 735 0010
Fax: 0171 735 0090
E mail: info@tec.co.uk
www.tec.co.uk

Terrence Higgins Trust
52–54 Gray's Inn Road
London WC1X 8JU

Tel: 0171 831 0330
Fax: 0171 816 4551
E mail: info@tht.org.uk
www.tht.org.uk

Treasury Solicitor
Queen Anne's Chambers
28 Broadway
London SW1H 9JS

DX: 123242 St James Park
Tel: 0171 210 3000
Fax: 0171 222 6006

Voluntary Euthanasia Society
13 Prince of Wales Terrace
London W8 5PG

Tel: 0171 937 7770
Fax: 0171 376 2648
E mail: info@ves.org.uk
www.ves.org.uk

Index